CLUTCH

||||||||||||||||||||||||

CLUTCH

WHY SOME PEOPLE EXCEL UNDER PRESSURE AND OTHERS DON'T

PAUL SULLIVAN

PORTFOLIO / PENGUIN

155.9
5

PORTFOLIO
Published by the Penguin Group
Penguin Group (USA) Inc., 375 Hudson Street,
New York, New York 10014, U.S.A.
Penguin Group (Canada), 90 Eglinton Avenue East, Suite 700,
Toronto, Ontario, Canada M4P 2Y3
(a division of Pearson Penguin Canada Inc.)
Penguin Books Ltd, 80 Strand, London WC2R 0RL, England
Penguin Ireland, 25 St. Stephen's Green, Dublin 2, Ireland
(a division of Penguin Books Ltd)
Penguin Books Australia Ltd, 250 Camberwell Road, Camberwell,
Victoria 3124, Australia
(a division of Pearson Australia Group Pty Ltd)
Penguin Books India Pvt Ltd, 11 Community Centre, Panchsheel Park,
New Delhi–110 017, India
Penguin Group (NZ), 67 Apollo Drive, Rosedale, North Shore 0632,
New Zealand (a division of Pearson New Zealand Ltd)
Penguin Books (South Africa) (Pty) Ltd, 24 Sturdee Avenue,
Rosebank, Johannesburg 2196, South Africa

Penguin Books Ltd, Registered Offices:
80 Strand, London WC2R 0RL, England

First published in 2010 by Portfolio,
a member of Penguin Group (USA) Inc.

1 2 3 4 5 6 7 8 9 10

Library of Congress Cataloging-in-Publication Data
Sullivan, Paul.
    Clutch : why some people excel under pressure and others don't / Paul Sullivan.
        p. cm.
    Includes bibliographical references and index.
    ISBN 978-1-59184-350-4
    1. Self-confidence.   2. Stress (Psychology)   3. Success.   I. Title.
BF575.S39S85 2010
155.9—dc22

                                        2010013789

Printed in the United States of America
Set in Fairfield Light
Designed by Victoria Hartman

To Laura for your love, patience, and never-ending support,

and to Ginny for sleeping through the night

CONTENTS

||||||||||||||||||||||||

CLUTCH

||||||||||||||||||||||||||||

WHAT'S CLUTCH?

WHAT DOES IT mean to be clutch? Most sports fans are pretty sure they know the answer. But consider these three classic moments in sports. They have all been called clutch moments, but only one of them actually is:

- In game seven of the 1965 Eastern Conference basketball championship the score stood at 110–109. The Boston Celtics led the Philadelphia 76ers by one point with five seconds left on the clock. The 76ers had been given possession of the ball and were ready to inbound it. Whichever player got it had time for one shot, to win or lose the game. As Hal Greer, the 76ers' All-Star guard, threw the ball into play, Johnny Havlicek spun and tipped it to his Celtics teammate. "Havlicek steals it!" boomed Johnny Most, the gravelly-voiced announcer of the Celtics. "Havlicek stole the ball! It's all over. It's all over . . . Johnny Havlicek stole the ball!" Arguably the most famous call in basketball, it has immortalized the play. What it leaves out is that Havlicek had his back to Greer and spun at just the right moment to tip the ball. This makes what he did even more extraordinary. He wasn't even looking at Greer. But his quick move sent the Celtics to victory.

- Two decades later, Tommy Lasorda, the Los Angeles Dodgers manager, decided to put Kirk Gibson in as a pinch hitter. Down 4–3 in the first game of the 1988 World Series, with two outs and the tying run at first base, Gibson would have been the ideal choice in the circumstance—had he not had a stomach bug and two legs in such pain that he limped to the plate. If he hit a pitch anywhere in the ballpark, he wouldn't have made it to first. He could only do one thing: hit a home run. Gibson, in that shape, looked like an easy out, even more so because he was facing Dennis Eckersley, the Oakland Athletics star pitcher and future Hall of Famer. But Gibson worked the count until it stood at three balls and two strikes. On the next pitch, he swung, all arms and no legs, and hit the ball out of the park to win the game. His hobbling around the bases, fist raised in triumph, remains a quintessential image of fortitude, determination, and toughness.

- Fast-forward another twenty years, and Eli Manning, the New York Giants quarterback, was facing a situation he had faced many times in his career: getting close to victory in an important game only to lose in the end. Tom Brady, considered one of the best quarterbacks of his era, had just brought the New England Patriots back from three points down to four points ahead in the last eight minutes of Super Bowl XLII. He had passed, handed off, scrambled—everything he could think of to get the Patriots into scoring position. When he threw to Randy Moss in the end zone, it seemed that Brady, with his nerves of steel, had engineered another come-from-behind victory. The score stood at 14–10 with two minutes left on the clock. Manning had led his wildcard team to the Super Bowl, but now it looked as though it was over. He had nothing to be ashamed of; it had been a great run. But it didn't play out that way. With the highest stakes of his career—win and beat a team that was expecting to go undefeated; lose and forever be overshadowed by his brother

Peyton, who had won the Super Bowl the year before—Manning refused to quit. He led his team down the field until he threw a short pass to Plaxico Burress in the end zone. The final score was 17–14, with the Giants as Super Bowl champions.

So which one of these amazing sports moments was clutch? There is only one right answer. Here's a fourth option that might help you decide: In July 2009, Roger Federer faced off against Andy Roddick in the Wimbledon final. Federer had had his five-year winning streak broken the year before. But this match was more than a comeback. If Federer won, it would be his fifteenth Grand Slam tennis title, more than any other player had ever won. Roddick, who had lost in the final three previous times, was in the best shape of his career, and he got out to an early lead, winning the first set. Federer won the next two. In the fourth, Roddick came from behind to force a fifth set to decide the match. At 8–8, Federer looked as though he might lose, but he came back, and the set stretched to 15–14 before Roddick faltered. Federer won 16–14. At the end of the four-hour match, the two had played 77 games—a Wimbledon record—and the longest fifth set in the championship's history. With his victory, Federer had broken Pete Sampras's Grand Slam record   with Sampras watching courtside.

So which of the four were clutch? If you picked the last two, you were right.

CLUTCH IS MORE THAN SPORTS

Most people associate clutch performances with a triumphant sports moment: the home run that wins the game or the basket or stolen pass at the buzzer. But each of these contains an element of luck, and clutch is not luck. Gibson could have easily struck out or merely hit a triple, and Havlicek's play was incredibly risky. However great these plays were, they relied on a good deal of luck. They were remarkable, but they were not clutch. The reason is being clutch is not the hole-in-one to win; it's the well-struck shot close to the flag and the putt that drops in with the tournament on the line. It's the precisely executed series of plays in football, not the Hail Mary pass. It's the fortitude to continue battling out a Wimbledon final as you always have—even though the whole world is wondering whether you are going to choke. Clutch, simply put, is the ability to do what you can do normally under immense pressure. It is also something that goes far beyond the world of sport. And while it has a mental component, it is not a mystical ability, nor somehow willing yourself to greatness. After all, every professional athlete is mentally tough or he wouldn't have made it that far. For that matter, every chief executive of a company has shown leadership to get where he is. But that does not mean he will be clutch.

Being great under pressure is hard work. This is part of the reason why we are so impressed by people who seem immune to choking. These people come through in the clutch when others don't. If they're business leaders, they become gurus other executives want to emulate. In politics, the person who runs the gauntlet wins the election, but if he can do so in a particularly cunning way, he becomes an example of strategic excellence. In combat, it is the leaders who come under fire and get their men to safety who are recognized as war heroes. If the people are sporting figures, their triumphs become legendary. We are so fascinated by these feats that we have created a nearly mythical aura around clutch performers. Think of what happens every time the Olympics roll around. People suddenly start rooting for athletes they have never heard of in sports they don't usually care about. We crave the feel-good story of the kid from nowhere who uses his one shot to win gold. But often we start to think of him as more than a great athlete, and this is when problems start. Such deification muddies how the greatest athletes, businessmen, politicians, and military commanders learn to perform so well under pressure.

Just because someone is clutch in one area of his life does not mean he will be clutch in others. Tiger Woods could be the pitchman for this. He was so great under the pressure of a golf tournament that his fans ascribed to him superhuman qualities. But when the world learned about his Las Vegas assignations, they felt betrayed: How could he make such good decisions in his professional life but such bad ones in his personal life? Yet if anything, I believe his double life made his ability on the golf course more, not less, remarkable. At the peak of his reputation for being a clutch performer, a few months after he won the 2008 U.S. Open on a broken leg, I sat down with Tiger at a golf course in Arden, North Carolina, ten miles outside of Asheville. When I asked him during our interview how he always seemed to win a tournament when the pressure was greatest, the simplicity of his answer struck me. "I've put myself there, in that situation, more times than anybody else," he told me. "I've also failed more times than anybody else. But along the way, you do succeed."

I found in writing this book that his explanation only goes part of the way to understanding why some people excel under pressure and others do not. What it means to be clutch for the rest of us is far simpler and far more difficult to achieve than just putting yourself out there. Think of it a different way: Tiger hits perfect shots on the driving range. He hits them pretty much any way he wants, left, right, low, high. But in this he is not so different from anyone else on the PGA Tour. They can all hit those shots on the practice range. When the tournament starts, Tiger does something different, particularly if he is in contention to win: He swings as though he is still on the range. He swings just as fluidly in moments of intense pressure when other pros can tense up like average golfers. He hits the ball on the eighteenth hole to win the way he would if he were playing with friends. This is why being clutch is difficult. Transferring what you can do in a relaxed atmosphere to a tenser one is not easy—or else everyone would be clutch.

THE QUEST FOR CLUTCH

When I set out to discover what made some people great under pressure, I had few preconceived ideas about the subject. My goal was to find people who were clutch across a range of professions and deconstruct what made them so good. Instead of devising a series of tests, I hit the road. The one thing I knew for sure was that no one had ever been clutch under laboratory conditions. I also had a healthy skepticism of the existing theories that purported to explain how people could become better under pressure. For one, most of them carried New Agey names that made my skin crawl. I distrusted the idea that your mind was an extra club in your golf bag, that putting yourself in the zone (wherever that was) would do much good, or that the "mental edge" was something sharp. I had interviewed or met enough great athletes to know that their minds were not always their greatest assets. The reverse was true for business leaders: I'd interviewed some very smart, interesting people who were doing less than I thought they could be doing and, conversely, some real buffoons who were running the show. I was pretty sure that the link between intelligence and rank at many companies was not always there, and I had no idea if the two had any correlation with a person's ability to perform under pressure.

On the other end of the scale, I was equally skeptical of finely crafted academic studies after my time as a graduate student at the University of Chicago in the mid-1990s. I was studying history, but I became fascinated by the success and stature of the Chicago School of Economics. My adviser's office was one floor above where Gary Becker, one of the school's many Nobel Prize winners, taught a class. I often had to wade through a crowd of eager students surrounding him when his class let out. Becker had won his Nobel for his work on the idea of "rational choice," an elegant concept that says, given the right incentives, people will act in the most productive ways. His work on marriage, labor choices, and criminal behavior is fascinating, but after some fifteen years as a business journalist, I came to see the flaws in the theory. Just because someone was well educated did not mean he was going to make the most rational choices about his job or his family. And if a theory created by someone as brilliant as Becker could be dinged in practice, I didn't have a lot of faith in sports psychologists and gurus of peak performance.

So I did what a reporter does when he has some questions. I found people who excelled under pressure and spent time with them. I observed them in pressure-filled situations. I sat with them. I interviewed them over and over again. I studied their past successes and failures. I looked over bits of research and turned to literature. But most of all, I asked them how they performed as they did. Many couldn't answer this question satisfactorily, so I spent more time with them and asked more questions. The result is this book, which looks at the good, the bad, and the surprising things people do under pressure.

CONFESSIONS OF A CHOKER

Long before I sat across from Tiger Woods, or even contemplated writing this book, clutch performers fascinated me. As a kid, I wasn't much of an athlete, but I was a great student, which meant much more to my future. I grew up in a rough neighborhood in an economically depressed town in western Massachusetts. My parents divorced and then spent the rest of my childhood hating each other, something they were wildly successful at doing. It sounds like the setup to a sentimental afternoon movie, but it was pretty grim then. My grandfather realized the pickle I was in and pushed me to apply to a nearby prep school. I was accepted, given financial aid, and with each test I passed, I began to move away from that childhood. From entrance exams and scholarship meetings to personal challenges and job interviews later in life, I had no choice but to be clutch. If I choked, I had no backup plan. So, I went forward. I learned to stay calm and remain articulate when it counted, but mostly I pressed ahead. Because of this, I've lived a much better life than I could have ever imagined as a kid coming home to an empty apartment on a truly bleak street. (My only friend in the neighborhood robbed our apartment when he turned sixteen!) Without really thinking about it in these terms then, I had to be clutch to get out.

But there has always been one area of my life where I have been a world-class choke artist: golf. It may seem like a minor thing, but this was the sport my grandfather taught me on the public courses he played with his friends. Our bond grew over the thousands of hours we spent out there together. I loved the discussions we had; he loved the sight of me hitting soaring tee shots to parts of the fairway he had never reached. I could hit those shots with him. I could hit them, too, on the driving range, where most every shot was crisp and accurate. But tournaments were a different story. I choked, sometimes mildly, sometimes in a soul-crushing way. Once I was eight up with ten holes left to play. For nongolfers, this meant I didn't have to win any more holes, just tie two and I would win the match. I lost all ten and was eliminated from the tournament. A similar moment came in a citywide junior tournament where I had played so well on the first nine holes that I was sure I was in the lead. I ran into the club-house to call my grandfather, and he rushed over to watch me finish. But before he got there, my game had started to fall apart, and I was lucky to finish in the middle of the pack. My prize that day—three golf balls—was worth less than my entry fee.

My choking streak has continued into adulthood, as I've turned in poor performances on most of the prestigious courses where I've been invited to play. I'll always remember the first hole at Oakmont Country Club, site of eight U.S. Opens. I hit my drive out-of-bounds—the only out-of-bounds on the entire course. When I had a great round going at The Country Club in Brookline, I put my final tee shot on the driving range—a place few ever see from that angle. It is even worse when I'm asked to play in a member-guest tournament. One of my wife's colleagues said her husband was thrilled to have me join his team at Kittansett Country Club, a gorgeous seaside course in Marion, Massachusetts. I had played a lot of golf that spring and I was regularly shooting in the mid-70s. He was convinced we were going to whoop the competition; we finished second to last. The list goes on, interminably. Yet put me on my home course or out with friends, and I'll shoot one of the low scores that keeps my handicap a single digit. It drives me crazy.

THE ROUTE TO BEING CLUTCH

My golf course frustration drove my initial (selfish) interest in the idea of a book about being clutch. I became more serious about the sub-ject as I began thinking more deeply about clutch performers and why they could do what so many of us cannot do: react in a pressure-filled situation the way they would act normally. Throughout this, I clung to the same two questions. The first was, Why are some people so much better under pressure than other, seemingly equally talented people?

The reality is that most people fail in extreme situations. They may be able to do what they do just fine under everyday conditions, but when the pressure mounts, their ability leaves them. They choke. Yet there is a small subset of people who not only succeed but thrive under pressure. What was most intriguing about interviewing them was so few thought of themselves as clutch. This astonished me because we are a country that lionizes performers who come through under pressure.

The first part of the book is the result of my quest to discover the key traits that make people clutch; I found five. I began by looking at focus, the basis for all great performances under pressure. The second trait is discipline, which in chapter 2 I look at through the stories of a psychiatrist and a banker in make-or-break situations. Chapter 3 discusses the need for adaptability by examining Special Forces leaders and Secret Service agents in the field. The need to be present—and block out everything else—is told in chapter 4 through an actor preparing for the stage role of a lifetime. Chapter 5 looks at the fear and desire that drive entrepreneurs to succeed under the constant pressure of their businesses. Chapter 6 applies all of these principles to what I call the double-clutch moment: when a woman beats a man at his own game, be it sports or business. In those victories, there is much more at stake because of the perception that women cannot be clutch.

Of course, just because someone is successful does not mean he will be good under pressure. High-profile chokers are the car crash we can't take our eyes off of. They fascinate us, largely because we expect high achievers to do so much better. If the clutch performers didn't think of themselves as clutch, the opposite was true for chokers: Before their fall, they held themselves in very high esteem. The second part of the book looks not only at the seemingly star performers who choke under pressure but at the three traits all chokers have. The first is an inability to accept responsibility for what they have done when something goes wrong. I illustrate this in chapter 7 through two tales of the financial crisis. In chapter 8, I look at how overthinking an opportunity can paralyze a person under pressure and cause him to choke just when everyone else thinks he will come through. In chapter 9, I talk about overconfidence by examining the common characteristics of leaders who bring down major companies—and have spawned an entire industry to deal with their mistakes.

This brought me to the second question I wanted answered: Can people be clutch if they are not regularly in high-pressure situations? The answer is yes, and I show how in the third part of the book. Chapter 10 is about a businessman who found himself in a financial bind he did not cause and looks at the series of painful decisions he had to make—or risk losing everything he had built. In chapter 11, I focus on a professional golfer who had been making his way on the PGA Tour without a victory and suddenly found himself leading a major tournament on the last day. Their stories illustrate the two areas where people choke the most—with money and in sports—and explain how all of us can learn to make better decisions under pressure. This, at the end of the day, is the goal of *Clutch*: to show people how to become better under pressure and avoid the simple mistakes that cause most of us to choke.

PART I

||||||||||||||||||||

WHY PEOPLE ARE CLUTCH

[1]

FOCUS
The Morality Plays of David Boies

BILL GATES LOOKED comfortable as the questioning began on August 27, 1998. The founder of Microsoft, then forty-two, was the leading entrepreneur of his generation. He was wealthy beyond belief, and love him or hate him, most people used his software. That day, he took his time answering the questions put to him. Occasionally he glared back or looked exasperated, as if he could not believe how stupid his questioner was. Other times, he took a sip from his can of soda. Such a gesture may have made other people look relaxed, but it had the effect of portraying him as combative, smug, and thoroughly unapproachable. Dressed in a brown suit, a tan shirt, and a wide, chocolate-and-brick striped tie, Gates mostly seemed perturbed, as if the answers to these questions were completely obvious and sitting there was a waste of his time. Condescension was his default emotion, and he did little to hide it.

When asked if he was familiar with a dictionary of computer terms Microsoft had published, Gates shrugged off the question. Then when the attorney began asking him to define various terms from a Microsoft-produced computer dictionary, he became pedantic. When asked if he agreed with a definition of "Internet Explorer" in the dictionary, Gates twisted up his face and said, "Did you actually read what was in there?

If you're trying to use the dictionary, you might as well read what it says." It went on in this vein, the attorney asking a question and Gates being evasive or snide in his response. When asked if he thought Microsoft was the most respected computer software company in the world, he said, "Some people would agree with that; some people wouldn't." When pressed for his own opinion of the company he had founded, he smirked and said that "on a statistical basis" it probably was the most respected. The deposition seemed to amuse him.

Yet the questions being asked were probing at something far more serious than Gates's glib answers revealed. He was being deposed because the United States Department of Justice had brought antitrust charges against Microsoft, alleging that it had acted like a monopoly in installing an Internet browser in its Windows operating systems. If a judge ruled that Microsoft was, indeed, a monopoly, the company could be broken up. Gates was being billed as the Rockefeller of the day, making his company the equivalent of Standard Oil. Yet he was acting as if these questions were a nuisance, not a deposition being taken under oath. At one point, he asked the court reporter to read back to him an attorney's question, as if he were the judge running the trial.

Toward the end of that day of questioning, David Boies, representing the United States, took over the questioning. "Prior to the December 27, 1995, meeting, had a decision been made to advise the world that not only would the browser be free but it would be forever free?" Boies asked Gates.

"Well, it's always been the case that when we put a feature into Windows that it remains part of Windows and doesn't become an extra cost item," Gates answered, bobbing in his chair and shaking his head. "So it would have been kind of a silly thing for anyone to ask, including about that particular feature. And by this time, of course, browsing is shipping with Windows 95."

"Exactly sort of the point I wanted to come to, Mr. Gates," Boies said with a catch in his voice. "When you put things into the operating system, generally, you don't announce that they're going to be forever free, do you?"

Gates jumped at this, seemingly cutting Boies off. "Yes we do. If anyone asks, that's obviously the answer we give."

With Gates rocking harder in his chair, Boies took advantage of the pause. "You finished, your answer?" he asked.

Gates said nothing. He stared back at Boies, blinking for ten, eleven seconds, an eternity on videotape. He was clearly trying to figure out if he was being set up. "Yes," he said.

"OK," Boies said. "Could you identify for me the products—other than browsers—that Microsoft has announced that they would be forever free?"

Gates put down his can of soda and drew himself up. But then something remarkable and unsettling happened. He looked down. He looked to his right. He rocked, but not as confidently, in his chair. He said nothing for a good twenty-five to thirty seconds. For the first time, he looked defensive.

Six days later, Boies was questioning Gates again, still for the deposition. This time, Gates looked shell-shocked, more like a soldier who had seen the horrors of a brutal battle than an executive who had spent days answering lawyers' questions. He was no longer cocky; he was rocking back and forth in his chair as if he were experiencing the aftereffects of a particularly traumatic shock.

"Mr. Gates, let me show you a document marked as government exhibit 390," Boies said. The sound of his voice caused Gates to look up, then around, but not to stop rocking back and forth. Gates reached out and took the document, his face twisting. "The first message here," Boies said, slowly, "purports to be a message here to you . . . on February 24, 1997, at 11:07 P.M. Do you see that?"

Gates hadn't looked up since Boies began his question. He answered with a mumbled yes.

"It talks about a focus group report, and it says that most of the people in the focus group were Navigator users, and then it goes on to say about those Navigator users, quote, 'They said they would not switch, said they would not download IE4 to replace their Navigator browser. However, once everything is in the OS and right there, integrated into the OS, in their face, so to speak, then they said they would use it because there would be no more need to use something separate.'"

The deposition had veered into the arcane areas of operating systems, Internet browsers, and how to market and sell them. Gates was still looking down and bobbing. He was, without knowing it, playing into what Boies would tell me was a career-long strategy: He makes all trials into morality plays, and this one was about credibility. Boies and his team handled Gates so well, made him look alternately unlikable and unstable, that his defense attorneys did not put him on the witness stand. Given how he did during the deposition, the concern was he would repeat the performance or make it worse in front of a judge. Yet without Gates on the stand, Boies was given a gift: the opportunity to play that deposition in court over and over again. Had the defense called Gates, Boies would have only been able to use his deposition to challenge statements he made. Most of the damning, embarrassing stuff probably would have had little relevance, because it came out during relatively benign questioning. But without Gates on the stand, that deposition became his word for the most high-profile antitrust case of the 1990s.

From the start, Boies told me he was never going to make the Microsoft case about the technology. He decided early on that he was going to focus on credibility. This may seem strange in a case that hinged on whether Microsoft embedded its browser in its operating system to force it on consumers, but Boies believes the key to winning any case is not to make it a long slog through facts and figures. "The technology is so hard that the natural reaction of everybody is to say I ought to stay out of this and judges should not be second-guessing software designers," Boies told me. Had he tried to win by focusing on the technology, he would have had to describe a simple scenario in which a programmer could have sunk his case. "If somebody from Microsoft comes in and says, 'Look, the reason we did this is because it makes it go smoother and faster and it's a better experience,' the judge doesn't have any idea about that. His inclination is to believe them. But if you undercut their credibility so when they come in and say that, the judge says, 'Wait a second, this is the same person who doesn't know what the word "compete" means, and he said he had never even read the complaint,' or 'this is the person who spliced that tape together.' At that point, the presumption of credibility disappears." Boies was willing to concede that Gates and the top engineers at Microsoft knew far more about browsers than he did. But as Gates's deposition showed, all of this knowledge had made them arrogant. Gates did not answer the questions like a person who was being prosecuted by the U.S. Department of Justice, a person who in effect was facing the full force of federal judicial power. Not being nervous might have helped him, but being arrogant and condescending certainly did not. The better position to take would have been a more humble, helpful approach. Even better would have been for Gates's counsel to put him on the stand, which might have humanized him but would have definitely neutralized Boies's deposition. "If they could have dropped that deposition into a black hole, it would have been fine not to call him," Boies told me. "But to leave me with it, to play a little bit over time, instead of having him appear once and be done with it—that was bad judgment." Yet that was exactly what Microsoft's defense did, and it played perfectly into the morality play Boies constructed. "They came in saying, 'I know something you don't know.' True. But if I can't believe you, it doesn't matter," Boies said. "It was very important from Day One of the Microsoft case to attack their credibility."

THE POWER OF FOCUS

Focus is the foundation for any clutch performance. It is the basis on which the other traits of pressure performers are built. Yet being focused is not as simple or obvious as it may sound. The reason is, many people confuse focus with concentration. The two are very different. In the Microsoft trial, Boies could have concentrated on the minutiae of browsers, the competition among browser makers, or even the underlying antitrust principles. His preparation would have been just as intense, but his arguments would have been subject to the vicissitudes of the witnesses. As he said, one programmer could have blown his case out of the water by telling the judge that the browser was bundled into every operating system because it worked better that way. Instead Boies focused on the issue of credibility. And that was why pressing Gates on seemingly insignificant details—like his definition of "Internet Explorer"—was so important. Whatever issues arose in the trial itself—from how browser software was developed and installed in operating systems to how Microsoft competed against other browser makers—could be related back to credibility. The crucial question throughout was: Are Microsoft's assertions believable?

Boies has defined his career through high-profile cases that have been as intense, pressure-packed, and public as any trials in America. But he has always handled the underlying issue deftly, even when that issue might be arcane and boring. To prosecute or defend someone for a crime against another person, you need to know how to litigate, but to be able to successfully litigate corporate cases—involving trusts, monopolies, libel, patents—you need to be able to bring the jury and sometimes the judge up to speed quickly. It's as much education as litigation; you have to make it compelling enough to keep even the knowledgeable juror awake. Framing each trial as a morality play helps Boies do this. It is his way of focusing himself and the jurors, and it keeps him from getting bogged down with—or concentrating too much on—arcane detail. By casting his cases in this seemingly folksy format, he has made them something all judges and juries can understand: right and wrong, good and bad. He does not talk down to them; he presents the issues in a way they can grasp. Browser technology in the 1990s, for example, was not widely understood, but colluding to crowd out your competitors was— and that is the real issue in any antitrust case.

When Boies was hired by the Department of Justice to try the Microsoft case, he had a long list of megatrials in which he had proven his ability under pressure. At thirty-two, he had made partner at Cravath, Swaine & Moore and had risen through the ranks to become one of the top litigators at that top corporate firm. In 1984, in *Westmoreland v. CBS*, he defended the network against libel charges brought by General William Westmoreland over a documentary about his command in Vietnam. "The theme of the trial then became not whether he is a bad man—which, if you ever saw or listened to him, would be extremely hard to get across—but did this patriot lie in the name of patriotism?" Boies told me. The focus of the morality play in *The Republic of the Philippines v. Westinghouse* was entirely different. The issue was bribery, and it looked very much as though Westinghouse, his client, had bribed Ferdinand Marcos to get the contract to build a nuclear power plant. A morality play with seemingly immoral actions is difficult to tell, but Boies focused not on right and wrong but on a more abstract point: How could you bribe an absolute dictator who looted the country's coffers when he fled?

By the time of the Microsoft trial, Boies had become so successful that he opened his own firm, Boies Schiller. Few would have expected this of Boies early on. He was born in 1941, in a small town west of Chicago. His father was a high school civics teacher. Although he would later graduate from Yale Law School, Boies did not learn to read until he was in the third grade. He suffered from dyslexia, which forced him to try harder than the rest of his classmates, and this meant that his ability to focus, to make sense of the world in his own terms, was essential from a young age.

Early in his legal career, he started to focus on the same two questions for every trial. "First, what are the facts," he told me. "And then, second, what are the basic principles of law here—not what were the detailed holdings of fifty cases, but just what are the basic principles of law that apply to this area." Such an approach seems too simple to have led to Boies winning a half-dozen major cases in his career. But Boies's focus on having a clear understanding of the issues and laws creates a solid foundation. He builds the morality play around that. However, it is not the play that helps him excel under pressure but his focus on telling the story in court. That ability allows him to withstand the immense pressure of any high-profile trial.

A CLASH OF TITANS

Ten years after the Microsoft case, I watched David Boies face off in a lower Manhattan courtroom against a formidable opponent in Ted

Wells, the head of the litigation department at Paul Weiss, a major New York law firm. The two sides were fighting over $4.2 billion and whether Hank Greenberg, the longtime head of the insurer AIG, essentially had the right to the money when he was ousted as chief executive. The case seemed like an easy victory for Wells, who was representing AIG: The money had been in shares of AIG stock that the company used to pay bonuses for senior executives, and the simple answer seemed to be that Greenberg was not entitled to control it. However, not only was it not simple, but Greenberg was not about to back down. That money had been held for three decades in a trust created by a separate company, Starr International, or SICO, which Greenberg ran. Through an esoteric arrangement, SICO paid those bonuses to AIG executives. Those executives thought that the pool of money was theirs; Greenberg, who set it up, said it belonged to SICO and as SICO's chairman he had discretion over it. The case turned on what the original trust documents said, and this was where it became complicated. AIG and SICO had once been one and the same, two parts of an insurance empire built by C. V. Starr and reorganized by Greenberg after Starr's death in 1970.

Wells opened his argument by trying to explain how the documents and the trust worked. But from the start, he set a high bar for himself. "The facts of this case are fairly simple," he said in his opening statement. "In 1970, a company called Starr International, commonly known as SICO, acquired about $120 million worth of stock in a corporate transaction. SICO was supposed to take that stock and put it in trust. And that is what SICO did." For the next thirty-five years, SICO used that money to pay AIG "retirement plans"—which was a folksy way of saying, very large executive bonuses. "Then, in 2005, something happened. SICO broke its fiduciary duty," Wells boomed. "It stopped using the stock to fund the retirement program. Not only did it stop using the stock to fund the retirement program, it started to use the stock for improper purposes. SICO started to sell the shares of the stock. SICO one day took a private plane, flew from out of the country into the United States, and took the stock out of the bank in New York and flew the stock certificates to the Island of Bermuda and put them in a bank there. And then, after taking the stock out of New York, it began to sell the stock, and it sold over $4.2 billion worth of the stock shares. Totally improper sales. Totally improper. And then, with the $4.2 billion, SICO started investing in all sorts of wild investments. They invested in things in *Russia*, in *China*."

He was on a roll, building momentum as his opening went on. The case suddenly sounded like an espionage thriller, with private planes and Bermudan dealings. At least that was the seed he was trying to plant in the jury's imagination. In a trial set to last for a month, he was laying out an opening that promised intrigue and excitement, two things not commonly associated with arcane trust documents. Then he took it a step further and made an impossible promise to the jury. "Now, some of you may be thinking, 'Oh God, I've been picked on a jury, I'm going to hear about a case involving trusts, fiduciaries,'" he said, drawing out the syllables to emphasize the anticipated tedium of it all. "At first blush, it sounds kind of boring. This case will not be boring. There is nothing boring about this case." This was a tough statement to live up to. For the jury to render its verdict, it was not only going to have to learn about trusts but also decide if something called "conversion" (a legal term involving unauthorized acts with someone else's property) had occurred. The facts of this trial would most definitely prove to be complex and sometimes boring to any juror who wasn't an accountant or a tax lawyer. Still, at the end of Wells's opening, if you heard not another word, you probably would have sided in favor of AIG and forced Greenberg to pay back the $4.2 billion at once. Wells's presentation was not that of an attorney about to litigate a complex corporate trial but one who was out to dazzle, who was promising hot facts and a sexy case. It was something out of an episode of *Law & Order*. And that was what Wells was known for: his star power and willingness to take on tough cases

Boies stood before the jury, but before he spoke a word, his style stood in stark contrast to Wells's. Boies was as sedate as Wells was forceful, as disheveled—known for wearing only navy blue suits—as Wells was dapper, and as folksy as Wells was urbane. Standing next to each other, Wells was the stiff-legged version of the college football player he once was at Holy Cross, while Boies was the thin, cerebral bridge champion. Of course, Wells was not merely a jock and Boies not simply a nerd. Yet they played those roles well for the jury. They both had the sparkle of master litigators who use a jury's assumptions about them to their advantage and their opponents' disadvantage. As far as legal face-offs go, this one was a clash of two titans.

"Good afternoon members of the jury," Boies began, avuncularly. "It will not come as any surprise to you, I suspect, to know that I disagree with a great many things that Mr. Wells said, but I want to start with one thing that we are in agreement on, and that is that the trust was formed in 1970 and the May 14, 1970, memorandum of intent is the critical document for you to look at in this case. And I want to put it back up on the board, because you'll remember Mr. Wells said this is where the pledge is. This is where these people pledged this trust."

It was Boies's belief that there was no pledge or second trust, and he was focused on teasing that out. "Ted's theme was you're going to hear this conflict between Hank Greenberg's speech, in which you hear about a trust, and the courtroom, in which you hear there is no trust," Boies told me afterward. "I get up there and say of course there's a trust. We've all heard about it, but the question is, was there a second trust, which they claim no one ever wrote anything down about? That's the real issue. So all of a sudden all of his best evidence became much less powerful because I was embracing it. If I had run away from it, the jury would have given up on my credibility."

While he was concentrating on the trust document at the outset, his focus was on asking one question in various forms: If you had $4.2 billion, wouldn't you keep track of it? Boies planned to prove his case using some of the same documents Wells was using. He was focused on showing that although a trust existed for this stock, the beneficiary was SICO, and SICO could do whatever it wanted with the stock. Even though it had been paying out AIG bonuses for over thirty years, it was not obligated to do so because it, not AIG, owned the stock. It was all perfectly legal but complicated. And it was a tough argument to make. That was why, Boies told me later, he had decided his focus would be on keeping tabs on your money. It went something like this: If members of the jury had bank statements telling them how much money they had in the bank, surely a company like AIG would have volumes of papers noting that the shares in the trust belonged to it and not SICO. If there was nothing explicitly saying this, was it truly plausible that AIG had owned the shares for thirty-five years and not put that in writing? Or was this case really about sour grapes against Greenberg for investing SICO's money some other way? That was the morality play—keeping track of what was yours.

In his opening remarks, Boies foreshadowed what might come the jury's way. "It's going to be a long trial," he said. "I'm probably going to bore you from time to time, because I'm going to be pushing the documents, I'm going to be pushing this memorandum of intent at you, I'm going to be pushing this big volume of documents at you. This is the 1970 reorganization volume, and I'm going to be saying, 'Tell me, Mr. AIG, where in here it talks about your trust.'" This was a strategic way to close, because in admitting he would bore them and then talking about documents that would almost certainly do just that, Boies took some pressure off himself. He was managing expectations but also establishing a rapport with the jury. He might end up boring them less than they feared, but it was going to be tough for Wells to keep them as enthralled as he had promised.

On only the second day of the trial, both attorneys' strategies were put to the test. Wells called Hank Greenberg as his second witness and began to hammer away at him. Wells wanted to show that speeches Greenberg made and memorandums he sent out talked about SICO shares being only for AIG employees. His plan was to juxtapose what he said then with what he was testifying to now and show that he was lying. It was a solid strategy. The only glitch came when Wells angered Judge Jed Rakoff, who felt Wells was quoting segments of Greenberg's speeches out of context. To rectify that, he made Wells play or read the speeches in their entirety into the court record. Right then, Wells broke his promise to the jury: These speeches were repetitive, long, and extremely boring. Worse, Greenberg, elfin and grandfatherly at eighty-four, was unflappable. He was giving complex answers to simple questions—not unlike what Bill Gates had done—but he was doing so in such a genial tone that Wells was the one looking bad.

Boies admitted to me that this was a lucky break for him. Wells bored the jury first in having to read everything into evidence, and by putting those speeches into the court record he also allowed Boies to quote select parts when he got Greenberg as his witness. Since the whole thing was in the court record, Boies would not have to reread it but could just pull out parts that, naturally, supported his argument.

When it was Boies's turn to cross-examine Greenberg, he used his first questions to let Greenberg talk about his background. What emerged was a man who had been married to the same woman for fifty-eight years, had four children and ten grandchildren, landed in Normandy on D-Day, won a Bronze Star in Korea, and earned honorary degrees and accolades for his philanthropic work. Boies was humanizing him, playing the grandfather card to his advantage and making him the good guy in the morality play. Was he really the kind of man who would redirect money that belonged to someone else?

Boies kept Greenberg on the stand for over a day as a way to level the playing field and get his version of the story in front of the jury much earlier than he would normally be able to do. "By doing that, I was able at the very beginning of this case to explain to the jury what my case was and show them the documents," Boies told me after the trial. In the process he was educating the jury about what he thought was important—that Greenberg was clearly an honorable man and if those SICO shares belonged to AIG, there would have been something in writing. Boies's focus also let him slow the trial down for the jury and defuse the pressure Wells was putting on Greenberg. He was focused not so much on laying out his counterargument as on humanizing Greenberg. If the jury came to believe that Greenberg was a businessman following the letter of the law and not the rapacious thief the prosecution would have them believe, then Boies was off to a good start.

PREPARATION ALLOWS FOCUS

Before Boies can craft his morality play, he needs to find the thread of the story. In SICO, he found it in a deposition—the same place where he caught Bill Gates flat-footed. This time Boies did the same thing with Martin Sullivan, the man who pushed Greenberg out as chief executive and took over his spot. Sullivan, a short, fat man with a plume of white hair, had himself been ousted from AIG in 2005. In the deposition, Boies asked him if he had ever heard anyone say there was an agreement between AIG and SICO over how certain shares would be used. Sullivan replied: "To the best of my knowledge, no." If the man who pushed out and succeeded Greenberg as head of AIG had never heard of the trust that AIG was trying to prove existed, was the jury really going to believe one existed? Shouldn't Sullivan have been keeping track of this? Just as good, Sullivan's deposition was deemed to have gone sufficiently badly by the plaintiffs that they did not call him to the stand. This let Boies project Sullivan's quotes on the screen without him there to rebut them.

This was where Boies's skill in the clutch came back to his focus on two things in every trial: the facts and the principles of law. Explaining to any jury that is not stacked with accountants and tax attorneys the intricacies of a trust would be a hard slog. For one, trusts only exist on paper. A trust is not a place where things are physically stored, which a jury could grasp. It is a legal construct meant to protect and shield what is inside and allow those assets to be used only for specific functions. It was an imaginative leap for anyone not familiar with them. Yet this was the tack Wells was trying to take. Boies, on the other hand, continued to shy away from delving too deeply into the minutiae of the trusts. He focused instead on the *location* of the trust, which went back to how AIG kept track of it. After all, if this trust existed as AIG said it did, and if Hank Greenberg removed the stock from it as the company alleged, there would surely be documents detailing the nature of the trust. Boies worked hard to convince the jury that no such documents existed. That was his focus, for he knew every juror received a monthly bank statement. If they kept track of their accounts, how could AIG not have better proof of its right to $4.2 billion?

Boies only knew there was no second trust document through overwhelming preparation. That was why he had the confidence to challenge the foundation of AIG's case—the existence of that second trust—from the start. The hard work he put in ahead of the trial gave him the confidence under pressure. "There are no surprises for me, but you can't imagine how few people that's true for," Boies, sixty-eight, told me. For the AIG-SICO trial, there were hundreds of boxes of briefs, literally millions of pages of exhibit documents. "When we showed up for the opening statement, I had read every single exhibit we had marked before we marked it. I had read every single deposition excerpt that we had marked for offering into evidence before we marked it. I had read every single deposition line they had offered. There is no way most lawyers do that." The reason they don't is that it is time-consuming and tedious. Standard practice would be to have the second- and third-tier lawyers in the firm go through everything and brief the lead lawyer. But for Boies, having read everything gives him the chance to recall a document when his side needs it. He knows where his argument will be supported and where it will not be. He can focus on the story he wants to tell. "When I get up there, I have the confidence of knowing what the total evidence record is, and I know how far I can push it and how far I can't. I know what the limits are, and that's the way you maintain your credibility."

Getting to a level that allows him to be at ease under the pressure of a trial is not easy. There is no shortcut for putting in the work. He admits that all lawyers shade things, because that is their job as an advocate for their client. But his goal is to find facts that can stand alone. Boies has seen how quickly a misstatement can turn a jury's opinion against an otherwise honest lawyer. "Most good lawyers lose credibility in a trial not because they intentionally mislead but because they make a statement that they believe is true at the time and it is not," he said. "By being sure that I know all the stuff that's out there, I know that when I say something, I'm not misleading anyone. And I also know when I have to admit something—when they have a good fact and you have to accept it. In the AIG case, you know that there is overwhelming evidence of a trust, so you can't deny it. You need to find a way of explaining its existence that is consistent with your theory."

ENTERING THE BUBBLE

Boies worked on the SICO case for four years. Still, when he found out the date of the trial, he canceled an annual cycling trip to Europe, which he had missed only twice in twenty years. It fell a few weeks before the trial was set to open, and he told me he could not imagine how he would have felt if he had gone and lost the case. Boies is a firm believer that a person's focus can continually get sharper with preparation.

"When I was in school, I'd be cramming, and people would say, 'If you don't know it now, you'll never know it.' I always thought that was really dumb," he said. "The stuff I learn at the last minute is always the stuff I remember best. The time you have immediately before the trial is really the golden days. It's when you really know everything and you're putting it all together. You've got all the information in the world, and you can really organize things and pick your targets. Those are the days you can't replace."

Once the trial starts, Boies's focus puts him into a bubble. At times, he told me, the only people he will socialize with are lawyers on his team and the opposing team. He doesn't want to lose his edge and start thinking of other things. In the courtroom, he said he not only has no idea how the trial is going on a broader level but he does not care. "It's totally irrelevant," he said. "I judge it by how the evidence is coming in—whether you can support what is being said. You sometimes get a sense from the judge, sometimes the juries, but that's very hard." This may sound like a flip, if not patently false statement. How can the progress of the trial not be relevant? How else would he know where he stood? But that is actually one of the keys to being clutch. If Boies stopped to congratulate himself on a particularly deft cross-examination or tried to tally up where he stood, he would lose his focus. He would be out of the bubble. He is concerned more with tangible measures. Is the argument he is making working? Is it true and will it hold up under scrutiny from the opposing lawyer? Whether he is winning or losing at any given point, he said, is "a very abstract concept while it is going on. What you're really focused on is the next step, the next witness, the next argument." He joked that if the other attorney starts quoting from a document, he will often look at it again, "even though I've looked at it ten thousand times." His focus does not make him myopic. It allows him to follow the tack that he or his opponent is taking at that moment and recalibrate his argument. That is what he can control. "When you're doing a trial, you're so focused, you're not thinking about anything else," he said.

In front of the jury, none of the underlying intensity shows. He speaks to the jurors as if he were a social studies teacher and they were a gifted class. He explains the issues without condescension. He laughs for emphasis; he jokes a bit. He very rarely raises his voice. And if he really wants to drive home a point, he will have it put up on the screen so the jury can read along. "If you take something you know a lot about, you just need to get up and talk to somebody about it," he said. The first level of focus is the morality play, but the second is its direction. It has to be compelling. "By the time I've gotten to trial, I know as much about what I'm doing as people know about the things they are most used to talking about," he said to me. "All I have to do is get out of my mind the idea that it has to be structured in an artificial way. All I have to do is talk to people the way you would talk to people if they were in your living room."

THE ENDGAME

By the closing arguments in the SICO trial, nearly a month after it began, two jurors had been excused and those left looked tired. One juror had actually been sent home for repeatedly falling asleep in the jury box. It was not hard to see why. They had been listening to witnesses discuss shares and trusts. At this point, the AIG-SICO trial felt like the college survey course you could not drop—dry, boring, and long—and all the while, the beautiful summer weather was painfully visible through the jury-room window. Boies had stuck to his morality play as his way to make sense of the case and, more important, to sway jurors to his side. Wells's strategy had also remained consistent, but his way of arguing his side was closer to a fast-paced thriller, with tales of betrayal and broken promises. Their closing arguments were their last chance to jolt the jurors awake and drive home the essential points in the cases.

As I watched the two litigators square off on the last day, Boies's theory about lawyers in a trial existing in a bubble seemed to hold true. Despite the ups and downs of the past month, their closing arguments were essentially bookends, in style, tone, and substance, to their opening arguments. Before Judge Rakoff entered the courtroom, Wells, who would go first, was pantomiming his argument in front of the empty jury box. He gesticulated for effect, removed his glasses for emphasis, and walked stiff-legged back and forth in front of the imaginary jurors. Boies, who would not be up for hours, sat in front of the papers and computer screen at his table and looked to be cramming for that college final. Then the jury came in.

Wells began with a fury that only built as he went on. "SICO and Hank Greenberg breached their duty of trust," he said. "SICO and Hank Greenberg breached their duty of loyalty. The evidence of that breach is overwhelming. It is overwhelming, it is unequivocal, there is no room for doubt. It happened. The facts of this case are fairly simple." He then recounted the history of SICO and the AIG stock and delved again into the speeches Greenberg had made over the years talking about the bonuses SICO funded for AIG employees. He emphasized that this was how it had been—until Greenberg was fired. "For thirty-five years, everything worked smoothly. Stock was used to pay compensation benefits, stock was held in trust. Thirty-five years, and then something happened. What happened was that Hank Greenberg was fired. Hank Greenberg was terminated. Hank Greenberg was kicked out of the company that, as far as he was concerned, he had built. How dare they, how dare they kick me out of my company? And Hank Greenberg, when he was terminated, was angry. You heard him from that witness stand say he was angry. You saw him glare at me because first he tried to say, 'Well, I wasn't happy about it.' I said, no, you were angry. You were angry. He said, 'Yes, I was angry.'" And he glared at me. And when Hank Greenberg was terminated from his job, he struck back. He retaliated. When Hank Greenberg stepped down as chairman on March 28th, within hours—listen to me now—not days, not weeks, hours, he got on the phone, called a special meeting of the SICO voting shareholders and terminated, removed seven senior AIG executives from the SICO board. Within hours." And there it was: the CEO scorned and determined to exact his revenge. Greenberg had all the motive in the world. Wells told a compelling tale, as heated as some criminal defense trials.

To defuse Wells's very strong closing arguments, Boies told me, he decided to use some of his allotted time to begin his closing remarks as soon as Wells finished. Even though doing so meant he would only get through a small portion before the lunch break, he felt it was worth it. Why wouldn't he want to lay out his whole argument and not bits and pieces of it? Because he wanted to focus the jury on what he thought was important and dilute the power of Wells's argument. "I didn't want the jurors to go out with Ted's thoughts in their mind," Boies said. His focus was on making sure Wells's closing did not gain primacy. He had to replace the potboiler with the morality play.

"You've heard a lot this morning about lies and fabricated documents and made-up things," Boies said when he addressed the jury. "I'm going to talk to you about some of the evidence, and I think, as you will see, the evidence is real, the evidence exists, and the evidence is entirely inconsistent with the arguments from counsel that you heard this morning." In the forty-five minutes before lunch, he refuted the key points Wells had made—with a focus on who benefited from the trust, and if it was AIG, then why was there nothing in writing? That afternoon, he went through his closing arguments systematically, holding up documents, many that Wells had used, to show the opposite of what the plaintiff alleged. His style was as atypical as it had been the whole trial. He fumbled a bit, told a joke or two, laughed at parts of the case that he thought were absurd. This was his strategy, to talk to them as if they were in his living room. His focus was firmly on relating how implausible it was that AIG claimed a second trust existed without anything to prove it. He was telling a story.

Two days after the closing arguments, the jury returned its verdict. SICO had a right to the shares in the trust. Boies's focus on keeping track of your money had struck a chord with the jury, and he had won.

IT'S ALWAYS AN ORDINARY SERVE

"Drama is essential in a morality play," Boies said while relaxing at the Four Seasons Restaurant in New York a few weeks after the verdict. "But too much drama is melodrama, and nobody believes melodrama. In my view, you err on the side of less drama rather than more. It's like *The Price Is Right*—if you go one cent too high, you lose it all."

The morality play of a trial is *how* Boies focuses, how he organizes his arguments and brings together many different parts. It is a device for channeling his energies in a case and connecting with the jurors. More broadly, it shows how important it is under pressure to block out everything extraneous, every distraction, and focus on what matters. Working within the confines of a morality play about keeping track of your money is one way. Yet being focused under pressure does not mean you are oblivious to what is going on. Boies was aware of the magnitude of the AIG-SICO lawsuit from the day he took the case. If $4.2 billion had not been at stake, he knew he would not have had the resources he had, from attorneys and associates, to the technology that always pulled up the right document at the right time. In the four years leading up to the trial, he estimated, it had cost the two sides between $75 million and $150 million; each day in court cost the parties $300,000 in legal fees alone. That was a lot of pressure right there. But once the trial got under way, Boies thought of none of this. He was focused on the witness, the rebuttal, the document.

Had he thought of the magnitude of this trial or any of the megacases he has tried while he was trying them, he would have choked. "If you think in those terms, it can be disabling," he said. "You've got to try AIG against SICO just the way you would try a $100,000 case and not a $4.2 billion case, because the principles are the same. You've got to try *Bush v. Gore* just like you were trying a county commissioner's race. If you ever begin to pull back, if you ever say, 'I'm serving for the championship of the U.S. Open' as opposed to 'I'm serving in a game of tennis,' you're dead." This is an absolutely essential observation: The focus is on the task, not the glory that comes from victory.

But four years of preparation does not slide away instantly. At the end of our conversation, Boies imagined how he would have argued the case if he had been Wells. Throughout the trial, Boies had painted Greenberg as an American success story and steered the jury away from Wells's portrayal of him as a thief who had stolen money that belonged to AIG employees. Wells practically spit the words *Russia* and *China* when he talked about where Greenberg had invested the money from the SICO trust. It was a clear attempt to imply something untoward about where the money went.

"If I had been Ted, what I would have begun by saying is, 'Mr. Greenberg I want to begin by congratulating you on an exceptional life,'" he said in the same social studies–teacher tone I had heard often in court. "'You've been one of the leading business figures in the country, right?' What's he say? 'Yes.' Then I'd say, 'You built the hugest insurance company in the world right?' 'Yes.' 'And you were proud of that, very proud of that, weren't you?' 'Yes.' 'You've been a great philanthropist. You've given a lot of money away?' 'Yes.' 'You enlisted in the army in the Second World War. You landed in Normandy. You won a Bronze Star, right?' 'Indeed.'"

"In my opening, I would have begun by saying, 'This is a case about Hank Greenberg and a company he ran. I'm going to tell you right now, Hank Greenberg is an American hero. This is not a case about whether you like Hank Greenberg or don't like him, admire Hank Greenberg or don't admire him. This is a case about the fact that in 1970 Hank Greenberg and other people made a decision, and that decision was to put in trust shares that could be only used for the future betterment of other employees. That was a generous act. I commend him for that, just as I commend him for other things he did. There came a time, though, when Mr. Greenberg was asked to leave the firm he built. I'm not here to tell you if that was right or wrong. I think there were reasons for that. Mr. Greenberg was obviously hurt by that, and I can understand how he would be hurt by being asked to leave the firm he built. But this is not a question about whether you feel sorry for Mr. Greenberg or don't feel sorry for Mr. Greenberg. This is a question about the law. And the judge will tell you that you have to decide this case based on the facts. And the facts are, he set up this trust and then he violated that trust. And if you're a father and you're paying your child money and he gets mad at you, says bad things about you, damages your car, you're going to stop paying that child money. But if you set up a legal trust for that child, you can't say, "Now I'm unhappy with you" and take that trust back. Once you've put it in trust, you've given your word and given up your rights to take it away. This is just a question of saying Mr. Greenberg, like every-one else, has got to keep his word.'"

Boies was on a roll. To hear him spin out the other side was eerie. But part of his preparation had been anticipating what line Wells and his team might take. "I would not have tried to make him an evil man—*Russia, China*—that's a tough argument to make to a New York jury. They're international. They know about people investing in Russia and China, and most of the goods they get are made in China."

But then Boies paused and drew back, perhaps realizing he had argued the other side long enough: "Like everything, there are different ways to do it," he said with a wry smile.

That was a different morality play—one based on honoring your commitments. He had focused on telling a story about keeping track of what was yours, and it had paid off for his client. Under pressure, Boies had a solid foundation to be ready for whatever tack Wells took, but he also never wavered in his focus. That is the basis for any clutch performance.

[2]

DISCIPLINE

When the Stakes Are as High
as They Can Be

THE SENATE PERMANENT Subcommittee on Investigations called Mark Branson to testify. It didn't matter that he worked in Zurich or that he was British. The committee wanted him in Washington for a hearing on offshore accounts, and he had little choice in the matter. Created in 1952, PSI, as it is known, has broad powers to investigate companies in the United States and abroad, with a particular emphasis on "investment fraud schemes, security fraud, computer fraud and the use of offshore banking and corporate facilities to carry out criminal objectives." The PSI, in the summer before the 2008 election season, was a platform for senators to posture and preen, take a few cheap shots at the witnesses, and make long-winded pronouncements in the guise of questions. For the person on the other side of the table, it wasn't as freewheeling. He generally had to sit there and take what came his way, invariably looking increasingly anxious and on edge the longer he was there. The best any witness could hope for, really, was a draw.

Mark Branson, the chief financial officer for UBS global wealth management division, which managed money for some of the richest people in the world, was there because the Department of Justice and the Internal Revenue Service were investigating the firm's offshore business. A former UBS banker had turned informant and was telling the government what he knew about secret Swiss accounts U.S. citizens had set up to shield money from taxes. As the CFO of the Swiss bank's highest-profile division—and the one where the secret accounts were kept—Branson had been called in to explain the firm's position. It was not a trip anyone would have made voluntarily, but with extensive operations in the United States, the bank had no choice. It had a U.S. banking license, and Carl Levin, Democrat from Michigan and the committee's chairman, had made noises about reevaluating it. The U.S. government had already detained Martin Liechti, a Swiss citizen and UBS's Zurich-based head of wealth management for the Americas. His passport had been confiscated when he tried to change planes in Miami. Branson, as a British citizen, may have been worried about the possibility of his own detention, but his primary concern was about the future of UBS. Its banking license was literally hanging on what he had to say.

The morning's testimony in the Dirksen Office Building was like a game of whack-a-mole: Each witness, an accused tax evader, stood up in turn and got slapped down by the presiding senators. The exception was the new IRS commissioner, Douglas H. Shulman, who simply laid the blame for lax tax enforcement on his predecessor. Then again, a group of tax cheats could only say so much in front of a Senate panel, let alone one chaired by two men desperate to score points a few months ahead of an election. Levin needed to show struggling autoworkers back in Michigan that he was tough on Wall Street, while the ranking Republican member, Norm Coleman, was locked in a close reelection bid and needed to show voters in Minnesota that he had their interests at heart.

Early in the hearing, UBS was not doing well. Liechti, tan from his Miami confinement, had already choked under the pressure of Senate scrutiny. Since being picked up, he had been living in legal limbo: not charged with a crime but detained in the United States with no way of knowing when he might be released. His testimony consisted of invoking the Fifth Amendment in a garbled, accented English that belied his role as a private banker to the world's richest families. It was tough to fault him for that: Aiding and abetting criminal tax fraud carried serious penalties, and broken English was probably the best way to deliver a halting defense.

After making someone as sophisticated as Liechti stumble and mumble like a child, Senators Levin and Coleman looked poised for an all-out victory. The pressure was on Branson: He could win it or lose it for his employer. He began humbly, thanking Senators Levin and Coleman for the chance to testify and giving his background at UBS. "I am the chief financial officer of our global wealth management and our Swiss businesses located in Zurich," he said, speaking fluidly but deliberately. "I have been with UBS since 1997 and in my current position for five months. Prior to this, I was chief executive officer of UBS in Japan."

This was a masterful setup. Branson had not been at his role long enough to have known what had happened. Instead of hiding behind this, as the IRS's Shulman had done, he accepted full oversight responsibility for what PSI was investigating: "I am now responsible for finance and risk control, including financial reporting of our performance, and our maintenance of a strong compliance framework for our wealth management business worldwide." In other words, he would have been the person to answer for all of the problems the bank was in, had he been in the role at that time. He wasn't, but he could fix things going forward.

Senators Levin and Coleman were listening intently. Branson was reading from a carefully prepared text, but it sounded as if he were speaking extemporaneously. I knew that he and his team of spokesmen and attorneys had been sequestered in a Washington hotel room preparing until well past midnight, but his statement did not sound scripted. Branson's voice was clear and strong; he was completely composed. Earlier in his career, he had been UBS's chief communications officer—the man charged with getting the bank's message across in the best light or shielding it from scrutiny when it did something wrong. One of Branson's former colleagues told me later that he imagined he had written the entire speech himself, so great was his reputation for spinning bad news to the firm's advantage. This wasn't said in a derogatory manner; it was said as a compliment from someone envious of his skill. What Branson clearly had here was remarkable discipline, in both delivering his message and saying precisely what he meant. Discipline served him well in the clutch.

"I am here to make absolutely clear that UBS genuinely regrets any compliance failures that may have occurred," he said. "We will take responsibility for them; we will not seek to minimize them. On behalf of UBS, I am apologizing, and committing to you that we will take the actions necessary to see that this does not happen again."

This was the type of full-out mea culpa the senators wanted to hear. It took discipline to pull it off, and it stood in stark contrast to the cavalcade of Fifth Amendment pleas and the desperate attempt by the IRS commissioner to blame someone else. Here was Branson, on behalf of UBS, saying his firm had done wrong. And now he was going to offer details on how it would fix things. First, it was closing the offshore banking business to U.S. citizens. And second, it would work with the U.S. government to determine the clients "who may have engaged in tax fraud." The disciplined wording of this second entreaty was key. Part of UBS's many problems stemmed from being caught between two legal systems: The United States expected UBS to recognize its subpoena power, even in Zurich, and turn over the information it wanted. But Swiss law made it a crime to disclose any client information unless there was an indication of tax fraud, a higher bar than just tax evasion. His carefully worded concessions allowed him to thread the needle between two legal systems while making the presiding senators feel as if they were extracting something from him. In doing so, he acknowledged the committee's power and stroked the senators' egos. He also lulled them into thinking they were achieving more than they were. That was when he dropped the boom.

"Chairman Levin, I know that you and Senator Coleman object to banks providing cross-border services to U.S. clients with accounts that do not require the filing of a Form W-9 with the IRS. But, respectfully, this cross-border business was—and is—entirely legal in both Switzerland and the United States," he said in the same calm, direct voice he had used throughout. "Unless or until those rules are changed, that is the framework with which we and other banks must comply."

He was pushing back. He had given ground, then reasserted the bank's prerogatives. The subtext was that the bank had gone right up to the line of legality, but it was a line that had been drawn by the IRS. If they drew it wrong or did not draw it clearly enough, it wasn't UBS's fault. The bank had adhered to the letter, if not the intent, of the law. Whatever one thinks about the merits of the charges, about tax evasion and Senate inquiries, about corporations skirting responsibility, Branson showed tremendous discipline in making his case and defending his firm. Then, to drive home his point, he made sure the senators understood just what UBS meant to the faltering U.S. economy: "UBS is committed to taking both corrective and disciplinary measures. Mr. Chairman, as you know, we have nearly thirty-two thousand U.S. employees out of some eighty thousand around the world. They are understandably alarmed by the reports of misconduct that they have seen. They want to know that such misconduct does not belong in UBS, and that the firm's ethics match their own. I am here today to tell you and to tell them that no, that kind of misconduct does not belong in UBS. And further, that by exiting this business, we have taken a major step, designed to ensure that this misconduct will not be repeated and that this matter can be properly resolved." Branson had made it clear that UBS was willing to make changes, but he was willing to concede only so much. And then, for good measure, he reiterated just how many people the firm employed in the United States, lest the senators go on some rant about foreign companies. The implication was clear: Nearly half of UBS's employees were voting U.S. citizens, and their jobs would disappear if anything happened to the bank's license.

Senator Levin had little more he could say. But after the hearing, he sent out a chest-thumping press release, reiterating his praise for his committee's good work. "UBS's surprise stance at the hearing provides a dramatic example of how Congressional oversight can help stop offshore abuses," Levin said. "If UBS lives up to its promises, it is prepared to trade in bank secrecy for transparency, the rule of law, and tax cooperation. The rest of the banking industry in Switzerland and elsewhere should follow its lead."

THE PRACTICE OF DISCIPLINE

At the outset of the hearing, UBS seemed to be in deep trouble and possibly on the verge of facing a full-blown Senate inquiry. By the end of his testimony, Branson had made his firm look honorable and, just as important, let the senators feel that they had accomplished something. This outcome took extreme discipline and rested entirely on Branson's testimony. He had prepared for his statement just as David Boies does for his trials. He was focused on retaining UBS's banking license. That was paramount. But then he showed tremendous discipline under Senate scrutiny. He knew he had to give the senators something, and he did. But he was careful not to give too much. Consider how he introduced himself to the committee. It was full of nuance. The term "Swiss businesses" was code for offshore, non-taxpaying accounts. They were held by the tax cheats the Senate wanted to track down, but he certainly did not highlight that. Like the IRS commissioner, Branson also admitted that he was new to the job of CFO; but this was part of his strategy to lower expectations, not skirt responsibility. He did not use his brief tenure to pass the buck back to someone who was long gone. What Branson promised UBS would do in front of the Senate PSI was equally masterful. Closing the offshore business for U.S. clients sounded like a magnanimous gesture. It made the senators feel that their hearing was accomplishing something. What they didn't know was that the firm had announced it was closing this business almost a year earlier and that it made up about 1 percent of the firm's earnings. Frankly it had become a massive headache to UBS. Yet Branson made a grand spectacle in announcing the closing of a business that was for all intents and purposes already closed, and in doing so, he let the senators feel they had forced the bank to do this. It was a particularly savvy move and made the early, Fifth Amendment–invoking witnesses the only target of the Senate's wrath.

Branson was only able to accomplish what he did because he maintained an unshakable discipline. This is a skill that builds on focus and is a constant among people who are great in the clutch. It is often the difference between success and failure when someone is under intense scrutiny. Had Branson grown defensive, Levin and Coleman would have pounced. But he maintained his discipline. He stayed on message and he ran the gauntlet. In doing this, he bested a Senate committee and ensured that his firm would make it through this set of problems scathed but with its most important asset, a license to continue to do banking business, intact.

THE PARADOX OF SHOOTERS

Discipline is almost always a battle against yourself. You may be in front of a Senate committee, but the true battle is against your own will. Members of the Olympic riflery team in the 1970s realized this when they sought out Ari Kiev with a simple question: How could they calm themselves enough to shoot as well in competition as they did in practice? As the first psychiatrist on the U.S. Sports Medicine Committee, his task was to teach top amateur athletes how to perform under the stress of elite competition. At the time, sports psychology was little known and less understood. Many were suspicious of psychiatry in general, and several athletes begged off working with him. One exception was the riflery team. They went to him because they knew their success was based on becoming more disciplined. They knew they needed to master their emotions to achieve success under pressure. Unlike hockey or soccer players, riflemen had no opposing player and no team to fall back on. What they did was not physically strenuous like skiing or track and field. A rifleman simply had to stand in competition and shoot the same way he stood and shot in practice. And the setting never really changed: A shooting range was a shooting range, and it was not as if spectators were cheering or jeering when the riflemen shot. There should have been no reason why a person could not shoot a target in competition just as easily as he hit it in practice.

But the best in the world missed. In the clutch, the pressure got to them. And that was where Kiev, a Harvard- and Cornell-trained psychiatrist, came in. The reality was that target shooting was akin to sports that had a moment where all the pressure was on someone to execute a simple, repeatable action: the basketball free throw, the extra point in football, the tennis serve, or the tee shot in golf, where you could set the ball up however you wanted it.

"I was interested in learning how to help them manage stress," Kiev told me. "I looked at what helped them focus and not get distracted."

Working with them, he gained a greater understanding of how pressure affected someone at the highest level. What they did was a pure example of how being disciplined affected their success or failure in competition. He found that the key for the riflery team was to learn to shoot between breaths. This was something they could focus on and, with discipline, control. But he learned as much from them as they learned from him. Kiev began to develop a series of weekend seminars that he called Life Strategy Workshops. They lasted for two days and gave participants a chance to "explore what was going on in their lives, what was working, what was not, how things could work better, what were the life principles they brought from the past that colored their worldview," Kiev said. He wanted to show people that the baggage they carried from their past could hold them back in the future. Kiev argued that it distracted them and hurt their ability to make key decisions in the present. While such thinking may seem quaint today, it stirred debate in the early 1980s. And there was a broader lesson to it. Kiev was a serious medical scientist, not some snake-oil salesman. He was trying to get people to realize that when it came to making big decisions under pressure, they failed because they lacked the discipline to evaluate their choices in the present, without interference from the past. This interference could come from a family crisis—a bad childhood, a difficult relationship—just as it could come from a decision that had not turned out as the person thought it would—a missed shot.

After one of these seminars, a little-known options trader named Steven Cohen approached Kiev, and that meeting changed both of their lives. Initially Cohen wanted to know how he could become better at what he did. Cohen managed a team at Gruntal & Co., an old Wall Street trading house. Legend had it that he made $8,000 on his first day, fresh out of his undergraduate years at Wharton. That was 1978, and he was soon turning six-figure profits daily at a time when this was a substantial amount for a trader. Yet when the two met, Cohen was like Tiger Woods at age twenty, vastly talented but still a few years away from becoming dominant. That transition began in 1992 when he founded his own firm, SAC Capital Advisors, in Stamford, Connecticut, with $25 million and nine employees. He asked Kiev to come in and talk to the firm. And then he kept bringing him back. When Kiev left the firm seventeen years later, SAC had eight hundred employees and managed some $15 billion. Cohen himself had an estimated net worth in the billions. "Their emphasis has always been on cooperation, hard work, digging, reviewing the game films, and staying focused," Kiev told me.

Bald, fleshy, and five feet eight inches tall, Cohen would not be mistaken for an Olympic athlete. He grew up in an average family on Long Island but with an abiding interest in how the stock market worked. With his piercing blue eyes and fierce intellect, though, he became one of the most successful hedge fund traders of all time. His firm became known as much for its outsize profits year after year as for its secrecy and hardball tactics. Each day, he and his colleagues had to make clutch decisions that earned or lost the firm tens, if not hundreds of millions of dollars. Yet it was their continued profits, through good economic times and bad, that drew acclaim and scrutiny.

At the center of it all was a fierce discipline. At least once a year, Kiev told me he sat down with each trader in the highly secretive firm and asked him what his goal was. How much money did he want to make that year? There was no wrong answer. But it was a useful measure to see who was too cautious and who was too optimistic in his assumptions. It also helped give those traders longer-term goals. That was important to keep them from becoming fixated on what happened in one day of trading. "The plan gives you a target," he said. "It gives you a sense of how many positions you need, how big each one has to be, how much risk management is involved, how much work you need to do. It provides a framework." Yet, he added, the plan was not everything and could be limiting. "Sometimes people get hung up on the goal," he said. This was why creating a culture of discipline was important. It gave the person something else to concentrate on. It was more finite. It was also easier for someone to think about making 5 percent on a single trade than it was for them to make 40 percent for the year. Discipline allowed them to break down the goal into its component parts.

Everything else radiated out from that conversation. Under the fluctuating pressures of daily trading, a person needed to set a goal for a particular trade. Let's say it was 15 percent. The trader would then have to have the discipline to sell when the trade made 15 percent. The gain could come in an hour, take all day, or not materialize for several days, weeks, or months. Whenever the trader made that 15 percent, he had to sell, particularly if he made it quickly. That was essential. If the trader made the 15 percent in an hour, the tendency would be to wait and see if he could make even more. Sometimes he would, but other times he wouldn't. Either way his discipline had failed. He had information that told him the trade should go up 15 percent. That was when he should sell. Making more than that was not a good thing because there was no data to support that gain. Let's say the trade went to 17 percent and the trader stayed in because he now thought it would go to 20 percent, but then it suddenly dropped to 14 percent because of information he did not have or simply because of the vagaries of the marketplace. Now the trader might feel he needed to remain in the trade to get back to 15 percent. But what he failed to see was the scenario had changed. The previous one, which made him believe the trade could go to 15 percent, was not the one that he was in now. The information driving the trade had changed. This left the trader with two options. He could either sell at 14 percent or hope the trade went back up. The risk was, it could fall further, and the trader would get sucked down.

On the other hand, the trade might fail from the start. After all, not every trade works out as planned. Kiev stressed that the best traders are right only 60 percent of the time. So they need to adhere to what is called a stop-loss provision in their trades. Simply put, the stop-loss provision sets a level of loss at which they must sell regardless of why they think the trade has gone down. If their limit was negative 20 percent, they needed to have the discipline to sell if the trade went down 20 percent, even if they were convinced the trade could come back. This discipline, Kiev said, highlighted the difference between a good and a great trader. The good one is still right half the time. The difference is, when the great trader is right, he makes more money than he loses when he is wrong. He has the discipline to sell, and that is clutch.

"You've got to consider what's changed," Kiev said. "The best traders are the ones who are willing to set a target and are willing to do the work to reach that target."

When it came to a trader's overall portfolio, goals were set for that, as well. The simplest was, How much did the trader want to increase his portfolio in, say, six months? If it was 30 percent, the question then became Was it easier to have one trade that added 30 percent, three trades that added 10 percent each, or six that added 5 percent? The answer varied, depending on the trader himself and what he was doing, but it pointed to the essence of decision making under pressure: To be clutch again and again, you needed to have discipline. "That model gives you a tremendous capacity for dealing with the inherent stress of the unpredictability and fluctuations of markets," he said. "It gives people a target."

Having the discipline to stick to the target was important because Kiev knew that the ability to make clutch decisions became exponentially more difficult as the pressure mounted. "In this high-stress activity, how you manage the process is critical to managing the stress," he said. "As the stress gets greater, the ability to think rationally declines. Some people can pull themselves out of this by themselves." But others could not. And that was where discipline helped people sell and buy within a set of parameters. That takes a lot of the emotion out of it. Instead of eliminating the stress that clouds clutch decisions, discipline helps manage it and, in this case, allowed the trader to achieve the desired outcome. Until the bull market collapse of 2008, investors in SAC were earning a 40 percent annual return on their money. This was the amount *after* SAC took its 3 percent annual fee and 50 percent cut of the profits. This meant that some years the firm made close to 100 percent on the money it managed, something few other investment vehicles have ever approached over such a prolonged period of time.

THE WIZARD OF DISCIPLINE

The culture of discipline at SAC came from the top. Cohen, according to a rare interview with Jack D. Schwager for his book *Stock Market Wizards* in 2001, sits in the center of a massive trading floor. He has eight computer screens open in front of him and calls orders out to the traders around him. In that interview, Cohen made it clear that he gives his traders autonomy: "I don't want to tell my traders what to do. I don't have a corner on what's right," Cohen said. "All I want to do is make sure they have the same facts that I do, and if they still want to do the trade, then they can. I encourage my guys to play around. I have to."

Implicit in this was the expectation that his traders be immensely knowledgeable about what they were trading. This knowledge removed some of the gut instinct that traders once beat their chests about having. Instead of saying they felt something, they could say they knew something. It is a subtle but important difference. Still, if that something turned out to be wrong, they needed the same discipline to reverse their position. Cohen spoke of the "catalyst" that motivated each trade. "Most traders want to trade everything. One minute they are trading Yahoo!, the next Exxon," he said. "My place operates very differently. I want my traders to be highly focused. I want them to know a lot about something, instead of a little about everything."

This is where Kiev's system of discipline was meant to work for the withdrawn and the flamboyant trader alike. For a firm like SAC to be successful year after year, it could not have only one type of person trading all types of securities. It needed the cautious and the reckless, the plodders and the grandstanders, the person who was an expert on interest rates and the guy who knew everything about exotic securities. And then the firm needed to create a culture so they could coexist and—since what they were doing was not pediatric oncology—make a lot of money. That was the reward for their discipline. "As much as you think these guys are risk takers, they tend to hold back more than overcommit," Kiev told me. "They want to win."

Someone who looked to trade across many industries and types of securities could not have that same cool confidence that comes from so much specific knowledge. If something wasn't going well in one area, the impulse would be to switch to another one. That is the complete opposite of the discipline needed to be great. Still, Kiev did not think someone who was overly cautious could be good as a trader. By choice of their profession, they had to be risk takers. The objective was for them to be *informed* risk takers. That way when the pressure increased, Cohen's band of traders would have the discipline to make clutch decisions backed by knowledge. This was not the case with the traders who existed on gut instinct: They may think of themselves as being more heroic, even clutch, but in the long run they were setting themselves up to lose more. That was the difference. "Steve Cohen is very intense, very focused, unflappable, continually willing to raise the bar," Kiev told me. "He's not driven by trying to outdo other people. I think he's driven by the need to do it as well as he can do it."

CONFUSING DISCIPLINE AND INSTINCT

To understand how essential being disciplined is to being clutch, you have to consider how trading was conducted before huge hedge funds like SAC changed the landscape. This is not ancient history, and at many less specialized firms it is not even history: Trading from the gut continues to get mixed results.

It was certainly the mantra in the mid-1990s when William Mumma was a partner and global head of derivatives at Bankers Trust. At the time, BT was a well-regarded firm, particularly for its trading of derivatives, instruments that were then used mostly to manage a risk or exploit an opportunity. Mumma was a gut guy by training but came to see that discipline, over many other attributes ascribed to traders, was key to success in the clutch. His problem was that not everyone had come around to this line of thinking.

"We wanted Delta Force guys, chess masters, Olympic gold medalists," he said of his early hiring strategy. "We went hunting for these guys. We thought there had to be some makeup for people who would be great traders. There isn't. I never found any pattern in the people."

What he found was a level of resilience that all good but not necessarily great traders have. Any trader who made a lot of money would whistle his way into the office the next day, but that did not make him a great trader. The best ones were the ones who could lose a lot of money and still be ready to trade when the markets opened again. Their common trait was they didn't like to fail, which is different from disliking losing. All traders lose at some point, but it doesn't mean they failed. It means they lost on a particular day. The better traders figured out how to avoid losing strategies, those that not only lead to losses in a single day, but failure down the road.

Mumma reversed his assumptions. There were two reasons people got A's at Harvard or became Navy Seals, and only one of those reasons made them good traders. Some prepared and studied harder, which would not necessarily help them. They did not expect to lose ever—in life, in school, in work. This was not possible in trading. But others, he told me, were innately better at pushing themselves to succeed. They didn't fear failure; they hated it. What this meant in practical terms was, the great trader who lost millions of dollars one day would come in the next morning having thought about what had happened and determined not to make the same mistake again. This doesn't mean he changed his strategy or that the one that day worked perfectly either. But if this person was a great trader, he would have the discipline to discard a bad strategy and find a better one—and even if that one failed, at least it failed in a different way. The distinguishing factor was between the trader who got A's at Harvard because he was super-prepared and the one who did so after faltering along the way. The latter was the trader who was truly resilient. The former had succeeded in avoiding failure. That is not possible in trading; everyone makes a bad trade at some point. The more resilient performer understood that and was able to remain disciplined and adapt to the changing situations.

"People won't exit a trade because they have a fear of being inconsistent," Mumma told me. "It's an irrational commitment. People lose a lot of money because they don't back away."

What makes Mumma's assessment so interesting is that it was a lack of discipline and a good deal of irrational behavior that hobbled Bankers

Trust in 1996 and arguably opened the door for Deutsche Bank to acquire it. At the time, BT was the subject of an intense investigation into how salesmen in its derivatives operation misled clients. An investigation into the firm commissioned by four regulatory bodies cited systemic wrong-doing. It said: "To a few of these employees, the customers' interests were often secondary. Others were well intentioned but inexperienced and undertrained for their positions. A few were venal and engaged in mis-conduct to further their self-interest." Mumma faulted senior manage-ment for not seeing the magnitude of the crisis. He believed they should have been more involved in order to see firsthand what was happening.

When I spoke to Mumma before the Great Recession had bottomed out, he had come out of retirement to head the brokerage unit and be the chief executive officer at the U.S. arm of Mitsubishi UFJ Securities. He was still in a temporary office, and his trading floor was still under con-struction. (This is only relevant because, spend any time with a trader at any trading house, and the first thing he will want to show you is his trading floor, like an exotic sports car or expensive watch.) Mumma was reflective and talked about how he knew when a trader was in over his head. His theory lacked the academic foundation that Kiev's approach had, but it got to the same issues.

Mumma had been a trader before he became a manager. He said there was a feeling you'd get when you were in over your head and your trade was not working out. Time slowed down. It became difficult to breathe. The room literally began to swirl but in slow motion. That, Mumma said, was when money was being lost. The longer this feeling lasted, the more money could disappear. "There's this moment of intense fear—even though you're not going to be taken down to the basement and tortured," he said. No trader got flogged, but if he wasn't seasoned enough to know he had to start selling whatever was overwhelming him, someone had to do it for him. He had lost his discipline. The best ones knew the feeling and knew what to do—sell—until it passed. The less experienced ones froze in the clutch, like a small child who has slipped into water above his head: No matter how much that trader tried to get out, he would thrash around until someone reached down to save him. That was Mumma's job, to pull people out. He could see the "stress signals" then. "I'd talk to them about kids, sports, games, office furniture, anything but trading," he said. "That's how you tell if something's wrong. I did my risk management by walking the floor." This was based on how he himself had felt as a trader. When he was losing money, he couldn't eat. "Most people will let their stomach or their stress determine their risk," he said.

Yet this response was based on a sense. It was quite literally a gut response. But just because you felt you should sell didn't mean that you should. "The feeling to get out is a false signal unless the catalyst has changed," Kiev told me. "Past ideas are holding us up. Oftentimes it's some fantasy or unrealistic notion about themselves or their concern about other people's expectations. It has nothing to do with trading. Self-doubt holds people back. Or they're not fully engaged in what they're doing."

This is where Kiev's approach to being disciplined is agnostic. It does not depend on what or how you trade, because at the end of the day, you always need to have the discipline to buy or sell under pressure.

A VARIATION ON DISCIPLINE

Eight months after his initial testimony, Mark Branson was back before the Senate PSI. This time, the mood was different. The election had come and gone, and the Democrats were one Senate seat away from Filibuster-proof control of both houses of Congress and the presidency. That seat happened to belong to Senator Coleman, and he was back in Minnesota, mired in a recount. Senator Levin, on the other hand, felt he could take an even harder line on Wall Street. By March 2009, the financial crisis had deepened, with no end in sight. His constituents—autoworkers and union bosses—were angry. A part of the country was against the bailout of General Motors and Chrysler, but his constituents were against anything that reeked of helping Wall Street.

Even in this more hostile environment, Branson was unflappable. He reiterated that UBS officers had made good on their commitments, but he used the strictures of Swiss law to explain why they had not been able to provide the United States with more information more quickly. He leaned hard on his previous testimony so as not to be contradicted. "We've acknowledged there are clients who used inappropriate structures," he said. When his statement was read back to him, Branson just listened. When asked a question, he answered. At times, he looked appropriately uncomfortable, but he never said more than he had to. Nor would he discuss other tax havens—he was there, after all, to speak for UBS. At one point, Levin tried to twist him up with a hypothetical situation about UBS handing over client information if Swiss law did not prohibit it. Branson responded that the exchange of information between governments was always governed by treaties and he would not speculate on something that could never happen. Whereas his first testimony was about keeping UBS's banking license and seeming cooperative, this appearance was about not contradicting what he had already said. If anything, it required even more discipline to stay on message than it had to confront the initial questions about UBS's offshore accounts. The senatorial posturing was far greater this time, but UBS's banking license was not on the line, and the firm had nothing new to offer. Branson had already made it through the truly clutch moment; if he kept calm in this appearance before the Senate committee, the only thing at stake was his feelings.

Having the discipline to withstand a Senate grilling and to make millions of dollars trading securities may seem to be very different skills. But they are both exercises in immense self-control. The trader who deviates from his plan could find himself losing far more than he expected, just as Branson would have found his firm drawn into more Senate questioning had he been riled up by Levin's badgering. Instead of taking the bait, Branson remained disciplined and calm. He answered the questions posed to him, but he said no more. He knew, with the U.S. economy and job market at their worst levels in decades, there was no longer a real possibility that UBS could lose its banking license. That would cost thirty-two thousand jobs. Levin just needed to look tough for the voters back home and Branson had the discipline to be his whipping boy.

That UBS would eventually turn over names of some tax cheats did not diminish Branson's effectiveness. It could have been much worse.

Like Steve Cohen and the other traders Kiev worked with, Branson made a reasoned decision based on the information available to him, and he had the discipline to see it through to the end. It was not all that different from getting out of a trade when it went up the amount you expected, no sooner, no later. That is why discipline is the second core principle of being clutch. It helps you stand your ground and see yourself through a situation when the pressure is intense. "You've got to begin to trust yourself," Kiev told me. "The truly great ones are less distracted." They are less distracted because discipline helps them maintain their bearings and that allows them to be clutch when others choke.

[3]

ADAPTING
Fighting the Fight, Not the Plan

ON APRIL 7, 2004, a U.S. Marine convoy was driving through the Sunni Triangle in Iraq. At that point in the war, this area, south of Fallujah in Al Anbar province, was considered one of the deadliest parts of the country. The Marines guarding it, part of the elite First Reconnaissance Battalion, were used to being sent into dangerous spots. They are the equivalent of Navy Seals or Army Special Forces and, like them, are trained to be alert and ready for battle at any moment. As the convoy moved through the desert, the morning was like any other: hot, dry, and stressful. Then the ambush began. From along the Euphrates River, some forty to sixty insurgents fired on the fifteen-vehicle convoy. A rocket-propelled grenade crippled the lead vehicle, causing the other vehicles to stop behind it. The convoy was under massive enemy fire. Mortar and machine-gun fire had disabled the Humvee carrying Sergeant Willie Copeland, a team leader, and his men. Before they could get pinned down, Copeland jumped out and led the five men out of the line of fire and toward an open field. Firing as they ran toward the wide, murky river in front of them, they started to counterattack the insurgents' position. But the insurgents had been waiting for them and were well entrenched. Since they had the upper hand in the ambush, there was no reason for them to retreat. Even by laying down a stream of fire, Copeland and his men could not dislodge them.

Copeland knew this. He knew firepower wasn't enough, so he continued to advance across the field. Leading his men across a deep, muddy canal, he got close enough to the insurgent positions to lob hand grenades into their machine-gun nest. Ten were killed, and the force of the counterattack prompted others to beat a retreat. Still under sporadic fire, Copeland noticed his men tending to Captain Brent Morel, his commanding officer. Morel had been hit in the chest and was barely moving. Copeland ordered the rest of his men to take cover while he lay across Morel to protect him from additional fire. Once he was able to move him to a safer spot, Copeland tried to bandage up his CO, tried to do anything to stanch the flow of blood until an armored Humvee arrived to evacuate him. Instead of getting in himself, Copeland led the withdrawal of his men, providing hand grenade cover as they retreated.

A year later, on April 21, 2005, Copeland was presented with the Navy Cross, the highest honor the Navy gives for valor and second only to the Medal of Honor, in recognition of his "extraordinary heroism." The citation detailed his actions during the firefight and ended with this commendation: "By his bold leadership, wise judgment, and complete dedication to duty, Sergeant Copeland reflected great credit upon himself and upheld the highest traditions of the Marine Corps and the United States Naval Service."

Yet to call his actions heroic is to understate how remarkable they were. Heroes put themselves at risk to save children trapped in buildings or throw themselves on grenades to save their comrades in war. What Copeland did involved strategic decision making under the most extreme pressure. Think through his actions. One, his Humvee was hit by enemy fire, and he led his men out of the vehicle to attack the enemy. They did not seek cover. They began to move strategically across an open field, over the berms and through the muck that lay between them and the insurgents. Two, he led from the front yet maintained the presence of mind to keep his team tightly behind him. He was throwing grenades right along with them. Three, while his goal was to stop the insurgents, he realized the more important task was saving his commanding officer,

Captain Morel. Four, he alone shielded Morel and bandaged his wounds, ordering his men to seek cover. Five, instead of getting into the armored Humvee, he stayed with his men and led the withdrawal, lobbing grenades for cover. Six, his team killed thirty insurgents at the cost of only one U.S. life. Seven, and most important of all, throughout all of this, Copeland maintained presence of mind. He wasn't calm. He was operating at maximum alertness but doing so without letting the stress of the situation overwhelm him. And he was doing this through a variety of unrelated actions: evacuating, running, attacking, shooting, throwing, tending to Morel, ordering his men to cover, leading the withdrawal. In short, with bullets flying around him, he never lost the ability to adapt under the pressure of a life-and-death situation.

RESPONSE AND ANTICIPATION

Copeland possessed an exceptionable ability to respond to a rapidly changing situation. This ability to adapt is the third component to being clutch, but his ability to adapt so quickly was particularly remarkable. How did he do what he did under such extreme conditions? Was it his training or something more? Before answering these questions, let's consider a different type of adaptability, one built more on anticipation than response.

Early in the 1992 presidential campaign, Christopher Falkenberg, in his second year as a Secret Service agent, found himself assigned to guard a Southern governor named Bill Clinton. This might seem like a plum job, and it was, especially for someone so young and inexperienced. But he got the assignment largely because no one thought Clinton could win. At the time, he was not the leading Democratic contender, and few expected him to be. The front-runner was Paul Tsongas, the former Massachusetts senator, followed by either Jerry Brown, the former governor of California who was derisively called Moonbeam, or Bob Kerry, the rakish businessman-senator from Nebraska. Clinton was an unknown outside of Arkansas when he made his first appearance on CBS's *60 Minutes* to rebut an allegation of an extramarital affair, his wife, Hillary, at his side. Falkenberg did not care whom he was guarding; he was thrilled to be part of his security detail, even if he figured it wouldn't last long. He had wanted to be a Secret Service agent since he was a kid growing up in Westchester County, New York. Guarding anybody at that point was a stepping-stone. It was a way to get noticed and secure a promotion later. Granted, as soon as Clinton conceded defeat, Falkenberg would be sent back to the New York office and resume his days doing the less glamorous job of the Secret Service—monitoring counterfeit currency. But there were not many twenty-five-year-olds who got to guard a presidential candidate, even one who was a long shot.

Then the improbable happened. The large crowds at Clinton's events started to translate into better numbers in the primaries. And by the time he won California in June, he had turned his campaign around, with very little time to spare. A month later, the Democrats held their convention in New York and nominated Clinton, the unlikely Southern governor from a town called Hope, to be their party's presidential candidate. Falkenberg's detail suddenly got a boost.

It was during a California campaign stop that it ran into trouble. Every Secret Service agent knows there are no such things as routine stops when they are guarding someone. If they are assigned to protect that person, he is by definition a possible target. While Falkenberg made it clear to me that a candidate was not a president and certainly not the president of the United States, the protocols are still tight. The service only began protecting candidates after Robert F. Kennedy was shot while giving a victory speech in Los Angeles after winning the California primary in 1968. At the time, candidates had to provide their own protection, and Kennedy had All-Pro defensive tackle Rosey Grier guarding him.

At the USC event in the spring of 1992, the Secret Service had protocols in place to keep people like Sirhan Sirhan out, but no outdoor event could be totally secure. Once Clinton was in motion, his detail began to check who was around him quite physically. "You're always touching people—'Hi, how you doing? Thanks for coming out today, great to see you. Can I look in there?'" he told me, while patting down my shoulders and torso as he would anyone in a crowd around his protectee.

"People are genuinely excited when they're meeting someone famous," Falkenberg said. "What you're looking for is the person who is distant, who is completely inside of himself. That's the person who is planning something." Clinton's greatest asset as a politician—his desire to mingle and talk to voters—provoked the greatest fear among his protectors. A rope line, as the meet-and-greets are called, opened the protectee up to potential threats all around him. It was a difficult situation to control; there were too many variables.

"Everything was normal," remembered Falkenberg, who was number one that day. His number meant he was next to Clinton. Each agent on protection knows his role by the number he gets. There are no *Reservoir Dogs* debates in the Secret Service: Number eight does what number eight is supposed to do, without complaining like Mr. Pink. The idea behind this numbering is to allow any agent to fill in for any other on a given day. While the weather and settings may be different, the person who was number eight always had the same role. This plug-and-play model was a great asset to an agent under the extreme pressure of guarding someone.

At the end of the line, Clinton should have gotten into the waiting SUV, but he saw more well-wishers to greet, so he drifted off course. This was not in itself a problem. The Secret Service system is built to adapt. The agents protecting their person know how to move out and continue to secure an area. As Clinton walked down a side path, a person in the crowd held on to his hand and would not let go. "He was saying stuff like, 'C'mon, you inhaled, I know you inhaled,'" Falkenberg recalled. "I was pretty sure the guy was stoned." Falkenberg didn't do anything, yet. If a member of Marine Recon was at risk of making a policy decision anytime he shot his rifle in an Iraqi street, a Secret Service agent was under similar pressure when free speech was layered over his responsibilities. Their job was not to filter out hecklers, stop protests of any sort, or censor what their protectee hears; it was simply to protect that person. If an agent ever has to take out his gun and fire into a crowd, Falkenberg repeatedly emphasized, something has gone seriously wrong.

"I heard Clinton say, 'He won't let go,'" Falkenberg told me. "That was the only thing I heard. I know that's not possible. There were thousands of people cheering around me. But I remember those words, and I reacted."

Within seconds, the overzealous supporter or opponent—it didn't matter what he was—was writhing on the ground, and Clinton had been whisked down the rope line and shunted into a waiting SUV. Falkenberg, who is five feet seven inches tall and weighs 150 pounds, grabbed the man's forearm and pulled his thumb back with such force that the man collapsed, his thumb dislocated and his radius bone fractured, Falkenberg would find out later. This was what he had been drilled to do until it had become instinctual. The only thing that mattered was that he had freed Clinton's hand and moved him safely along. He had adapted in seconds.

When I asked Falkenberg what happened to the guy whose thumb he shattered, he paused as if I had asked him the stupidest question imaginable, as if I had completely missed the point. "I don't know. I didn't care. My job was to get the protectee out of there," he said. And that was what he had done, followed by numbers two and three, who fell in behind him. The job of rounding up the guy, now writhing on the ground, fell to agents behind them. Falkenberg said the man was arrested and questioned, but he stressed that this did not matter. What mattered was protecting Clinton. That had been his sole focus, confident that the other highly trained agents behind him would do their jobs.

"Someone gets shot, the police show up and try to figure out who shot him," he said. "That's reactive. That's after the fact. The goal of the Secret Service is for that to never happen."

The Secret Service's plan is for nothing to happen, but that is not always realistic. Adapting is key. How Falkenberg reacted to an overzealous handshaker may seem extreme, but that was how it had to be. The man could have been John Hinckley, who emerged from the press pool and shot President Ronald Reagan in March 1981. That he succeeded in shooting the president was an enormous failure on the Secret Service's part, but how they adapted showed the service's strength. Each man fell into his role. Timothy McCarthy stepped into the line of fire and took a bullet meant for Reagan. Jerry Parr and Ray Shaddick threw the president into the bulletproof limousine. The one, though, who stood out most was Drew Unrue, the driver. He was initially told to drive to the White House, but when it was clear Reagan needed immediate medical attention, he was redirected to George Washington Hospital, finding it quickly in an era before every car was equipped with a global positioning system. Every man had a job to do and did it. They did not bemoan the enormous breach of security that had enabled Hinckley to fire five shots. That would be handled later. They fell into line to save the president, allowing the others to clean up afterward. Their plan of protecting the president had failed completely when he got shot. But they didn't focus on that. They adapted and saved his life.

THE PLAN VS. THE FIGHT

So how did Willie Copeland and Chris Falkenberg know how to react as they did? In these situations they kept the goal, not the original plan, in mind. The plan for Copeland's Marine Recon unit was to guard a convoy so it arrived at its destination safely. Falkenberg's plan was to make sure nothing happened to Clinton while he was campaigning. When these plans failed, the people charged with implementing them adapted. Copeland responded to what happened, while Falkenberg anticipated it. These are the two facets of adapting under pressure. The key, though, is that they did not stick to their initial plans. They relied on their training to adapt to any possible scenario and focused on the outcome: surviving the ambush and protecting the candidate, respectively. This is a key difference between people who are great under pressure and people who are not. Those who wilt when the pressure is hottest fall back on what they expected to do ahead of time, as if it were a security blanket or the only way forward. Those who succeed under pressure readjust: They focus on the goal that needs to be accomplished, not a specific way to accomplish that goal.

This is what Colonel Thomas Kolditz, the head of the behavioral studies department at the United States Military Academy at West Point, strives to impress on cadets. "We teach our cadets to fight the fight, not fight the plan," he told me at his office in Thayer Hall at the center of the garrisoned campus. "There is a break point where the plan goes in the trash. That's the skill. The focus is on intent. It's outcome based."

Kolditz has his doctorate in social psychology, but he is a soldier first. For seventeen years, he was in an artillery unit. He served in Germany, commanded an 850-person battalion on the demilitarized zone in Korea, and worked on the ground in Iraq in 2003. This informs the research he does on leaders in extreme situations. (He refers to it as *in extremis* and defines the Latin phrase as "at the point of death.") His war-zone experience has made him intent on finding out how to make sure leaders lead when the pressure is highest and human lives are at stake. He said he has little time for business-school case studies about companies that have pulled themselves out of crisis. "They're amateurs," he said, not joking. His nexus is life and death. "From my perspective, a leader who puts people in dangerous contexts or makes decisions about dangerous contexts has a moral obligation to get that right," he said, leaning in for emphasis. "You're not allowed to be bad about that. It's not an option for you to be bad. We can be bad at golf; we can be bad at our office jobs. If you're going to put yourself in a position of putting people in dangerous contexts, you have to be good at it." This is a high bar, because the pressure is not only to make the right decision but to be able to make it when someone is shooting at you.

Kolditz's mantra is fight the fight, but he believes a leader should do everything he can to get his plan right. This is the Secret Service way of protection. Kolditz breaks the creation of the plan into five points. The first is "commander's intent." It stresses that all crises are ambiguous, so no plan, as the military saying goes, survives contact with the enemy. Kolditz calls the second the concept of the *Schwerpunkt* [focal point], which is a term from the blitzkrieg. In World War II, the *Schwerpunkt* was the critical point in the other army's line; the Germans would mass troops and tanks on it and blast their way through the front line. It is crucial, he said, for any leader to find that critical point and protect it. On an army mission, the *Schwerpunkt* could be an ambiguous turn where someone needs to be stationed to prevent the convoy from losing its way; at a company like Enron, he said, it was the accounting department. A leader should ask himself, "Where does my direct influence as a leader need to be exerted right now?"

"Practical drift" is the third step in creating a plan. Devised by Lieutenant Colonel Scott Snook after his investigation into how two F-15s shot down two Black Hawk helicopters in the First Gulf War, the concept is rooted in the need to revisit protocols. Those that are rigid—in the hope that they will keep workers more focused—need to be reviewed more often, because in the daily exercise of his job, a soldier or worker is going to find a more practical way to do something. When that happens, the leader either needs to reinstitute the original way or adapt the protocol to the new system. The fourth step in Kolditz's program is the "premortem," which is a check to make sure all of the available information has been gathered and checked before doing something. Last is "red teaming." In this, the army has institutionalized the devil's advocate, the person whose job it is to poke holes in the plan. This, Kolditz said, is a way to counter what happens to even seasoned leaders: "We fall in love with our plans." All of these points are aimed at making the plan as strong as possible, to give it the best chance of succeeding.

And once the plan is as good as it can possibly be, Kolditz says, it is time for cadets to prepare for all the ways it will fail under pressure. This is when they learn to fight the fight. Kolditz said there are four key areas that need to be addressed so that in the heat of combat, the soldiers will stick together and continue the fight. The first is "shared risk," or knowing that what your leader is telling you to do he can do himself. As the coach of West Point's elite parachuting team, Kolditz literally coaches by hanging on to the side of the plane—with fourteen thousand feet of air beneath his windblown feet—and the cadets know he will be jumping with them. "When you climb out, it's hard to climb back in. There is ninety knots of wind on your whole body," he said. "They know you're not coming back in. There's shared risk, and they go."

Another key for leaders in a pressure-filled situation is having a common lifestyle. If a leader uses a position of authority to gain an advantage—like better accommodations or food—those who are supposed to follow him won't. And once this trust is lost, Kolditz said, it is nearly impossible to regain.

The third area is demonstrating competence and engendering trust and loyalty, which seem obvious. Yet this is a fine line to walk. A leader needs to be bold, but he cannot be cocky or arrogant, nor should he be humble and self-effacing. A bold leader has to step forward and say he understands the situation. "You tell them, 'I've got it. I've been here before. The sun is going to come up tomorrow,'" Kolditz said. "You don't say, 'We've done everything we can, and we'll just go forward from here.' People pay attention to what leaders do and decide whether they're credible."

Yet it is the fourth of Kolditz's precepts that is the most intriguing for clutch decision making. He calls it "inherent motivation," which is slightly misleading. The idea is that in certain areas of life you need someone or something to motivate you. Running around a track is a good example: You are either trying to win or you probably have a coach pushing you to train. Without that extrinsic motivation, chances are you would take a few days off here or there and not become the best runner you could be. The situations soldiers—and, though Kolditz might disagree, leaders in non-life-and-death areas—find themselves in are so overwhelmingly stressful that there is no need for their leader to rev them up more. There is an inherent motivation in what they are doing or about to do. If someone had been shouting at Sergeant Copeland to shoot the Iraqis or at Falkenberg to save the candidate, it would have thrown them off their games. "Hollywood gets it so wrong," Kolditz said. "All of their leaders are screaming into a microphone. Nobody needs any of the boot-in-the-ass, Hollywood Drill Sergeant motivation. That's exactly the wrong thing. We want to teach our leaders to calm people down."

Interestingly, Willie Copeland had none of the buttoned-up West Point bearing. He was a kid from Smithfield, Utah, who liked to hang out and talk about the rodeo. "Willie was one of those guys who came to my Recon battalion and no one wanted him," said Colonel Michael Paulovich, a Harvard-educated Marine who was running the Recon School when Copeland came through in 2001. "He was skinny. He smoked cigarettes. He drank mugs of coffee." On the plus side, Copeland had a very mechanical mind. He had come over from an infantry unit and could fix anything by simply studying it for a while. "The truck is broken down, the machine gun stops working, you're looking at him in a panic, and he'd say, 'I can fix this,'" recalled Paulovich, who said Copeland intrigued him from the start. "He was cool all the time. Nothing flapped him."

Still, Copeland's physical appearance was not typical for a Recon Marine. These were usually strapping men. They were football quarterbacks and lacrosse players who were big and could take a hit but also had great instincts from their days scanning the field and assessing what was coming at them. Copeland did not seem to be one of them. "He wasn't the kind of guy who was taking vitamins and eating the best food," said Paulovich. "We had some guys who were ultimate triathletes. They metered everything they ate. Then you have the other guy who had a Big Gulp mug of coffee."

What Copeland lacked in physical attributes and diet, he made up for in his focus and discipline. He was resolute in the intense Recon training. To simulate conditions these Marines would face on the battlefield, they were sent as part of their training into the woods for days with nothing other than a compass; they were submerged in fifty-degree water, and they were forced to parachute when they were exhausted. The aim was to create environments in which the levels of fatigue and physical discomfort would approximate the mind-scrambling fog that an unanticipated attack creates. "You could have a guy fully rested on eight hours of sleep, and the convoy blows up," Paulovich said of combat situations. "Suddenly he has to Medevac people out of there, in a mine field, and, oh, someone is shooting at him." That was why extreme conditions were necessary in training and how Paulovich came to suspect Copeland would excel under pressure. He may have been skinny, but he was solid and tough. He swam hard and trained as fiercely as the rest of the Marines. What he lacked in strength and stature, he made up for by gutting it out.

Paulovich knew from experience that the most unlikely men could be molded into Recon Marines. He himself was only five feet six inches tall and weighed 150 pounds. Once he remembered a bugler trying out for Force Recon, the more covert of the elite Marine units. Copeland's smoking and coffee drinking were accepted quirks in a group whose binding characteristic was the desire to be part of a high-risk, high-pressure battalion. They were all adrenaline junkies. And as the initial twelve-week training course wore on, Copeland continued to impress Paulovich and his fellow trainees.

Still, telling me about Copeland's actions in Iraq, Paulovich sounded amazed, if reluctantly so. After all, he had trained him. "You wouldn't have picked him out of the lineup that he would have been the hero," he said. "It throws off your thinking. I went out of planes in the dark, but he knew exactly what to do: Get guys to safety, engage the enemy, protect his leader." By every measure, his actions were clutch, not least of all for the extreme pressure under which he carried them out. When he was presented with the Navy Cross, Copeland summed up what he had done simply. "Nothing's natural about running into bullets," he told the Associated Press. "It's more important for me to make sure my men are OK."

In the fog of war, Copeland did what was most important to being clutch: When he had to adapt his plan, he focused on something other than himself. To Kolditz, this is everything. "When you're focused outward, you can't focus inward on your emotions," he said. "It's not a matter of teaching cadets how to control their emotions. What I try to teach them on the parachute team is not to feel their emotions at all. I say, 'Look at the wingtip as hard as you can.' What it does is take them out of their own arousal, and they can function. If you try to teach someone to control their emotions, they focus on them and it gets worse." Copeland focused on saving his CO and his men; Falkenberg focused on protecting the candidate. Retreating inward in either situation would have been a recipe for choking. Instead they adapted to the task at hand—the fight—and that allowed for the quick responses they needed.

FIGHTING THE FIGHT THAT MATTERED

Matthew Bogdanos is the archetype of the soldier-leader who could respond and anticipate, adapt and lead. On the cusp of the U.S. invasion of Iraq in 2003, Colonel Bogdanos was commanding a group of one hundred men inside the country. They were part of the Joint Inter-Agency Coordinating Group, created after the September 11, 2001, attacks on New York and Washington. They were a real-life A-Team, composed of veteran Special Forces and black ops soldiers but also agents from an alphabet soup of enforcement agencies—FBI, CIA, DEA, IRS, even NYPD detectives. Colonel Bogdanos, a Marine, had been given clear instructions from the commanding general: Find and eliminate terrorist cells, sources of their financing, and any prohibited weapons. He had been part of a similar covert operation in Afghanistan, where he was awarded the Bronze Star. (When we met shortly after he returned from Iraq in 2004, he said matter-of-factly that Al-Qaeda had put a bounty on his head, which required him to be armed at all times.) But this was the first mission he was leading. He had no problem being in charge. Handling the pressure of a mission came naturally to him. He was also a middleweight boxing champion and assistant district attorney in New York City. He was proud of this combination of fighter and thinker.

In the midst of his mission, he got word from locals that the Baghdad Museum was being looted, and he realized he had to change his plan. Bogdanos also has an advanced degree in classics from Columbia University, and he knew how important the museum's collection was—it was no less, as he told me many times, than the shared foundation of humankind. These were the first artifacts from Mesopotamia, the cradle of civilization. He feared they would be spirited out of the country. There was an underground network of antiquities collectors that he was familiar with from his work in the DA's office. They would pay top dollar for a sought-after item, and that piece of civilization would never be seen again.

There was only one problem with changing his plan. He did not have the rank to do it himself. "This was a general's decision," he told me about his desire to take fourteen men from the task force and race from northern Iraq to Baghdad. His new plan was to pile into their heavily armed Humvees and drive through the desert night. He knew this was not the typical way to move through an Iraq on the verge of chaos, but he did not have another option as he searched for a general to approve his breakaway mission. One after another rejected him, starting with General Gary Harrell, a legendary Delta Force commander. Their rejections were the same: The mission was too dangerous, given the plan he had formulated. Yet Bogdanos knew he had to stop the looting, and he was convinced that his group was the one to do it. Within a few hours, he had racked up a half-dozen rejections, but then he got through to General Gene Renuart, director of operations for U.S. Central Command. "Had I not had my background, had I not had the feel for this stuff, would I have gone to General Renuart after a half-dozen nos? Probably not," Bogdanos told me. Renuart granted him permission, and Bogdanos was ready. He had already sold a group of his men on the value of saving the museum's holdings, and thirty-six hours later, they rolled into Baghdad.

When he went to Iraq, Bogdanos had had an important plan—stop terrorists. He changed it not because he had accomplished it but because he knew the looting of the museum had to be stopped as soon as possible. In an environment of overlapping and immense pressures, he realized that his original plan was not the most important one in the short term. Racing to Baghdad like a modern-day Dirty Dozen also meant more to the image the United States was trying to project: They were supposed to leave the country better than they found it, and the disappearance of three-thousand-year-old treasures would not count as better.

With a new plan came a new goal. When he entered the Iraq Museum, he sought out the directors and assured them that he was there to find lost antiquities. "I'm not here to investigate war crimes or political ideology," he told them. "Frankly, I'd rather we never talk about it. Except to the extent that it proves necessary for the investigation, I have no interest in anyone's contact with Saddam Hussein or the regime."

Under extreme pressure, his focus narrowed to the essential task: Save the antiquities. If he succeeded, these artifacts would stay in Iraq, not be locked away in some private home in Zurich. He would also be able to show that the U.S. military was a liberating force meant to bring good to the region. And that was what made Bogdanos's decision so clutch: There was a practical and a political motivation to his actions, and he had to navigate his way to that end.

Within days Bogdanos's team had its first success: The Statue of Shalmaneser, a vase of a Syrian king from 858 B.C., and a Sumerian bronze bull from the Temple of Ninhursag, the first such bull in relief, were returned. The man who returned the pieces was a violinist who said he had wanted to protect them. Bogdanos may or may not have believed him, but he arranged for the man to be interviewed on television so other Iraqis could see him keeping his word to provide amnesty. After that, goods poured in. Soon, members of Bogdanos's group were being sought out on the streets.

The decision to offer amnesty was Bogdanos's. He quoted the Geneva Convention to me and the responsibility of an occupational force to govern, yet he also admitted that such a sweeping proposal should have, again, come from a general. "I told my men, 'This one's on me,'" he said, meaning that if anyone up the chain of command objected, Bogdanos would take the heat for it. "You know the old saying that it's better to beg for forgiveness than to ask for permission? It was the right thing to do. Would General Renuart have said yes? Sure. But what if it had gone south?"

Far from insubordination, Bogdanos demonstrated the decision-making skill under pressure that the military hopes to inculcate into all its officers. It also solidified his leadership standing with his men. But most of all, his idea of granting amnesty worked. In an environment in which Iraqis did not trust anyone, even the forces sent to liberate them from Saddam Hussein, Bogdanos showed from the start that recovering the antiquities, many of them objects of world historical significance, mattered more than listening to the banal excuses of how someone came to possess each object. He tapped his shoulder and said, "I got these eagles for a reason, and one of them was to make a goddamn decision and stick by it. And if you're wrong, be a big boy and take the consequences. As George Patton said, a good plan executed now is better than a perfect plan executed too late. Everything was judged by that: the amnesty, the nonprosecution and recovery, the raids—it wasn't like we asked permission to go on the raids."

His decisions paid off. The greatest success came in June 2003, several months into the recovery operation, when the Sacred Vase of Warka appeared. The meter-high Sumerian vase from 3200 B.C. is one of the most important antiquities in the world for the way it depicts human life. One day a man walked up to John Durkin, a member of Bogdanos's team who ran the New York Police Department's emergency services unit in civilian life. He showed him a picture of the piece among dozens of vases and jars; he wanted $500 to return it. "Clearly, the guy didn't know what he had," Bogdanos said. "[If he had], it would have been the only thing in the photograph, and it wouldn't have been $500." The next day three other men drove up to the museum with the vase in the trunk of the car and returned it without asking for a cent.

Bogdanos's plan had worked under pressure because it had matched his goal: Recover as many artifacts as quickly as possible. And that remained his focus even when circumstances changed. A few months into living in the Iraq Museum—he and his men wanted to be there to broker deals at any hour—Bogdanos became convinced that the looting had been an inside job. There was too much selection in what had been taken. It was almost as if certain pieces were stolen to order. Of twenty-seven cuneiform bricks arranged high on a wall, for example, only the nine most important ones were stolen—and they were interspersed at various levels up the wall. "A looter is going to grab the stuff that is on the ground," he said. Still, Bogdanos maintained his amnesty program: Anyone who returned an antiquity would not be questioned and would be allowed to walk back out. If Bogdanos began to prosecute while he was still recovering artifacts, he knew he risked the whole operation collapsing. "What you have to do is suspend moral judgment," he said. "Nothing gets in the way of an investigation more than moral judgment."

In the end, Bogdanos turned out to have made a clutch policy decision, for both moral and public relations reasons. But if you go back to Colonel Kolditz's four precepts for scrapping a plan and leading under pressure, Bogdanos followed all of them. He certainly shared the risk with his men—he was in the convoy with them and out front in the negotiations. He had a lifestyle in common with his soldiers, sleeping in the museum with the rest of them. His training in antiquities as much as, if not more than, his rank of colonel made it clear that when he said something was important, it was. And given the speed with which he and his men initially got to Baghdad and how quickly they began recovering antiquities, he managed their inherent motivation. His success, though, was far from certain when he began calling generals to beg permission. Yet he knew he was right, and because of his training, he was confident he would succeed. It was no different from the way Willie Copeland knew how to react to an ambush and Chris Falkenberg swiftly handled a man accosting a presidential candidate. All three adapted their plan and carried out an effective, new plan. This was fighting the fight.

[4]

BEING PRESENT
Opening-Night Jitters and
the Role of a Lifetime

IN DAVID RABE'S *Streamers,* the actor who plays Sergeant Cokes only appears onstage twice. The play takes place in 1965, and the Vietnam War is about to heat up. Set in a barracks in Virginia, it tells the story of a group of recruits contemplating going off to Vietnam as their fears, prejudices, and innocence rise to the surface. The first time Cokes, a career soldier with combat experience in Korea, comes out, he is drunk and full of himself, reminiscing with his good friend Rooney as they barge into a room of new recruits. The second time he is even drunker. Rooney has just been killed, stabbed by one of those recruits, but Cokes has no idea that his friend is dead. He meanders through the barracks in the wake of the stabbing, talking to soldiers who saw Rooney killed, and in doing so becomes both introspective and expansive. The twenty-minute monologue he delivers, the last words of the play, has become one of the most important in contemporary American theater. Whether the play succeeds or fails rests on the shoulders of the actor who plays Cokes, making it a moment ripe for stage fright.

On a late fall night in Boston, the play opened at the Huntington Theater, a respected regional venue, and Larry Clarke was playing Sergeant Cokes. This was the first major revival of *Streamers,* considered by many to be the best of Rabe's four "Vietnam Plays," in thirty years. It was being put on in the fall of 2007 as the United States was fighting wars in Iraq and Afghanistan. Clarke knew that Rabe had been reluctant to allow the play to be staged. Rabe feared that the current military had changed too much and that the ongoing wars would overshadow what he had wrought about Vietnam. He had agreed to the production, though, and that meant it was up to the actors, and Larry Clarke in particular, to convey the haunted meaning of his work.

The popular image of opening night is one of actors pacing and full of nerves as they wait for the curtain to rise. For seasoned profession-als, it is different: That pressure charges them up. It signals that this is not a rehearsal, this is what they have been working toward. They are completely committed to the present. Regardless of what their fellow actors or the audience throws their way, they're prepared to react under the pressure of live theater.

Clarke, a veteran stage actor whose everyman look became widely known through a recurring role on *Law & Order,* was excited for the curtain to rise in Boston. "It's just like hitting the field," he told me. "I say, if we miss a line, if we fumble, just do another down and don't let it ruin the whole play. My job is to keep trying. David wrote the play, and I'm going to do it. It's no small thing. This is where it all has meaning. I feel that. I'm not nervous. We're going to affect an audience." And the rambling, tension-filled twenty-minute discourse that is crucial to the play's success is the whole reason he wanted to play Sergeant Cokes. "That monologue, for a character actor—it's *Hamlet,*" he said. "And if you're going to come in and do it, you'd better be good."

BECOMING PRESENT

It might seem hard to believe that Clarke was not nervous to take on such a risky and important role. But he had long ago mastered the art of being present. This ability to be prepared to respond to anything that comes your way is the fourth component of excelling under pressure. What does it mean to be present? The phrase itself has an almost New

Agey feel to it, but that is not what I intend by it at all. Being present is a learned behavior. It is partly the result of the previous three clutch traits I've discussed—focus, discipline, and adaptability. Think of how Clarke described his feeling before the curtain went up on opening night. He said it felt like "hitting the field." He was obviously focused. As you will see in this chapter, he had been disciplined in his rehearsals, and his admission that his job onstage was "to keep trying" showed he knew how important it was to be adaptable. But being present is more than the aggregate of these other traits. Being present is a state that makes someone ready for whatever comes his way. It is a heightened awareness that prepares him to respond. It can be a bit edgy, but it is more that feeling of being aware of nothing other than what you are doing.

Clarke was completely present by the time he stepped out onstage as Sergeant Cokes. But it took him a month of rehearsals to get there. He told me it was not something he could always do. There was a time when he struggled to be present. A self-admitted "class clown," Clarke had wanted to be a stage actor since high school. He was naturally gifted, but in some ways that was a hindrance. He did not have to work as hard as others, and he became overconfident in his talent. When he landed a leading role his freshman year in college, he told the head of the theater department that he would skip the beginning acting class. Yet within two years, Clarke was landing roles at the regional theater in Baltimore, and he got his Actors Equity card while still a student. But then he started to party too much, and it looked as though he was going to squander his ability.

His nadir was an audition in the early 1990s for a Las Vegas review that would have paid $5,000 a week at a time when he was shuffling restaurant jobs. "I figured I would get this," he recalled. He breezed into the audition room, dreaming of success. "I was still cocky. I walked in there without preparing. I hadn't sung with a piano in years. It was a dismal failure." It was that disaster that convinced him he needed to rethink how he approached acting. He realized he might not waltz into the roles he wanted. So, he stopped drinking, and at thirty he met an acting teacher who worked with him. Three years later, Clarke landed his first film role, in In & Out, directed by Frank Oz and starring Kevin Kline.

"Once you start to achieve success, another type of pressure enters your life," he said. "Your ego takes over, and you start to get expectations." So while he was taking his craft more seriously, he still wasn't totally present. At times, he allowed himself to be distracted by what his success could mean—the fame and fortune.

Then came a casting call for *Law & Order*. By that point, an audition no longer gave him stage fright. He had done too many. But when he landed a role as Detective Morris LaMotte in 1997, he arrived on set as nervous as he had ever been. He had never done anything on this level before. "I had watched these guys on the show," he told me. "I was nervous." When his scene began, he just stood there. He was supposed to move around but he did not know when. He had never heard the term "background action" before, so he was waiting for someone to shout "action" as they do in films. "I was so embarrassed," he said.

He was asked back, but that next episode went worse. He had more lines, but he had rushed to learn them. "They gave me the script the night before," he said. "It was a chunk of dialogue. The hard thing with these action dramas is, you're not going back and forth. It's these dry facts. They had me in the witness interrogation room. I'm talking in this mirror room. Benjamin Bratt was right next to me. They have a cameraman a couple inches from my face, dressed in black like a monk. I freaked out. I started mumbling. I couldn't do my lines. I started looking at the ground. There are thirty people on the set waiting to go to the next scene."

It seemed that classic stage fright had seized Clarke. At that point, the director stopped the scene. "Do you know your lines?" he barked at Clarke and then made him say them out loud, as if this were a high school production. From the director's point of view, every take was time lost, and if Clarke kept mumbling, they were going to fall behind. Television is not theater—rehearsal, then performance; it is scene after scene, shot out of order on a tight schedule and stitched together later. "I was thinking in my head that I don't know these lines like I should," Clarke said, the memory still vivid over a decade later. But he did know them. He had just memorized them in his apartment. What was keeping him from saying them? The problem was he was thinking about all the great actors around him, and wondering how he was there. He had watched them on television; they had probably never heard of him. Moreover he had not rehearsed his lines with a camera in his face on the set of the most popular drama on television. He was completely out of his element. He was not in the present, and he was flailing.

"They did take after take," he said. "It has to be perfect. In my head, I said, 'This will never end.'" It did, though, and the scene from a viewer's perspective turned out fine. Clarke went on to film twenty-one more episodes as Detective LaMotte. Yet he told me that when he watches that episode, if he slows down the film, he can hear his nervous inhale, a telltale sign that he was feeling the pressure. "That was my acting that day, pretending not to be nervous," he said.

From that day on, Clarke began to prepare differently. He got the script earlier and worked through the lines. When he returned to the set, he knew how it would feel. The other actors were no longer people he watched on a hit television show; they were his colleagues. He stopped being in awe of them and started concentrating on getting himself ready. They were all working together. Still, it was a precarious existence to be a featured actor and not one of the stars. "At the end of these takes, no one is coming up to you and saying how you're doing," he said. "You're always waiting to be killed off or written off."

Being there regularly gave him a different perspective: It made him less serious on the set. He concentrated on what was happening the moment the camera started rolling, not what it meant in any larger context of his career. "I looked at Benjamin Bratt on set and wondered, 'How is he so damn good?'" Clarke said of an early star of the series. "He was laughing and dancing and not taking anything so seriously. He was really smiling and enjoying life. This was a guy who realized, the looser I am, the better I'll do. The camera picks up all of this." Bratt's dancing was not meant to be entertaining, and it was more than staying loose. Actors have a term for someone who never stops acting. They say he is "always on." This is not a good thing. All good actors can switch from being themselves to whatever character they are playing quickly. They have a command of that role and know how important it is to inhabit that person. However, spending long workdays forever in character actually makes it more difficult to truly be that character. Bratt was dancing on set so he would not be thinking about what he had to do. That way, when he was called to shoot a scene, he'd get into his character and be ready, mentally and emotionally. He could be entirely present, and that freedom allowed him to block out any external pressure and concentrate on what he had to do. From observing this, Clarke refined his own technique, and things seemed to change. He realized he could act at this level and started feeling that he belonged.

His new routine worked but it wasn't pressureproof yet. Clarke had one of his most embarrassing auditions while working on *Law & Order*. He went in for the third season of *The Sopranos*. He had already shot a role in the first season, which put him on the short list to audition again. It gave him a leg up on other actors. When he heard there was an opening for an FBI agent, he thought he was perfect for it and reverted to being cocky. "It was my worst audition ever," he told me. "I had my wallet in my hand. I was going to flash it like a badge. As I'm pulling it out, it flips out of my hand onto the floor. Then I start to forget my line. I blew it. I was trying to be cute. It was so stupid."

Now forty-five, Clarke has crafted a routine that puts him immediately in the moment. He likes to walk in to an audition and crack a joke, show that he is relaxed and normal. Then, when told, he snaps into character. In landing a role on the television series *The Closer*, he had to cry twice in the audition, so he made sure he came in sunny. He did not want the director to think he was depressed—and so crying would come easy. He wanted to show him he could act, going from an everyday conversation to that role. Even if the part is comedic, Clarke said he needed to snap in and out of the role. He had to show he could become instantly present. Being always on can be off-putting to directors; going into character showed a professionalism as an actor. "Cocky is not being prepared but still feeling self-assured," he said of his old self. "Confidence is the same thing but being prepared. I try to remain confident, but it's good to remain humble."

That was how Clarke approached being cast in *Streamers*. Though he had worked previously with both Rabe and director Scott Ellis, he was their third choice for Sergeant Cokes. That did not matter to him. He knew the play, knew how to get ready for it, and most important, knew the pressure surrounding a revival of this magnitude. The challenging part was to make the role of Cokes his own. "This was going to be the highlight of my career," he said. Far from shrinking from the role, he saw it as something his work had been building toward.

KEEPING THE PAST AT BAY

Clarke was poised and confident before going onstage in *Streamers*. The very thought of doing that makes many nonactors cringe, particularly those who struggle with public speaking. They imagine being afflicted by stage fright and see the actor walking out, forgetting his line, and bringing the play to a grinding halt. If you're at the top of your profession as an actor, though, you have found ways to remain immune to this. Clarke said he feeds off the crowd's energy and uses the pressure to his advantage. He tries to feel what they're reacting to and either speeds up or slows down his performance accordingly. It is a collaborative effort. But not everyone can do this, and that is why stage fright paralyzes many smart, articulate people. Think of those nightmares of addressing a crowded room naked or showing up to something in your pajamas, or the one I still have: sitting for a college test without having studied. These are all versions of what is more generally called performance anxiety, and it is not limited to actors. This anxiety causes usually capable speakers and leaders to clam up under pressure. They cannot move or think, and all of their worst fears take hold.

"If you have performance anxiety, you don't calm down during the event," Joyce Ashley, a Jungian analyst and the author of *Overcoming Stage Fright in Everyday Life,* told me. "Other people calm down if things are going well, but not the person with stage fright. It gets worse. A certain amount of adrenaline means you're up; too much, and you're paralyzed."

Ashley knows this firsthand. She had been an actor before becoming an analyst, and she suffered horribly from stage fright. Even though she told me she had done some four hundred commercials—"floor cleaners, beer, national airlines"—and acted in summer stock and on soap operas in the 1960s, she was never comfortable in front of the camera. "I hated being the center of attention as a girl," she said. This seems completely illogical. Why, then, would she go into acting? She said it had been a compromise. She never thought the commercials or soap operas were important, so they did not make her anxious. What she really wanted to do was sing, but she couldn't muster the nerve—without a few glasses of wine. Like many old-school analysts, she came to see the root of this anxiety in childhood. "If you were nurtured and got approval, you carry that with you," she said. "If you weren't, if you felt scorn and derision, you project that on the audience. You walk out and see that audience as hostile, and you know they won't like you." In her case, Ashley said her parents wanted her to "disappear into the woodwork and get married"; singing was not something they approved of at all.

Placing the root of anxiety in childhood might seem outdated. But there is some logic here: If you are anxious about disappointing someone, what is the audience if not that person, multiplied, sitting in judgment? If the audience is your partner, as in Clarke's case, the relationship is more productive. If you believe the people there are waiting for you to stumble over a line, it's going to be more difficult.

How Ashley helps people overcome their anxieties points to why being present and avoiding stage fright is so hard but so key to being clutch. If it were not, public speaking would be a breeze: People would figure out what they were going to say and say it. That's not how it happens for many. "The only way to neutralize performance anxiety is to identify and confront the inner sources of your fears," she told me. As she wrote in her book: "No one is born afraid of being seen and heard. Therefore, something must have happened to those of us who suffer from performance anxiety to convince us that being the center of attention would bring us psychological and/or physical pain." She has a strong belief in the brain's adaptability, but adaptation cannot happen without acknowledging the source of the pain first. "It won't ever be completely gone," she said. "But something different will happen. A new set of experiences will counterbalance it."

To her, its most pernicious effect is that it keeps someone from doing what he or she wants to do and is capable of doing. These people have skill and talent, but if they cannot sing or act in front of an audience, that talent is trapped. Ashley told me about working with a great tenor who was stuck in the chorus. He should have had a brilliant career, but he could not audition: He saw his father, living vicariously through him, whenever he stepped out into the lights. The key was to replace that negative association with a positive one. She calls this part of the process "confronting your inner critic." But she stressed that the essential part was moving on after finding the source of the stage fright. "There's no resolution," she said. "Life goes on."

In rehearsals for *Streamers*, Scott Ellis was well aware of the inner doubts the actors had. As an award-winning theater and television director, he tried to make his cast relaxed. He did not want them thinking they were preparing for a play that was going to put them in front of hundreds of people who had paid a lot of money to see them perform. He wanted to coax them along. He thought of what he was doing in terms of a circus act. "It's the analogy of an actor who is tightrope walking," he told me between shots for a Showtime drama he was working on. "You have to first get them from one place to another. Then they're going to have to do tricks before they get to the other end. They're going to fall. If there's a safety net, they're going to get back up and do it again." But his goal is to bring them across gradually. "They're all going to work differently," he said. "Some you can prod. I had worked with Larry before, so I knew how to work with him." But he demanded one thing of all of his actors: "The only thing I say is, we don't talk about the critics or reviews. Sometimes you get lucky and they like you; sometimes they don't."

This might sound like a cop-out, something a parent might tell a roughed-up kid. But there is a truth here that any person who crumbles under the pressure of giving a presentation can learn from. Ellis has no way of controlling a critic's opinions, any more than he can influence the weather on opening night. Like an actor, playwright, or director, a critic has his own preferences and his own baggage, particularly when he is considering a revival. He may be trying to stake his own claim to a play like *Streamers,* or he may love or loathe Rabe. Unlike a new play, there are preconceptions. This is where being present counts for so much: The only thing you can control is what you are doing, not what someone did in the past or is poised to write when the curtain is lowered. And if you let that reviewer's voice into your head, whether it is positive or negative, it is going to take you out of the moment. Like the criticism of an over-bearing parent, it will rattle around in your mind, and the pressure will cause you to choke.

With *Streamers,* Ellis had to block out a lot of thoughts himself. He had to think of only that production or else he risked being overwhelmed. The original 1976 production was iconic, as much for how it shook up the theater world as for the problems with the production. When it was staged, Rabe was without question the hottest, most important young playwright in America. His "Vietnam plays" would come to define the 1970s the way Arthur Miller's social realist dramas framed the post–World War II years and David Mamet's tough-guy talk was shorthand for 1980s greed. Rabe won a Tony Award in 1972 and was revered at New York's Public Theater. But when *Streamers* opened, the New Haven critics hated it. "The shock of the initial production did not help people understand—it blinded them," Rabe told me. "It was truly terrifying." Part of this was the violence; another part was the way racial tension was presented so frankly. Worried that the play would close because it was misunderstood, Rabe and Mike Nichols, the director who was just as influential in his profession, invited a group of New York critics up, figuring they had nothing to lose. That was the turning point. They grasped what the play was saying and understood the symbolism in its violent, confrontational dialogue. Suddenly *Streamers* had extremely positive reviews from some New York newspapers, making a move there inevitable. But the process had left Rabe exhausted. He retreated into a period of writing screenplays in Los Angeles and rejected many offers for a full-scale revival. When Ellis approached him in 2006, he was still hesitant, after three decades, to revisit such a tough time in his career. "I was very leery of doing the play again, in New York," Rabe said. "When Scott first came to me, I turned him down, as I had a series of other directors. I wasn't comfortable with it because of the war in Iraq. I said I didn't know the contemporary army. I didn't feel comfortable doing the play. Then Scott said, 'Can I do it in Boston?'"

Ellis appreciated both Rabe's hesitancy and what Nichols had done directing the original play. But he tried not to let it weigh on him. "In a brand-new play, more of the pressure is on the writer than the director," Ellis told me. "But in a revival, it worked once, and if it doesn't again, then you've fucked it up. I was under a lot of pressure with *Streamers* because of David's whole relationship to the play and the people involved with it. I certainly felt it."

Ellis focused instead on something that would be totally his: casting. It went great until it came to finding Sergeant Cokes. The role had to be played by an experienced actor. But Ellis knew it was not going to be easy to convince a veteran performer to live in Boston for two months, away from his home in New York or Los Angeles. He was right. His first choice dropped out because of scheduling conflicts. A few weeks later, he found another actor and thought everything was fine. But right before rehearsals were set to start, the second actor pulled out, citing artistic differences. Ellis put it bluntly: "With that role, if you don't get it right, you're just fucked." It was probably the moment of most intense stress for him. "The pressure from David, the pressure I put on myself—I had been pushing this for years," he told me. "When I got that call, I said, 'What the fuck am I going to do?' I had two weeks and that was it. I was also in the middle of putting together the tour of *12 Angry Men"*— another revival that had met with great acclaim.

For a director, the greatest pressure comes from the weight of expectations, and that can make it particularly difficult to be present. Ellis had made a promise to Rabe but also one to the Huntington Theater, and he was struggling to fulfill both. "Who is Scott Ellis to be doing this?" he said. "That was the biggest pressure. All I kept telling myself was, that was thirty years ago. Several generations hadn't seen it, and people needed to see that play." Most important, he told himself that he would direct it without letting the past influence what he was going to do.

REHEARSALS

"How am I going to start a monologue saying hi to everyone and end with singing a song in gibberish Korean about a guy I killed ten years earlier?" Clarke joked, recalling his first reaction to the magnitude of the monologue that ends *Streamers*.

An actor as accomplished as Clarke has the ability to become present for any role. But even though he has done it many times before, he still has to achieve that state again each time. That does not happen all at once. With Detective LaMotte on *Law & Order*, becoming that character was much easier as the role went on. In the case of *Streamers*, this was where the rehearsals were key. Just as someone preparing to give a speech in front of a large or important audience would practice it over and over again, Clarke used the rehearsals to ask Rabe how he had envisioned Sergeant Cokes. This was essential, Clarke said, to his getting to a point where he would literally *be* Cokes onstage, reacting within the play as if he were in a Virginia barracks in 1965. "What creates a guy who has done three wars? What's 'Beautiful Streamers'? What's this war cry they do?" Clarke told me these were all questions he had asked Rabe about Sergeant Cokes. "This is a guy who doesn't have a family, who only has his war buddies. For the first time, he is being haunted by death." Clarke credited Rabe with helping him to get the tone right. "My first drunken-sergeant routine, I was doing it very drunk," Clarke said. Rabe told him that he needed to work on the tenor more. These men had drunk heavily their whole lives and could handle their alcohol. Cokes may have been drunk, but he was not stumbling down. "That helped me, but it hurt in front of the other actors," Clarke recalled. "The thing about process is, you can't impress people all the time. You have to try different things. When you're crafting a performance, it isn't pretty. You have to make bad choices and look ugly for it to come out." He was willing to open himself up to this because of what was at stake: "These guys had two scenes and they had to knock it out of the park," he said of Cokes and Rooney.

Watching Clarke on opening night in Boston, I never thought of him as anything other than Sergeant Cokes; his monologue felt totally organic, and everything he did as an actor was as if he was an army sergeant with a head full of war memories. "It's hard to get the audience there," he told me. "The hardest part is to keep the guy laughing and smiling through it. It got easier the hundred-odd time I did the play."

This is not unlike the pressure people feel delivering a speech or making a crucial decision with all eyes on them. It gets easier the more often they do it. But even after the hundredth time, if they are thinking about anything other than what needs to be done, they are going to choke.

Whether Clarke thought one night's performance was better than another was a matter of degree. Each time he stood there, he was Cokes. He was thinking of nothing else. He was in a barracks in 1965, reminiscing about his old friend. And as an audience member, that was what I believed. Clarke was in a difficult role, but he was not thinking of the people who had done it before him, of failing and taking the play down with him, or of what he was going to do after the show. He was present, and that was why he could be clutch with one of the most challenging roles in contemporary American drama.

Yet beyond preparing for the role, there was another challenge that could have kept him from being present. He had to be his *own* Cokes, not the one from the original production, and he could not become fixated on the history of the monologue. When the play was originally performed, in 1976, Nichols was concerned that the Cokes monologue was a tough way to end a taut, two-act play. He based this on the audience's reaction. "They were crawling out of their skin," Rabe told me. But Rabe resisted Nichols's pressure to remove it. Rabe could see something they could not. "In the first preview, at the Long Wharf, the audience was like, 'What the fuck? Get me out of here,'" he told me. "I was in the light booth with a bottle of gin. But I believed the issue wasn't the speech—that if we could get the violence under control and deliver it in a terrifying but controlled way, the speech would provide comfort of a kind. Perspective. A vantage. Without that monologue, the play has a certain power but no resonance outside the room. But with the monologue and leading to the song, you're no longer in the room."

Getting the audience to that transcendent place is the sole responsibility of the actor playing Cokes: You have to feel the need Cokes has, that everyone has, for connection. This is why the speech is so crucial and why the actor giving it cannot think of anything other than being a Korean War veteran in 1965. Clarke accomplished this by never watching

the play, by pacing backstage with his headphones on. If he was following what was going on, he knew he would have trouble being present.
He had learned this the hard way during one rehearsal; he watched
from the audience and was so overcome by Cokes's loss that he was
in tears by the end of the monologue. ("Don't do that again," Ellis told
him.) Instead, Clarke became a play within a play. "It felt like a one-man
show," he told me. "The audience has to think all of these characters are
going to talk to me and it's going to be over. If they think it's going to be
a twenty-minute monologue, it's not going to work."

By the time the curtain went up in Boston, there was no chance he
would suffer from stage fright because he wasn't Larry Clarke anymore:
He was Sergeant Cokes. His friend Rooney and a young recruit had been
stabbed. The audience, having witnessed this, was in total shock and
unprepared for the jovial Cokes. His first line, addressed to the recruit
who had just mopped up the blood in the barracks, was: "What a day
gen'l'men. How you all doing?" The men did not know how to respond.
He followed this by asking where Rooney was, but before they could
answer, he started regaling them with stories about his war buddy. As his
monologue went on, his friendship for Rooney became more apparent and
his loss more pronounced. The other soldiers said nothing to him; they
were some combination of transfixed and paralyzed by Cokes's speech.
But through his rambling stories, Cokes took the audience to a different
place—he made them feel that they were there with him. "I gotta find
him," Cokes said. "He knows how to react in a tough situation. He didn't
come up here looking for me?" The audience's shock registered on the
other actors' faces as the monologue built to its gruesome, famous ending.
This was where Cokes described in excruciating detail how he wrestled a
Korean soldier to the ground, stuffed him into a foxhole with a grenade,
and sat on top of the trapdoor so the man could not escape. He equated
the whole incident to a Charlie Chaplin movie that ends when the other
soldier blows up. About to lie down to pass out, another soldier asked
Cokes, "You think he was singin' it?" The "it" was "Beautiful Streamers,"
the song paratroopers sang when their chute did not open. "Oh, yeah. Oh,
yeah; he was singin' it," Cokes said before doing his rendition in made-up,
Korean-sounding words to end the play.

BRIGHT LIGHTS, BIG CITY

A year after the Boston run, *Streamers* transferred to the Roundabout Theater in New York. After initially ruling out such a move, Rabe found himself more interested in the prospect as the Boston run progressed. There was always a higher level of pressure on any production that was taken to Broadway: Careers, reputations, and a lot of money were at stake. At the Roundabout, there was the added pressure of bringing this iconic play back to New York exactly thirty years after it had been nominated for a Tony Award. This was a big moment in the theater world. There might not be another staging of *Streamers* in Rabe's lifetime.

"It's not about the reviews or success—there is just a pressure about exposure," Rabe told me late one night. "There's the rawness of whatever you've written, and you're sitting there while they experience it. Watching it closely and coming off their expressions, it's a psychic reaction. I don't like it, ever. You can't separate from what they're experiencing, whether it's going well or not." While he never actually saw the production in Boston, only attending two days of rehearsals there, he worked closely with the actors and with Ellis in New York.

For Clarke it was different. He had been doing other roles in the intervening year and had not thought much about his character. "I scared David when I said I hadn't looked at my piece until I did the read-through in New York," he told me. Clarke had let the character go after each show, so it made sense that he would put him away, as it were, in the year between stagings. "When you open it, you commit," he said of his decision to try to forget about Sergeant Cokes. "It becomes part of your life. I don't like to do that all the time. It was more about relaxing and getting intuitively connected again."

This was what Clarke had learned in his early episodes on *Law & Order,* and it is what people who are clutch on any grand public stage know: You have to have the ability to block everything else out, but you cannot always exist in that state of readiness. A person who will be clutch has to develop the ability to snap into the present. Clarke could do this under pressure, but just as important, he could turn it off and forget what had happened. That was why he was so comfortable with the audience. He was there with them.

Only years later was Clarke willing to reflect on how well the staging had gone and what Rabe had accomplished. "The play is considered his best play, and it is studied mostly because of that coda at the end of the play," he told me. "It's a ballsy move. To have two people get murdered and then have a character come on and talk ad nauseam. You can fail grandly doing that as a playwright and as an actor." Under that level of pressure, being anything other than present would lead to failure.

[5]

FEAR AND DESIRE
Living Life Without a Plan B

WHEN MARK STEVENS'S father died of a heart attack at age forty, his mother was left with $84 in the bank. The year was 1965 and, as an eighteen-year-old college freshman, Stevens suddenly had to figure out a way to take care of her and his younger sister. He had no idea how the family was going to pay the rent, let alone the rest of its living expenses. At first the family thought Mark's father had a $5,000 life insurance policy, but the insurance company would not honor it, claiming he had lied on his application. Without any work experience or educational credentials, his mother would have trouble finding even the most basic job. So he went to the New York Department of Education and lied. He knew her high school had burned down, so he thought he could finagle a diploma out of them. At first they said they would just mail a copy, but then someone checked their records and realized his mother had never graduated. (She told Stevens she had left school because she wanted to go to a Frank Sinatra concert and just never returned.) After months of back-and-forth, Stevens said he was no longer asking for a diploma: He was telling them to send one immediately or his widowed mother and her two kids were going to starve. This was an exaggeration, but improbably the threat worked: The diploma arrived, and the next day his mother got a job as a clerk shelving books at the New York Public Library.

During this time, Stevens was making money busing tables, which in his mind ranked just below shoveling snow—his winter job—on his personal list of the most boring jobs in the world. To keep from going numb or becoming embittered, he told himself he was going to be the best busboy in the restaurant. If another boy bused six tables, he was going to triple that and clean all of the tables better. His strategy paid off: The waitresses for those tables appreciated what he was doing and were more generous in sharing tips with him. Better still, the plan he had cobbled together after his father died began to work. His mother was able to pay the rent and eventually remarried. His sister was handling what had happened well enough. He had moved home to finish college at C. W. Post University on Long Island, not far from his family's apartment. And as soon as he was done, he packed a bag and took off for Paris.

Today Stevens owns a marketing firm called MSCO in White Plains, New York. He lives in a seven-thousand-square-foot house in nearby Bedford and drives a white Mercedes SL 550. He has written a dozen business books that have sold well, and he appears regularly as a television commentator. His marketing firm has a list of top clients, including Nike, Starwood, GE, Guardian Life, Intrawest, Wolfgang Puck, and Estée Lauder. By any measure, Stevens has done well for himself. Add to this the fact that he has been married to the same woman since 1974 and raised two sons who are doing well in their own careers. Yet he has never forgotten the day his father died and he had to concoct a plan on the fly for his mother to survive. "I've carried the trauma of that, but I've recycled it into a discipline," Stevens said. "It's like an alcoholic who can't drink anymore—one drink and you'll go back to being an alcoholic. You need to use your instincts and bearings to change things."

There is little risk Stevens would go back to the cold-water flat in Queens where he grew up. He knows this on a rational level. But he also knows that plenty of successful people have been laid low by overspending and thinking a surge in success would always continue. Stevens knows life can change quickly, and he has woven that knowledge into his professional life, however successful he has been. For this reason, he is open in talking about his father's death three decades later. He has come far, yet when you hear him tell the story, it is as fresh as if it happened last week. Listening to the story of his success, I never felt he was bragging about what he has done. Nor does it come across as if he is trying to trump anyone—as in, "You think you had it hard, listen to this." Stevens tells people that his mother had $84 to her name when his father died because it motivates him but it also keeps him grounded. The memory of that moment, of having to find a way out of the situation under such intense pressure—no money meant no food—has informed the personal and professional decisions he has made since. From that day, any backstop he might have had was gone.

Yet his father's death affected him in another way, one that made Stevens a more complex person. His father always had expectations for him. He wanted him to be a doctor because it had been his dream. "He used to say that if I was not a success, it would kill him," Stevens told me. His father had spent his life in various sales jobs, bitter that he had had to leave Cornell University when his own father died to run the family's bookbinding business. He ran that company into the ground before Stevens was born and spent the rest of his life thinking about the great doctor he could have been but for fate. "He was a good, natural salesman, but he wanted respectability," Stevens said. "He drove me not to make money but to be a doctor. He never talked about money, but he always talked about being a success." The result was predictable. Stevens refused to live out his father's dream. He wanted to live out his own dream, even if he had no idea what it was at the time.

Stevens was driven by the twin fears of his past: that apartment in Queens and his father's vicarious expectations. That sent him on his own path. "I vowed never to be ordinary," he said. Millions of unmoored teens surely swear something similar each year, but Stevens acted on it. He admitted that he was afraid to end up broke like his father. "There are certain things we can't control, but I didn't want life to happen to me," he said. "I wanted to be able to control my destiny as much as possible, and money was important for that. It was important to have a bulletproof layer of money for whatever happens—you lose your job, your company goes bankrupt." From that frank admission, Stevens drove himself. His fear of the past coupled with his desire for a future different from the present informed the decisions he made, always under pressure both external and from within.

WHAT MAKES ENTREPRENEURS RUN?

The classic Hollywood image of the fear-driven, hard-charging leader is Sammy Glick, the protagonist in Budd Schulberg's novel, *What Makes Sammy Run?* It begins with this sketch of Glick:

> The first time I saw him he couldn't have been much more than sixteen years old, a little ferret of a kid, sharp and quick. Sammy Glick. Used to run copy for me. Always ran. Always looked thirsty.
> "Good morning, Mr. Manheim," he said to me the first time we met, "I'm the new office boy, but I ain't going to be an office boy long."
> "Don't say ain't," I said, "or you'll be an office boy forever."
> "Thanks, Mr. Manheim," he said, "that's why I took this job, so I can be around writers and learn all about grammar and how to act right."
> Nine out of ten times I wouldn't have even looked up, but there was something about the kid's voice that got me. It must have been charged with a couple of thousand volts.

The novel, published in 1941, was an unflattering portrait of Hollywood. Controversial at the time, it charted, uncharitably, Glick's sharp-elbowed path from nowhere to the top of the moviemaking business. From it, the name Sammy Glick has become synonymous with a sort of archetypical striver, a person willing to do anything or say anything to succeed. One of Glick's most memorable lines comes midway through the book: "Going through life with a conscience is like driving your car with the brakes on." And that was not for Glick. He was full speed ahead, running, and he continued to rise, from screenwriter to producer to studio head to son-in-law of a well-connected financier. He ran a long way from the Lower East Side of Manhattan, and when all he ever wanted seemed to be in his grasp, he pronounced, "Everything's mine. I've got everything. Everybody's always saying you can't get everything and I'm the guy who swung it." All seemed great until, on his wedding night, he found his bride in flagrante delicto with a handsome young actor. She was unfazed and let Glick know that their marriage was a business arrangement, between her father and him. She'd play her part, but she'd play it by her rules. This was cosmic payback for Glick's mercenary striving. He had worked hard, strived for more, cared about no one, and never looked back. He had navigated his way through every pressure-filled situation that came his way, but he could not control love.

The book, though, belies Schulberg's class prejudice. He was the son of a successful Hollywood producer and had been sent to Deerfield Academy and Dartmouth College. Right out of school, he landed one plum screenwriting job after another. When I spoke with him in 2004, he recounted the story of traveling to his alma mater with F. Scott Fitzgerald to write the film *Winter Carnival* in 1939. Fitzgerald was near the end of his career and hardly the man who had written *The Great Gatsby* and *Tender Is the Night*. But Schulberg was only twenty-five and realized his good fortune to be working with Fitzgerald, even if his best writing was behind him. Yet Schulberg had no love for the Hollywood system that had given his father so much. Two years later, already disillusioned by it, Schulberg published *What Makes Sammy Run?* It was a fascinating but one-sided story. What Schulberg missed in Glick was how strongly the fear of where he came from—the rough, violent, poverty-stricken Lower East Side—had driven him as much as his desire for fame. Glick became entranced by the glamour and overnight fortunes of Hollywood. He was running away from his past as much as he was running toward anything.

Far from Hollywood fantasy, the force of fear is a remarkable factor in helping someone make crucial decisions under pressure. In 2007, researchers at the University of Bath, in England, found that fear of something less desirable provided great motivation under pressure. They studied 281 university students, two thirds of whom regularly went to the gym. The researchers were focused on physical fitness and what motivated some students to work out and others not to. It asked half of them to imagine themselves as overweight and unattractive. The researchers then further divided the sample by asking half of the group to imagine themselves failing at their workout regime—and thus becoming even less attractive—while telling the other group to see themselves succeeding wildly and in doing so becoming much more attractive. Over the course of the study, the researchers found that the group that was motivated by the fear of looking awful stuck to their workout better than the group that was doing it with the hope of looking better. The gap between the two groups was significant, with 85 percent who wanted to avoid becoming unattractive continuing their workouts when told they were failing compared to 65 percent who were told they were succeeding. Even if both groups started out going to the gym regularly, the ones that were doing it to look better than they already did dropped off, while those who felt, in essence, that they had to dig themselves out of a hole were the ones who continued.

The purpose of the study was to assess how marketing works on consumers. Brett Martin, the University of Bath professor of management who conducted the study, said at the time, "How consumers see themselves in the future has a strong effect on how motivated they are to keep using a product or service." In other words, if they saw themselves as slipping back into something worse than they were, they tried harder. If they saw themselves as improving marginally on what they already had, they tried less. There was not the same incentive. The same held true for Mark Stevens. At eighteen, he was not looking at how great his life could be; he was desiring something different.

Yet Martin's study also found that at a certain point, fear stopped working. "When people dwell on a negative future, fear motivates them, yet as they move away from their feared state—a flabby body or a wrinkled skin—they become less motivated. At that point, marketers should take advantage of another insight of our study—that of motivating people with a more positive outlook," he said. "Once someone moves away from their 'feared self'—in this case, an unattractive body—because they are successful in the gym, they lose motivation, so highlighting thoughts of being unattractive is unlikely to work. But at that point, as they become more positive in their outlook, good marketing will build on this and suggest they can do even better. That type of motivation works for those with a positive outlook." It would make sense that once someone has attained something tangible, like a degree of physical fitness, fear would not work as a motivator anymore. This is the story with so many people who lose weight, only to put it all back on again. They started out trying to lose twenty pounds, and when they accomplished that, they went back to their old habits. This was not the case with someone like Stevens and other executives who have motivated themselves through the push and pull of fear and desire. For them, the pressure is always on, and there is no end zone. They feel that they need to keep going, or else they will be drawn back to where they started. That combination of fear and desire allows them to be clutch when someone motivated by just one of these emotions might fold.

In previous examples, people showed skills that have made them clutch in particular events—a legal case, a congressional hearing, war, a play. But those who have navigated through pressure-filled upbringings to successful lives are different. Theirs is an overarching life strategy for being clutch. It is macro, not micro. Fear and desire enable them to be clutch, but these are not strategies they can turn off. Obviously not all people who had a lousy childhood or suffered a business setback will learn to succeed under the pressure of leading an entrepreneurial life. So let's look more closely at Stevens and then Bernie Marcus, who went from being unemployed on the cusp of fifty to starting one of the country's most significant retail chains in less than a decade, to answer the question Why can some use fear and desire to succeed under pressure?

THE RUBIK'S CUBE OR THE VIOLIN?

Mark Stevens sells himself as a renegade. He has promoted his marketing firm by writing manifestos with provocative titles: His book *Your Marketing Sucks* was followed by *Your Management Sucks, God Is a Salesman: Learn from the Master,* and *Rich Is a Religion: Breaking the Timeless Code to Wealth.* His blog on marketing is called Unconventional Thinking. Yet in person he is far from the gonzo evangelist you might expect. Even with his rectangular glasses and black shirt, he comes across as introspective and melancholy. He mumbles often but laughs easily. As the conversation continues, he seems to shrink from his outsize persona. In doing so, he becomes more interesting than the sales pitch.

"You shouldn't think small," Stevens said. "You can always have a plan B. Most people out there have a plan A. Successful people have a plan A, B, C, and D—that's the key to life."

His plan A was initially to become a doctor to please his father. "The autocratic determination and the hitting started when I was five," Stevens told me. "My plan wasn't for myself; it was for him. He told me he would kill me if I disappointed him. I'm lucky I'm not in a mental hospital." But as he got older, he realized that plan wasn't his. He rejected it as much because of his rocky relationship with his father as because of his lack of interest in medicine. He had realized from his father's mistakes that if he didn't think through what he wanted to do, if he just went along with what happened, he could end up someplace he did not want to be—like dying at age forty and leaving a wife to fend for herself in a rented Queens apartment. "What came out of it was, I had to have a philosophy," he said. "If you don't have a philosophy, life happens to you. If you have a philosophy, you can shape your destiny, to some extent." His philosophy was that he would never work for anyone, which was his way of saying that he would have control over his life and not be average.

Yet it was while working for someone else that he hit upon his first idea for a business. In 1969, largely ignored in his desk job at Texaco, he came up with the idea for a small-business column—even though he knew nothing about business, big or small. He called up an editor at *Newsday*, the Long Island newspaper, and pitched the idea. The editor told him to send in a dozen columns, and he would make a decision as to whether they would publish them. "The first one was on the occupational safety and health act, which I knew nothing about, so I called people up," he said. "*Newsday* liked them and agreed to publish them." It did not matter that the topics were boring; they were his start.

Most young men would have been thrilled with their success and been content for quite some time. Not Stevens. After three months of writing the columns, he called up the United Press Syndicate and asked them to syndicate his small-business column. "They said, 'Who are you?' But then they took a look at them and said, 'We'll take this on.' I was excited as hell." It got better: After a couple of months, the company built a sales package around the column. He remembers that "they called and said, you have a winner here." He was twenty-three and cruising along. Two months later, the editorial department called back. Stevens was expecting more good news, but instead they dropped the ax. He was crushed. At this point, the average young man might have hunkered down, licked his wounds, and been content that he was even writing for *Newsday,* a major daily newspaper at the time. But that would have gone against his mantra—not to be average—so Stevens syndicated the column himself, building it up to eighty newspapers a mere three years after his first column ran. "I was brought up with the belief that you have five minutes to cry and whine and then you have to find what you're going to do," he said. Around that time, he was recognized for his work. "I got a John Hancock Award for outstanding financial journalism, lucid reporting, and excellence in understanding the nation's business," he said, with a hint of disbelief in his voice. "That was when I quit Texaco."

As he told the story in a café in Rye, New York, I had figured he had quit Texaco long before then to devote himself full-time to his column. He hadn't. He wasn't the dreamy sort; he was completely pragmatic. He didn't want to risk not having the steady income, and besides, the company's bureaucracy was so dense that no one caught on to what he was doing. It was his fear that kept him in the job. Once he was on his own, he transitioned from a moonlighting employee to an entrepreneur. He noticed that he received the same question over and over again from readers: How could someone get a small-business loan? In the early 1970s, such information, particularly outside of a major metropolitan area, was hard to come by. So he started putting a line at the bottom of his column, saying for $1 he would send people information on small-business loans. He wasn't sure if this would work—and he surely didn't have a list made up. The first day, he received 1,800 letters, each with a dollar in them. So he got to work gathering up loan sources first and then added some context. By this point, he actually knew something about small businesses and how they got their funding. He sent it out and kept sending it out as the dollar bills came in. "I was living life by a high-wire act," he said. "I was not living ordinary, which was my goal. The problem was, I didn't have any counsel. I probably could have done more with that list if I had had some advice."

The key, though, was that he had the desire to keep at it. Soon he had the Associated Press syndicating his column, which took some of the pressure off him to do it himself. Yet Stevens wasn't going to sit back and relax. He started thinking of his next project, and writing books seemed natural. "The first books were horrible," he said. "I call them my porno books. I never want anyone to dig them up." Then he landed on one that made money: 36 *Small Business Mistakes: How to Avoid Them,* which Prentice Hall published in 1980. Still, he wanted more. He wanted to raise his profile. That was when he wrote *The Big Eight,* about the Big Eight accounting firms. The book opens with the Academy Awards and an accountant from Price Waterhouse coming onstage with a winning envelope. He tells a wide-ranging tale of just how pervasive the reach of these accounting firms was and how no one in America really knew anything about them, beyond one firm's appearance at the Oscars. Somehow, he managed to turn a history of accounting firms into a potboiler about a "world of infinite discretion and vast financial power" that landed on the best-seller lists in 1981. As he thought it would, that recognition opened doors for him. His questioning of the firms' tactics led him to become a consultant, though mostly on small business. That was fine by him. Stevens was eager to put his ideas to work.

Other books followed, including an early biography of corporate raider Carl Icahn called *King Carl.* At first, Icahn did not want to cooperate. "I called him up in Bedford. I was amazed he picked up the phone. I said I'm going to write a book about you, and he said, 'No you're not.'" Icahn threatened to sue to block Stevens from writing it, but Stevens wouldn't back down. For four months, they argued back and forth, he said. What was funny was, after the book came out, they became friends and started playing tennis together at Icahn's estate in Westchester. It was a long way for a kid from Queens to come.

When Stevens became interested in marketing in the early 1990s, he admitted he knew little about it. "I had no training in this, but I realized that what passes for marketing sucks," he said. "Their first question is always about what the budget is. No one has a strategy. It's like saying I want to retire on $5 million without an age in mind or a sense of how you're going to save that much money. After they know the budget, then they come up with the ideas. They don't know anything about the business they're getting into; they're trying to win a creative award when what the business wants is to grow." So he put a novel spin on it. He told clients that his firm would help their company in some tangible way, be it through gaining market share or increasing revenue. He put himself out there as being accountable to the client and disparaged his competitors, who in his view were more interested in winning advertising and marketing awards. In 1994, he started his firm, MSCO. Their offices are, fittingly, in a vast, white building that was once Kraft's headquarters, until the company realized it had overreached and sold it to a property developer. Stevens set out to change the business of marketing from the inside the way he had critiqued the Big Eight accounting firms from the outside. He did so by laying down the gauntlet for his firm: He told clients that he would increase the size of their business, something that was measurable but a lot more difficult to accomplish than writing a catchy jingle.

After ten years in that business, in true Stevens form, he wrote *Your Marketing Sucks*. He came up with the title after an unorthodox business pitch. He had been trying to reach the head of marketing for Smith Barney for weeks. He had decided that he wanted the brokerage firm as a client. But the chief marketing officer would not return his calls. After six attempts, he tried again at eight P.M., and the CMO answered his phone. When Stevens recalled the conversation, his retelling sounded as though it might be embellished. "He said he wasn't interested, and I said, 'You should be.' He said, 'How do you have the temerity to say that to me?' And without thinking I said, 'Because your marketing sucks.'" Stevens then told him that he was a client of Smith Barney's private bank, which he was, and gave him his account number as proof. But he told the man he had not invested in any of the company's products in years. "I said, 'You send me a statement every month that's thirty pages long, but why don't you put something in it to educate me about a new fund?' He paused and looked up my account. Then he said, 'Why don't you come in tomorrow?'"

This is a typical Stevens story. It sounds perfectly true and reasonable when you hear it, but then you wonder about it afterward. Could the chief marketing officer have access to his account data? Had Stevens really not invested in the firm's products in six years? But the point of the story was what mattered: Stevens was never going to take no for an answer. He couldn't. At the back of his mind was what might happen if he ever did. Other stories usually get punctuated, at some point, with Stevens's admission that he doesn't care what people think of him. Most people who say this really do care what people think about them; in fact, they usually care an awful lot. But when Stevens says it, he is stating it as a fact, if not a guiding principle. "Once you start caring what the world thinks of you, you become locked in," he said. "It's a matter of independence." Not caring about people's opinions has the added benefit of reducing the pressure over a decision: You can make what you think is the right one and not worry about how it will be perceived.

Of course, some of Stevens's career success might be ascribed to luck rather than being clutch. He began writing a small-business column at a time in America when there was a great need for that kind of information. The Smith Barney marketing officer happened to pick up his own phone. But Stevens does not see it this way. He put his head down and kept working. He didn't stop; he kept running. If it wasn't a small-business column, it would have been something else. If his father had lived and kept tormenting him, he said he would have moved to California. If he had not gotten the job for Smith Barney, he had other clients and would have kept finding more. In our many conversations, he never told a story about a company that rejected him. It's not possible to run a marketing company without rejections, but that does not fit into his personal calculus. He was always racing forward. "I just wasn't going to let someone say no to me," he said.

What made him so resolute was the desire to go up from where he had started in life. But what made him circumspect was the fear that if he did not put everything into what he was doing, he would end up broke like his father. And what allowed him to continue looking ahead was his desire to have control over what he was doing. He got it, and he succeeded. Fear alone would not have gotten him to that point; he needed a strong desire to pull him when the push of fear weakened. "I'm not a magician. I haven't been a juggler, a ballroom dancer, an opium dealer. It's a continuum," he said. "I have always followed the law, but from an early age, I said I would not follow the rules."

At age sixty-two, he is not relaxing; he is working more. He has taken to writing on his BlackBerry while he hikes, his favorite form of exercise. He started this after having open-heart surgery in 2006. This may paint Stevens as a cliché of the driven, self-made man who cannot let up for a moment. There is some of that to him. But it goes deeper, to a personal philosophy that can be summed up by a question he asks to provoke people: Would you rather master a Rubik's Cube or a violin? This is not a question that has two right answers. There is only one. The violin. This is because it can never be mastered. If you're trying to solve a Rubik's Cube, it is actually mastering you. "Rubik is playing with me," he said. "I'm trying to please Rubik. It's a dumb thing to do." Stevens does not play the violin or any other instrument, but it is his metaphor for life. "I'd rather do those things that aren't masterable," he said. "You can't master the violin or parenthood or CEO-ship."

THE RUNNING-SCARED PHILOSOPHY

Bernie Marcus's drive comes from a different place than Mark Stevens's. In 1978, he suddenly found himself out of work and wondering what he was going to do. He was forty-nine and had just been fired from the Handy Dan chain of hardware stores. Worse, he left with his professional reputation in question. The new owner had claimed Marcus and another executive, Arthur Blank, had funneled money to a fund that illegally fought a union at one of the chain's stores. The charge was inflated to get rid of them, but it made finding another job difficult. Before going into retailing, Marcus had received a degree in pharmacy, but he did not see working as a pharmacist, something he had only ever done briefly, as a viable option. He was on his second marriage, and there was no way he could support his family on that.

Marcus, born poor to Russian immigrants in Newark, New Jersey, had few options, so he finally did what he had been talking about doing for years: He started his own hardware chain. He knew the business already, from years on the inside, and he felt comfortable enough to go off on his own. It helped that he did not have another choice. The challenge was, he would have to be clutch at every turn. For the first time, he was not working for someone else; he was playing with money he had raised himself. "We were running scared," Marcus told me. "We knew everything was on the line. We knew what happened could have a significant impact on the rest of our lives. But we were always aware of the fact that we could go down."

From the start, the stores he dreamed up would be different from not only Handy Dan but all hardware stores at the time. They would not even be stores—they would be warehouses filled floor to ceiling with everything a person could need to fix or improve his home. The chain would use its ability to buy in bulk to offer the lowest prices possible, essentially undercutting all of the competition. Yet they would be staffed with knowledgeable employees who could keep customers from becoming frustrated in the cavernous spaces and mirror the service of a small hardware store, the kind where the proprietor knew everyone and what they needed.

Marcus and Blank had a great plan, except for one glitch: They did not have enough money to fully stock their first two stores. They had done the research and knew that Atlanta was the right market for them. They had arranged for financial backing. But they just didn't have enough stuff. When Marcus surveyed one store, it looked more like a going-out-of-business sale than a grand opening. That was when he came up with a solution born as much of his street smarts as of his two decades in retailing. "We bought boxes. We bought empty paint cans. A box costs us 50 cents. With merchandise in it, it was a lot more," he told me proudly. "We had to give the illusion that we had merchandise in the store." It worked. "Pretty soon," he said, "we had customers coming in the door and we could buy merchandise." In taking this outlandish step, Marcus made the place look like a fully stocked warehouse. By 1981, two years after the first store opened, the concept was doing so well that Marcus and his partners decided to take the company—The Home Depot—public. With that, Marcus and Blank were on their way to becoming billionaires.

The quick thinking behind the shelf-stocking story is emblematic of how the two ran The Home Depot. They made that apparent when they dubbed their management strategy "running scared." It emphasized what was not working, instead of congratulating themselves on the things that were going well. "We had confidence in our philosophy," he told me. "Correcting our mistakes became a major part of it. Every company makes terrible, tragic mistakes. How a company recovers and corrects the mistake can put you way ahead of anyone else." Marcus emphasized, though, that even when the economy was strong and they were opening stores at a rapid clip, they stuck with the running-scared philosophy.

This approach could also be seen as a commentary on where the two came from: Marcus grew up poor in Newark, and Blank came from working-class Sunnyside, New York. The success of The Home Depot gave them lives that were far richer than anything they could have imagined, but that did not stop them from always looking for ways to go forward and not back to where they came from. They were never content, and they never let up, even when they could have. Their focus was on the "character" of their employees, even when they had five hundred employees. And Marcus wanted to have contact with them. He wanted to be involved in the training of every senior manager and division head, but he also wanted to walk the floors with the workers. "They'd tell us where we were screwing up, and we'd fix it the next day," he said. That responsiveness was key.

Like every company, they published a corporate motto—"Doing the right thing instead of just doing things right." Most of these slogans are little more than clichés meant to show customers that the company appears to care. But Marcus and Blank were serious. They kept in touch with their associates on the floors of their warehouses. A key component of their management was to ask these employees what was working and what was not and then to act on what they were told. They feared losing touch—and going the way of Handy Dan, which eventually went out of business.

For Marcus, this philosophy has the practical effect of both encouraging individual initiative and expecting accountability. The first time we spoke, he told me how heartened he had been when The Home Depot employees did their best to pitch in after terrorists crashed an airplane into the Pentagon on September 11, 2001. Without prompting, the employees started shipping over timber to shore up the walls of the Pentagon. "I never knew about it," he said a few years after he had stepped down as chairman. "They just did it." The same was true, he said, when an associate would order more plywood for a store in advance of a hurricane. This was the kind of initiative he wanted to instill in his employees. "If there was a tornado, we would send people out to cut trees down. We felt it was something we had to do," he said. Yet it also helped the hardware chain ingratiate itself in the wider community. The founders hoped that if The Home Depot was helping just as a small hardware store would, then people might not complain that their neighborhood store had disappeared. This fear of failing, blended with a desire to fit in, help out, and succeed, allowed Marcus to build a successful brand.

But initiative without accountability would have been a disaster. The Home Depot ensured that each store had many layers of management to deal with problems before they reached the top. This was a business philosophy, but it was not a rigid one. Marcus told me a story the last time we spoke that captured the independent, almost insouciant, attitude he encouraged in employees. He was touring a rival executive's store, and he noticed that all of the employees were deferential to him. They were afraid of the chief executive and for that reason were never going to give him the right answer. Marcus knew that in a crisis, without the right information, he would have been sunk. They then walked into a Home Depot store, and Marcus said he was swarmed by employees. "Someone would walk up to me and say, 'Why do you let people buy this crap?'" he recalled. "I'd ask them what was wrong with it, and they'd tell me. I'd make a call right there and find out why we'd bought that piece of crap." He knew he needed them to spot things he couldn't. But what was more telling, he said, was that the other executive was shocked by this lack of deference.

THE RISK OF CONTENTMENT

The way Marcus and Stevens avoided becoming Sammy Glick characters is instructive: They never got too content with their success and were able to stay clear-eyed under pressure. For Marcus, the running-scared management approach kept him and everyone else focused on the goal. There could be no fearlessness when fear is driving you to stay vigilant. And since stepping down from the company with an estimated net worth of over $2 billion, his charitable work has kept him looking beyond himself, from building the Georgia Aquarium to funding the Marcus Institute to help children with brain disorders. "I'm going to keep going until they carry me out of here," he told me. He could sit back and do nothing, but it is not in his personality. He would not be where he is if that had ever been part of his personal philosophy. Desire won out over fear, but it kept pushing him forward.

Stevens does not have Marcus's wealth, but he is well aware of the garishness that many self-made men embrace and what it does to the clarity of their thinking. If you are maintaining vast estates, many cars, and several other big-ticket toys, there is a risk that you will become complacent in your decision making. "The fear of failure and the drive to succeed got me past the glitches I ran into," Stevens said. "It's been a series of 'Oh, God, it's going to end' moments. I've never feared that I was going to be found out as a fraud or incompetent, but that my luck would run out. I still fear it." Stevens told me a story about his car that illustrates this perfectly. He drives a Mercedes SL and has driven this model for more than a decade, buying a new one every few years. The car retails for $104,000, a vast sum for the average car buyer. Stevens knows it is a nice car, but he could buy a nicer one—if it did not make him uncomfortable. "There's a point where the pragmatic accommodation of reliability and comfort places me precisely where I am, but I'd never buy a Bentley or a Rolls-Royce—it would violate my Calvinistic sense," he said. "I test-drove a Bentley once, took it out for three or four hours. I was embarrassed the whole time. At first I felt like I was driving an apartment building; then I felt like a fucking asshole." Forty years later, his goal is still independence, not the trappings to let the world know he has succeeded.

Of course, people who have been motivated by fear to work harder and push themselves further are not always as good under pressure as Marcus and Stevens. After a remarkable run, their Achilles' heel is often self-congratulatory behavior—when they switch from fear to entitlement. Being clutch gets them to the top, but then they try to leave that behind. At best, they make decisions that are clouded by things other than the issues at hand, which shows being clutch is not a constant: The ability can be lost, particularly if you become complacent. At the very worst, these seemingly great leaders become stereotypical plutocrats: Bernie Madoff, John Rigas of Adelphia, Bernie Ebbers of WorldCom, Richard Scrushy of HealthSouth, Dennis Kozlowski of Tyco, Ken Lay of Enron. Out of the 2008 financial crash came Angelo Mozilo, a man driven by fear who became fearless. He built Countrywide into one of the nation's largest mortgage lenders, and then he went for even more— for even greater profit through exotic mortgages that made it seem as though all customers could afford the home of their dreams, and for political connections bought by sweetheart deals for "friends of Angelo." In this way, Mozilo was Sammy Glick: He had escaped from working in his father's Bronx butcher shop to become a leader in the mortgage industry, but then he stopped running away from where he came from and toward something unattainable, the respect of the well-heeled bankers who mocked him as the "tan man" for his permanently bronzed skin. His motivation flipped from being fear-driven to ego-driven, and he lost his way. As I will discuss in part 2, you cannot be clutch when you are making business decisions to advance your personal standing—or get revenge for being slighted.

Mark Stevens never rose to the level of Mozilo's wealth, and Bernie Marcus surpassed it. But when Stevens and Marcus talk about what tempered their fear and guided them, they sound remarkably similar. "I was formed with a shock to the system, and I developed a plan from there," Stevens said. "My life has been a built-in competition with myself—it's not just speed that counts; it's achievement. I never wanted to move laterally." Marcus credited his Home Depot success to an obsession with how his company was performing. "We never stopped worrying," he said. "Bad things happen. The economy changes. You've got hurricanes, catastrophe, people making terrible mistakes. This is a constant thing. There isn't a day in retail where you're not faced with some kind of problem that you have to deal with."

The combination of fear and desire, like focus, discipline, adaptability, and being present, can propel someone to be clutch. Unlike the other traits, though, fear is more dangerous. It is a great force for making clutch decisions when blended with desire. But it is at the fulcrum between being clutch and emotions that are far worse than choking. This is where the story of Sammy Glick comes back into play. He had everything he wanted. But on his wedding night, he broke down in tears when he saw his new wife in bed with another man. He had lost the moral compass that allows someone who is clutch out of fear and desire to stay grounded.

[6]

DOUBLE CLUTCH
What Billie Jean King Did for Women

ON SEPTEMBER 20, 1973, Billie Jean King and Bobby Riggs entered the Houston Astrodome in a procession worthy of gladiators. King, one of the greatest female tennis players of her day, was carried in on an Egyptian litter by four barrel-chested men in togas. Riggs, a player once ranked number one in the world, was wheeled into the stadium by a bevy of voluptuous women pulling a rickshaw. Some thirty thousand people had filled the stands, and the match was broadcast live to an estimated 48 million American homes as well as beamed via satellite to thirty-six foreign countries. Howard Cosell, the greatest sports broadcaster of his day, did the color commentary for what was billed as "The Battle of the Sexes." The whole thing had the feeling of a publicity stunt, except that its implications were serious. Riggs, fifty-five, had been shooting his mouth off about women being inferior athletes compared with men, and King, twenty-nine, had stood up to prove him wrong.

The "battle" actually began five months earlier when Riggs challenged Margaret Court to a similar match on Mother's Day. Court, thirty, was a top-ranked women's player, but in the prematch press conference Riggs started to psyche her out. "Do you realize, Margaret, that this is the most important match ever played?" he asked. "Just think how many women are counting on you." (On the day of the match, he handed her roses on the court, and she curtsied.) King had been worried about the match's significance, too. "This isn't about tennis," she told Court. "This is about social change, about women's sports and women's rights." Whether it was that pressure or the junk shots of a hustler, Riggs beat Court 6–2, 6–1, and worse, he did it in under an hour. *Time* magazine put him on the cover the next week, and his victory became known as the Mother's Day Massacre. The magazine branded him a "male chauvinist hustler," and with that he became the poster boy for men who thought women could never compete with them in sports, let alone the workplace. King had said that Riggs had been taunting her to play him for years, and after he beat Court she felt she had to accept his challenge. Riggs was so confident that he was going to beat King as he had Court that he said he would jump off a bridge in their home state of California if he lost. To back up his boast, the consummate hustler placed sizable bets on himself to win.

On match day in Houston, the rules were different from those in Court's match. Riggs had agreed to play King over five sets, the longer men's format, which seemed to be to his advantage. Riggs, considered great in his day, had won the singles, doubles, and mixed doubles titles at Wimbledon in 1939—the so-called Triple Crown. But King dominated the women's circuit. She had won Wimbledon four more times than Riggs had at the time of their match. (She would win six grass-court titles overall, in addition to four U.S. Opens. She had also helped start the Virginia Slims tennis tour for women in 1970.) Beyond the rules, the atmosphere was more suited to a college football game than to the more staid environs of a tennis match. Her fans were yelling "Atta boy, Billie" when she scored a point, while his were chanting "Kill! Kill!" (She, however, had George Foreman, the heavyweight champion, in her cheering section.)

From the outset, King ran Riggs all over the court. She served and volleyed to beat him at his own game. In the first set, the match stood at four games to five, with Riggs down but serving. When it reached 30–40, Riggs, the self-proclaimed hustler, double-faulted on his serve to lose. King won the second set 6–3. In the final set, she exhausted him.

At one point, down 2–4, he had to stop, complaining of hand cramps. She went on to beat him 6–3 to win. In the *New York Times* story the next day, King was lauded for her victory. The paper reported that she took just over two hours "to reaffirm her status as one of the most gifted and tenacious competitors in sport, female or male." It went on: "Most important, perhaps for women everywhere, she convinced skeptics that a female athlete can survive pressure-filled situations and that men are as susceptible to nerves as women." (Despite that summation, she was referred to as "Mrs. King" throughout, while Riggs was jocularly called "Bobby"—a nod to the backslapping men's-club culture of the day.) King, at the time, called the victory "the culmination of nineteen years of tennis." In the press conference afterward, she revealed that she had learned from Court's mistakes. She knew Riggs's weaknesses and how she could exploit them. And he admitted as much afterward: "She was too good, too fast. She returned all my passing shots and made great plays off them."

Had King lost the match to Riggs, though, all of her other accomplishments would have been overshadowed. It would have been the footnote that dogged her for the rest of her life. Her obituary would have certainly been headlined, "Pioneering Tennis Champion King, Lost Battle of the Sexes, Dies." For her, beating Riggs was more than the ultimate clutch win. There was more to it than just besting a former Wimbledon champion who was now fifty-five. She was playing to beat him—and shut him up once and for all—but that was only the first layer of pressure. She was also playing for the greater, heavier goal of proving that women could compete against men. That layer made this a double-clutch moment: There was the pressure of something she could affect—the match—and the far larger, more powerful pressure of being thrust forward as the bulwark of the women's equality movement. A year earlier, King had been instrumental in the passage of Title IX, which required colleges to fund men's and women's sports equally. If she then went down to Bobby Riggs, as Margaret Court had, the one-two punch would have been disastrous for the equality movement she had associated herself with.

Riggs, for his part, had nothing to lose but his own money. He had already gotten so much out of his gambit. While he may have been a former world number-one-ranked tennis champion, a *60 Minutes* interview before the match revealed that for decades since retiring from the sport he had worked in New York City like any other businessman-commuter. A return to tennis and the spotlight after a failed marriage was a return to an interesting life. After all, he won Wimbledon as the world was entering World War II. If he had beaten King, he would have dined out on his battle-of-the-sexes shtick for years. King stopped that, but more important, she proved that women, under extreme pressure, could be as clutch as men.

THE BURDEN OF DOUBLE CLUTCH

When a woman succeeds under the inherent pressure of what she is doing but also while being judged against men, she is double clutch. Here's why. If one woman beats another under the pressure of a major tournament, coming from behind to do so, against expectations, she is clutch. But transpose that to worlds where women have not historically been leaders—the business world, scientific research, the military—and the woman who succeeds there is double clutch. She first has to perform under the pressure of the task at hand as anyone would, but then she also has to navigate through an inherent bias that says women have not succeeded historically in these fields. She has combined all five elements that would make us say she was a clutch performer but then taken her skills to a higher level. She has made her sex irrelevant and her performance paramount. She has done this against the inherent pressure of the task and also the pressure of institutional bias.

Some thirty-five years after King's victory, the tennis world has changed. Venus and Serena Williams are the face of twenty-first-century tennis as much as or more so than Roger Federer. They are exciting to watch and have become off-court role models. Thanks to one of the reforms King pushed for in her career, equal prize money, women now earn the same as men when they win a Grand Slam title. The first tournament to fall in line was the U.S. Open—after King threatened not to defend her title in 1973 if they did not equalize the purse—and the last was Wimbledon in 2007. All would seem fine in tennis, if not in general. But the perception endures that women are not as clutch as men.

In 2007, Daniele Paserman, an economics professor at Hebrew University, published a paper that gained wider currency when it was discussed in an article on Slate.com. Paserman argued that female tennis players were worse than male tennis players under pressure. His sample was the Grand Slam tournaments in 2005 and 2006. "The set-level analysis indicates that both men and women perform less well in the final and decisive set of the match," he wrote at the beginning of the study. In other words, there was more pressure on playing to win at Wimbledon than at some run-of-the-mill tournament. "The drop in performance of women in the decisive set is slightly larger than that of men, but the difference is not statistically significant at conventional levels," he continued. "On the other hand, the detailed point-by-point analysis reveals that, relative to men, women are substantially more likely to make unforced errors at crucial junctures of the match. Data on first serves suggests that women play a more conservative and less risky strategy as points become more important." An unforced error happens when a player fails to return a shot that he or she should have been able to hit. Two classic examples are double-faulting on the serve and hitting an easy shot into the net. Men in the Grand Slam events made unforced errors 30 percent of the time regardless of where they were in the match, while women, the study of the eight tournaments found, made 6 percent more unforced errors on the most important points in a match.

From there, the paper used tennis to open a discussion on the labor force and wage inequality. One of the papers Paserman cited to set up his argument was a 2003 study entitled "Performance in Competitive Environments: Gender Differences" in the *Quarterly Journal of Economics*. It argued that women performed less well against men when pay was structured competitively, as in bonuses, than a straight payout. Paserman's paper concluded somewhat differently, hedging in the end from making a connection between tennis and the rest of life. "By contrast, here we find that women's performance deteriorates as competitive pressure rises, even when the competition is clearly restricted to women alone," he wrote. One interpretation, he suggested, was that women become more conservative and risk averse when the pressure is on and therefore make more unforced errors. Steven Landsburg, the *Slate* writer, laid out the argument statistically. He noted that only 2.5 percent of the highest-paid executives in America were female and that women accounted for only 9 percent of the members of the National Academy of Sciences. "Depending on your biases, you can read that as evidence that women are better at science than business, that corporations discriminate against women, or (if you believe that profit-maximizing corporations get everything just right) that the National Academy discriminates against men," he wrote. Then he ensured that Paserman's paper would attract maximum attention with this: "Women—especially high-achieving women—choke under pressure." He highlighted the difference in unforced errors, emphasizing the six-percentage-point difference. "That is almost surely too big a difference to be mere coincidence," he said. "What besides choking could explain these errors?"

This made no logical sense to me. And it turned out that many other things could explain the errors. The top contender was statistical accuracy and a small sample size—eight tournaments. Ian Ellwood, a physics professor, posted a detailed rebuttal. He dismissed the basis of the paper by saying Paserman was "comparing a dubious measure of choking with a fishy measure of importance." He noted first that the study was comparing unlike things—men and women have different styles of playing tennis—in a forum where there is no ability to have a control group. Tennis is always competitive, because you are playing against an opponent. Hitting golf shots on a driving range or shooting free throws in basketball practice can be done in environments with no external pressure, so you can measure the difference between practicing and playing. He also doubted the significance of the unforced error as a measure of clutch, as the greater athleticism of male tennis players could allow them to muscle shots over the net that female players could not. This is physiology, not psychology. He reserved his greatest criticism for the way Paserman extrapolated his findings in the conclusion beyond the tennis matches he observed, calling the research "fuzzy and muddled." What is central to the argument is how polarizing the debate is: One side is looking to prove scientifically that women choke more than men, while the other is appalled by the science that supposedly supports the finding and, by extension, dubious that such a distinction exists. I think of it as the difference between believing wholeheartedly in the science of economics, which is difficult to do at times, and caring deeply about social equality, which often leads people to overlook evidence that people are not inherently equal.

Marianne Bertrand, an economist at the University of Chicago Booth School of Business, found a different reason for the paucity of women navigating the pressure of top-paying corporate jobs: taking time off to have children. In a groundbreaking study, "Dynamics of the Gender Gap for Young Professionals in the Corporate and Financial Sectors," she looked at men and women who had received their MBAs from Booth between 1990 and 2006. In that time, 570 degrees were awarded, with a quarter going to women. The premise was that graduating with an MBA from the same top business school should put men and women on an equal footing as they went to work. She accounted for differences in the professions chosen—a top marketing executive will make less than a foreign-exchange trader with the same years of experience—so she was comparing similar sets statistically. What was so radical was that her study found no evidence of gender-based discrimination. What it did find was a serious drop in earnings for women who took more than six months off after they had a child. Their pay continued to fall if they worked fewer hours than their colleagues. Women who did not take time off did not suffer the same loss in earnings and maintained relative parity with men. The difference in wages, her research found, was most pronounced in the corporate and financial sector. Women who became doctors, lawyers, and academics did not suffer equivalent losses.

"We can identify the lower hours as the big driver between men and women and men and mothers," Bertrand told me, early one morning before leaving her Chicago apartment for class. "You may be assigned to different jobs than others who may need to be there twelve, fifteen hours a day. You take a man and a woman and put them in the same hour box, the same experience box, the same education box, and they look similar."

In other words, if as Landsburg suggested, companies maximize profits, then they believe women can handle the pressure. What may be a differentiator, though, is the relative lack of women in certain fields. Bertrand said the nature of jobs in finance and the corporate world accounts for the difference. They have longer, less flexible hours, which are tough for working mothers to accommodate. Whereas a doctor can have a level of control over her hours, a woman working for a bank or an industrial company is typically more confined to a set schedule that does not account for children. The issue is not that women do not rise up the corporate ladder because they cannot make the tough decisions; it is that they cannot put in the same number of hours that men and women without children can. She noted that the same drop in earnings would be expected for men who had been out of the workforce. "There is not a story here that investment banks don't give high-profile jobs to women because they fear women are going to have kids," she told me. "The difference happens after kids, when women work less. There is no difference between the men and women without kids, in terms of earnings." Bertrand noted that she herself had waited until later in life to have her two children—after she had put in the hours to establish herself as a leading economist of her generation.

This is where the question of women and pressure often gets lost in the broader discussion about women and equality. Bertrand's study does not, and reasonably could not, account for differences in perception. When Sallie Krawcheck and Zoe Cruz, two of the highest-ranking women in banking, were pushed out of their positions at Citigroup and Morgan Stanley, respectively, the news coverage focused on their being among the few high-ranking women in finance instead of on the jobs they did or did not do. In Cruz's case, a *New York* magazine profile entitled "Only the Men Survive" speculated that she was fired because she could be, not because the losses in her division were her fault alone.

When I spoke to Krawcheck after she had landed a top job at Bank of America, she did not want to go into the details of leaving Citigroup. She pointed out the obvious in any of these top corporate positions: "They're high-pressure jobs by their nature." This moots the initial implication that she and Cruz were not able to cope with the demands of the jobs.

They also both have children. Krawcheck, whom I found personable but steely and shrewd, offered insight into how she had continued to climb so high. "I'll be having a fight with my sister, and she'll cry," she told me. "You're never going to make it if you do that. She can't help it." It reminded me of the famous line from the film *A League of Their Own*: "There's no crying in baseball." The same can be said for Wall Street. What I found intriguing—and hypocritical—was the initial reaction when men like Dick Fuld of Lehman Brothers and Jimmy Cayne of Bear Stearns drove their respective banks into the ground in 2008. The coverage focused on management mistakes and market forces seemingly beyond their control. It did not, at first, say that these were men who had grown arrogant from prolonged power and so out of touch with what their institutions were doing that they had choked under pressure. (In chapter 7, I will look at how two other bank leaders weathered the financial crisis.)

Still, when Jack Welch, the former chief executive of GE, spoke on the subject of women and pressure, people listened—and were provoked by what he had to say: "There is no work-life balance. There are work-life choices, and you make them, and they have consequences," he said as a keynote speaker at the Society for Human Resource Management annual meeting in June 2009. Then he spoke directly about the pressure any leader must work under, saying the problem with women taking time off was that they were "not there in the clutch" to make decisions under pressure. "The women who have reached the top of Archer Daniels, of DuPont, I know these women. They've had pretty straight careers," he said, according to the *Wall Street Journal*. "We'd love to have more women moving up faster. But they've got to make the tough choices and know the consequences of each one."

What he said caused a minor kerfuffle at the time, not least of all because Welch's self-styled "straight from the gut" approach seems gruff, almost arrogant, at the best of times. He was not saying that women in general were not good under pressure but that they had to be in the workplace as much as everyone else to make decisions under pressure. His point echoed Bertrand's research: Women who do not take time off for kids do not suffer the same drop in income as women who do; they remain on par with men. That does not mean they do not have kids; it means they do not stop working. And, of course, few men who lead companies ever purposely take time off in their careers. The point, shown by Bertrand, is that a woman with the same educational credentials as a man can earn as much and rise as high, making all the pressure-filled decisions needed to do so—if she puts in the time. What is holding her back under pressure is not her gender, but the time needed to become clutch. Let's delve deeper into the Battle of the Sexes.

A GUIDE TO VICTORY

When Billie Jean King beat Bobby Riggs, she contended with both the pressure of the match and the pressure of the women's rights movement. Winning or losing matches was something she had been dealing with since she was a kid, but having the weight of a cause on her shoulders was entirely new. Riggs had made the most of his victory over Court, thumping his chest and crowing about male superiority. King knew that if she lost this match, the women's rights movement would suffer. It was a lot of pressure on one tennis match. But in her victory, resoundingly beating Riggs in straight sets, she showed that a woman could be clutch on the biggest stage of her time. How did she do it? King was clutch because she did everything it took to be great under pressure. In one double-clutch moment, she brought to bear all five of the principles we've discussed—focus, discipline, adaptability, being present in every moment, and keeping herself motivated through the right combination of fear and desire.

First there was her focus. King did not prepare for the match as if she was playing a man the same age as her father, which Riggs was. She prepared as she would have for any big match, and that meant she trained as hard as she could. She trained emotionally as well as physically. She treated the match as if her opponent was Margaret Court and this was a Grand Slam event. She actually consulted Court's coach and other coaches who knew Riggs's style of play so she could be as prepared as possible. She remembered that in 1939 he had won the triple crown at

Wimbledon, a testament to his ability under pressure. That was thirty-four years earlier, but she focused on his status as a past Grand Slam champion. "I always think it is far better to overestimate your opponent than to underestimate him or her," she wrote in *Pressure Is a Privilege*. All of this allowed her to keep the second layer of pressure at bay.

On the court, King's discipline was in her shot selection. She knew how Riggs had tied up Court with short, spinning shots, so she decided to play long rallies. This meant she would be running him back and forth, trying to tire him out. This was not her normal strategy as a player. She liked to win points quickly and move the match along. But if she did this with Riggs, she feared he could gain the upper hand. She was the one who had suggested they play the longer men's format—of five sets, not three—to guard against his getting off to a quick start, as he did against Court, and winning again. She was not sure what kind of shape Riggs was in or whether she could keep up if the match went on to four or five sets. Instead of hitting hard, sharp shots, she hit soft ones deep, so he would have to run for them and then put effort into returning them. She was using the simple physics of tennis to her advantage: A hard-hit shot is easier to return when you get to it because it will bounce off your racquet with the force of the ball plus the force of your return stroke. "It worked like a charm," she wrote later. "Within minutes he was covered in sweat."

At the same time, she said, she was not wedded to her strategy of tiring him out. If it became evident that it was not working, she would change it. Her goal, after all, was to win. This was where she was really being adaptable and fighting the fight, not the plan. Her plan was to win the first set to give herself a cushion, but if that did not happen, she was ready to adjust her strategy. As Colonel Kolditz said, being outer-focused keeps a person in the fight. If she had started to look inward, she would have risked becoming too conscious of the magnitude of what she was trying to achieve. It could have thrown her off her game. King was well aware of how important this event was in her career and for women's rights. Yet she kept her focus outward, on the match. "I was aware of its significance at the time, but in order to win I had to remain focused on the immediate goal," she said. "I just wanted to beat Bobby Riggs. So I totally embraced the opportunity."

Yet once she felt she had prepared all she could, she relaxed. She became totally present. Before the match she went to a cocktail party put on by the sponsors, to thank them. When she was asked if she would mind being carried in on the Egyptian litter, she agreed. "About two months before the match, I was very anxious," she wrote. "But because of all of the focused preparation I did, the closer the match got, the calmer I became." Her strategy in previous matches had been "one ball at a time," meaning what she cared about was the next point. She thought about that point alone, not about the set or the broader match and all of its implications. This was a difficult but essential tactic to use in her match with Riggs. After all, there were thirty thousand screaming fans and scores of television cameras all around her. Keeping her attention on the court was paramount.

What she feared, of course, was the impact her defeat would have on the women's rights movement. "If I lost, it was going to be an even bigger blow to women's rights—Bobby would now have proved his point by beating not one but two of the top-ranked women in the sport," she wrote. That was why her desire to win was so strong. It was hard to overstate the fixation on this match: The early 1970s was to the women's rights movement what the early 1960s had been to the civil rights movement, and a King loss would have fired the belief that women were not the equal of men. She feared she could lose support for Title IX, which had only been passed the previous year, and hurt collegiate athletes. And she was honest enough to admit there was a far greater downside than upside to the match: Riggs, by 1973 standards, was old, so beating him wasn't like beating Rod Laver, the top men's player of King's day.

What needs to be emphasized again is that King's double-clutch moment came after she had established herself as a top female tennis player. She already knew how to win against her peers under the toughest circumstances in her sport. At seventeen, she had accomplished her childhood dream of winning at Wimbledon when she captured the doubles title. As she wrote in her memoir, she had the added pressure of knowing her childhood coach was dying of cancer and had dreamed of coaching a Wimbledon champion. (He died the day after her victory.) She then won Wimbledon five more times before facing Riggs. In fact, by the time she met Riggs she had been in sixteen Grand Slam finals.

THE CHALLENGE CONTINUES

So why, four decades after King was clutch, do questions about women not being as good as men under pressure persist in sports and business? In so many ways, it is an emotional, not a rational argument. Men, on average, are physically stronger than women, but being clutch has nothing to do with strength. It is about focus, discipline, adaptability, being present, and in many cases being driven by fear. These are all things any woman can do just as well as any man. Krawcheck's continued success on Wall Street should end the argument about women and pressure. Yet the desire to pit the two genders against each other persists in unequal forums that are meant to prove something they cannot. Think of what happened to Michelle Wie. As a tween, Wie decided to compete against the top male professional golfers, and the outcome was not nearly as good as what King achieved. When Wie received her first exemption to play in a PGA Tour event, the Sony Open in her home state of Hawaii, she had only ever won the U.S. Women's Amateur Public Links Championship, not a top-rated event in terms of the quality of the field. What was remarkable was that she had won it at age thirteen and went on to make the cut at her first LPGA event, the prestigious Kraft Nabisco Championship. Then, in her first PGA Tour event, she shot a 69, or four under par, in the second round. Suddenly, she was a child prodigy, the female Tiger Woods. And she seemed to just keep going. The next year she finished just outside the top ten of the U.S. Women's Open. Two years later, she made an impressive run through the Men's Amateur Public Links Championship. The winner of that event traditionally got invited to play at the Masters in Augusta, Georgia—a club that did not allow female members—and she publicly said she wanted to win it for the invite. There was a certain youthful arrogance to this, given that she was only fifteen at the time. (Tiger Woods was nineteen the first time he played in the Masters.) But she was a solid golfer and seemed to be able to back up her boasts.

Then Wie's problems started. She had been tied for the lead in the 2005 U.S. Women's Open heading into the last round and was poised to become the youngest woman to win it, and younger than Tiger had been when he won his first Men's Open at age twenty-four. But on the last day, she blew up with an 82—ten over par—and finished twenty-third. This was a telltale sign of choking, of losing her focus and discipline, of probably dreaming of the victory before it was hers. The next week she found herself playing on the men's tour, at the John Deere Classic, where she missed the weekend cut by two strokes. In doing this, she beat forty-eight men. But she had also started to alienate female pros and golf commentators, who had begun to grow weary of so much focus on a fifteen-year-old girl. A few days before her sixteenth birthday, Wie turned pro, collected huge endorsement checks, and was promptly disqualified from her first professional tournament, for violating a simple rule about dropping a ball.

After that, in full public view, her stellar game started to come apart as her lack of experience showed through. And when it got bad, it quickly got worse. She withdrew from tournaments. She injured her wrist. She lost her long, smooth swing and started whacking the ball all over the course. She was choking under pressure that never had to be there. She was dealing with the regular pressure of playing tournament golf at the highest level, but layered on top of that was the pressure of winning any professional tournament with only one amateur victory, the pressure of being a girl competing against women, the pressure to play well in PGA tournaments because she was the main draw, and most of all the pressure, implicit or overt, from her parents. It reminded me of the story of Bobby Riggs approaching Chris Evert to play him. This was before he had beaten Margaret Court, but Evert's father—she was still a teenager—declined on her behalf. He knew that kind of unnecessary pressure could stunt her development. Lacking this kind of parental protection, Wie suffered. And as she choked in various tournaments, it was evident that she completely lacked the tools to be clutch. She was too young, too inexperienced, and too distracted by the pressure her family had created. Her failures led inevitably to commentators saying women could not compete on the men's tour. A setback had been dealt where none needed to be.

The year of Wie's one amateur victory was also the one and only time

Annika Sorenstam, the best women's golfer of her generation, played in a PGA Tour event. On a course almost a thousand yards longer than any on the LPGA Tour, Sorenstam played well. In the first round, she shot a 71, one over par. It was way off the leader, who was at six under, but it was respectable. If she shot a similar round the next day, she had a chance to make the cut and become the first woman to play on the weekend in a men's tournament in sixty years. It wasn't to be. On Friday, she shot 74 and missed the cut by four strokes but finished as an ambassador for her sport. There was pressure on her throughout, but it was the pressure of someone who was playing a tough course set up for a tournament. And in the end, she beat thirteen men. The way she handled it, there was no risk of making much of a statement. And the one golfer who criticized her openly, Vijay Singh, came across boorishly and withdrew from the tournament.

Such comparisons open up old gender wounds, even though like objects are not being compared. Golf is a game that accounts for unequal strength. Members of the Champions tour—men over fifty who for the most part dominated the regular tour in their youth—play shorter courses because they are older and cannot hit the ball as far. The same is true for lengths of the courses on the Ladies' PGA, but that is not a slight. It is an equalizer: They may not hit the ball as far as the men do, but they still have to hit all of the shots under tournament pressure and on challenging courses. That Sorenstam missed the cut at the Colonial and Wie missed it in many PGA events was not the point: Men who were regular members of the tour and used to playing courses of that length not only missed the cut those weeks but some also played worse than Sorenstam and Wie. King herself had made it clear when she played Riggs that the best male player in the world could beat the best female player. The reason was physical strength. Rod Laver, the greatest player of his time and Wimbledon champion in 1968, would have no chance at beating Roger Federer, the greatest player of today, who won Wimbledon five years in a row. Likewise, Laver in 1973 would have trounced Riggs and King. But again this is a matter of physiology, not psychology.

The debate over how women fare under pressure also regularly gets conflated with comparisons of compensation. Tennis is an anomaly in that women and men get paid equally in the Grand Slam events. The same, though, cannot be said for other women's professional sports, like basketball and golf. In fact, what King fought for in tennis is still glaringly absent in golf: equal prize money in major tournaments. In 2008, when Tiger Woods won the U.S. Open at Torrey Pines, he took home $1.35 million. Inbee Park, who won the 2008 U.S. Women's Open, got only $585,000 for her victory. In fact, the second-place finisher in the 2008 Men's Open won more, $810,000, and the third-place finisher received $491,995. The United States Golf Association runs both tournaments, just as the United States Tennis Association runs the U.S. Open for men and women. That the USGA decided the Women's Open champion should earn less is pay discrimination sanctioned by golf's governing body. But it has nothing to do with how Woods and Park played under the pressure of the most prestigious events on their tours. One thing to remember: Zoe Cruz may have been smaller than the men around her, but she earned more than all but a few; her reported compensation when she left Morgan Stanley was in the neighborhood of $30 million a year.

As for Wie, her time came. After such a fitful start as a teen, Wie retreated. She enrolled at Stanford University, but she was not eligible to play on the golf team because she had turned professional. At that point, there were questions swirling about whether she was ruined mentally and could ever play again at the highest level. She was shaping up to be the female equivalent of John Daly, not Tiger Woods. But in pulling back from the public eye, she began to work harder. Instead of skating by on exemptions from sponsors—which made her the show pony of the week—she went through the qualifying school for the LPGA Tour like anyone else, and when she came out on tour in 2009 as a full member, she was a steady, confident player. In the second-to-last event of the season, she finally won, seven years after her only other tournament victory. Most significant, she held up under real pressure. At the end of the third round at the Lorena Ochoa Invitational in Mexico, she was tied with Cristie Kerr, who had won twelve times in her professional career—including a U.S. Women's Open. She was a seasoned and formidable opponent. But paired together in the last round, Kerr shot even par to Wie's three under. On the green, with her victory sealed, Wie did a little dance. She had finally come through under pressure. She did so by doing all the things a clutch performer has to do. It was not a double-clutch moment for her but it was a step toward that. She had learned from her past mistakes. Given how publicly she had lived, it was hard to believe that she was still only a twenty-year-old college student.

WHAT DOES IT ALL MEAN?

How Billie Jean King prepared to play Bobby Riggs was a lesson in combining the five key traits of being clutch. While I pointed these out earlier in the chapter, they bear repeating because they show what a true clutch performer needs to do. One, King was focused on preparing for the match as if she were playing a top female competitor, not an old man. Two, she showed tremendous discipline in the shots she hit, picking the ones that would put Riggs at a disadvantage. Three, she had a plan to tire him out, but if after the first of five sets that plan was failing, she was prepared to adapt it. She was concentrating on winning the match, not winning it in any particular way. Four, after she had prepared, she put herself in the present, embracing the moment but never getting ahead of herself. Five, she was driven not only by the fear of losing to Riggs and the setback that would have been for women's rights but also by the desire to shut Riggs up. This was the total clutch package.

The flip side of this was Riggs, who made two of the three cardinal errors of people who choke. These will be examined fully in the next section. First, Riggs was shockingly overconfident—a trait more fully explored in chapter 9. He had beat Court and thought he would beat King just as handily. Second, he was already thinking of the accolades that would be bestowed on him when he beat her—before they had even played. This will be looked at in chapter 8. While he was talking, he was not training, and that showed in how quickly he tired out. Yet after his defeat, he did what many chokers do not or cannot do: He took personal responsibility for his loss. As King threw her racquet in the air to claim victory, he leaped the net, and in congratulating her, he said, "I really underestimated you." He expanded on this in a Tennis Channel interview toward the end of his life in 1995. "I made the classic mistake that anyone can make when they think they're so good and they underestimate their opponent," he said. "If you underrate your opponent and overrate yourself, you're in trouble right away." Accepting responsibility as he did is the subject of the next chapter.

PART II

||||||||||||||||||||||

WHY PEOPLE CHOKE

[7]

A LEADER'S RESPONSIBILITY

How the Reputations of Ken Lewis
and Jamie Dimon Fell and Rose
in the Financial Crisis

AT THE ONSET of the financial crisis in 2007, Jamie Dimon and Ken Lewis were in charge of two of the country's most respected banks. Dimon ran JPMorgan Chase, which had its roots in investment banking and securities trading but through its merger with Chase acquired an extensive network of consumer branches. Lewis ran Bank of America, the largest commercial bank in the country by assets and a frequent acquirer of local and regional banks. Dimon was Wall Street; Lewis was Main Street. But in their worlds, the two were highly respected, and since banking had become more intertwined in the late 1990s, the paths of their banks crossed.

On October 9, 2007, considered the stock market's boomtime peak, Lewis's Bank of America was a hairsbreadth away from being the largest U.S. bank, with a value of $236.5 billion, only $200 million less than Citigroup, the financial conglomerate. Dimon's J.P. Morgan was ranked fourth, with a value of $161 billion. Then came the financial crisis of 2008, and the worst recession since the Great Depression began. When the stock market hit bottom on March 9, 2009, J.P. Morgan was the largest bank in America, with a value of $59.8 billion, while Bank of America was fourth with a mere $24 billion. Two years after the peak, as the economy began to recover, J.P. Morgan remained number one with

$167.1 billion in value, as of September 11, 2009, while Bank of America had regained the second spot, albeit with a value of only $146.8 billion. It was a remarkable reversal.

The numbers, however, do not tell the whole story. In leading his firm through the recession, Dimon, fifty-two at the time, acquired two firms on the verge of collapsing—Bear Stearns, a trading house, and Washington Mutual, a commercial lender—and still increased the value of his firm by $6 billion. During the same period, Lewis, then sixty-one, acquired a storied financial firm—Merrill Lynch—that seemed sounder at the time, but then watched $90 billion in shareholder equity evaporate from Bank of America. The two men were operating in the same difficult economic environment with the same access to the best and brightest people in the financial world. Both also had support from the federal government in the darkest months of the recession. But Dimon made his firm better and stronger during a time in which Wall Street was under intense scrutiny. Lewis not only left his firm struggling to integrate what he bought but made himself a target of Congressional inquiry, judicial subpoena, and public disdain.

How did this happen? Deals like Bear and Merrill both carried the added pressure of being deemed crucial for the continued functioning of the U.S. economy. Yet in short order, the two diverged. What J.P. Morgan acquired benefited it and the U.S. economy, while B of A's deal for Merrill nearly brought down the bank and became a huge drain on the U.S. taxpayer. If not for massive government support, even by the standard of what the government had been giving to all banks, B of A might have broken apart under the weight of Lewis's bad judgment. It became apparent that Dimon had been clutch under the pressure of the financial crisis, and Lewis had choked. The explanation for why this happened lies in the old-fashioned notion of personal responsibility.

THE MIND-SET AT DEAL TIME

Just as there are five traits shared by people who are clutch, there are three common causes of choking. An inability to take responsibility for your actions is one of them. The other two are overthinking and over-confidence, which I'll explain in the subsequent chapters. But when it comes to choking, a refusal to accept personal responsibility is often the starting point. The unwillingness to take blame for bad decisions and tolerate criticism for tough ones is a telltale sign of a bad leader under any conditions. It becomes a critical flaw, though, if he finds himself in a situation where serious, tough, and probably unpopular choices are necessary, as Lewis did. The longer he has to navigate under pressure, the worse he is going to make the situation. His desire to dodge responsibility is going to become more apparent and magnify his choking. As Colonel Kolditz said in chapter 3, once a leader loses the trust of his subordinates under pressure, his ability to lead has been irreparably compromised. This was what happened to Ken Lewis.

Let's look at the two deals that defined these men in 2008. In March, J.P. Morgan was approached by the Federal Reserve and the U.S. Treasury and asked to save Bear Stearns from bankruptcy. Six months later, in September, Bank of America announced that it was going to buy Merrill Lynch after a weekend of negotiation and would not take any government money to do so. Bank of America's news came the same day Lehman Brothers filed for bankruptcy and was seen as a shrewd move on Merrill's part to avoid its own bankruptcy. By contrast, when J.P. Morgan bought Bear Stearns and its balance sheet full of assets that were hard to value, Dimon asked shareholders to withhold judgment for one year. He knew it didn't look good on the surface. Moreover, the Bear acquisition came in the spring when few imagined how bad the economy would get in six months; the Merrill deal came as the market was already pretty bad and about to get worse. The difference in the deals was not what was happening in the full glare of the media spotlight but what had happened before either deal was announced.

On Thursday, March 13, it became clear to federal regulators that Bear Stearns was in serious trouble and that it might not have enough capital to open for business on Monday. Timothy Geithner, president of the New York Federal Reserve Bank, called Dimon. Geithner wanted him to buy Bear, which was tantamount to saying he wanted

J.P. Morgan to save the firm from failing and wreaking havoc on the financial system.

"There was a lot of government pressure on us to do it," Dimon told me in an interview in his office, where he had sat throughout the deal. "I told them, 'We'll do everything we can in our power to do the deal. We understand the seriousness of it. But in terms of buying the company, it's got to make sense for us too. We can't leave this company in a teetering condition in this kind of market that could get worse.' It wasn't the pressure. I wasn't going to do a deal where we'd be a teetering giant with too much leverage and too much mortgage exposure. I said, 'We'll go as far as we can and no more, and I'm the sole determinant'—I'm telling the government this—'You can argue all you want, but I will take no more risk than what I tell you, and we need a huge margin for error.'"

These were bold words but not empty ones. Dimon has a strict moral code. He believed J.P. Morgan should help the U.S. financial system by buying Bear, but he also believed that he could not risk the failure of his own firm to do so. As soon as he got off the phone with Geithner, he called Steve Black and Bill Winters, the coheads of J.P. Morgan's investment bank. Dimon needed them to start the due diligence process to find out what they would get in a Bear deal. When he explained the situation, he said, Black and Winters got out of bed and went to the office. Soon, hundreds of other bankers had been roused and were streaming into J.P. Morgan's headquarters on 270 Park Avenue, a block from Bear Stearns's headquarters. They were there to go through Bear's books, to see what was there and what it was worth before any deal was agreed on. They wanted to know where the danger lurked.

"We sat in a room and they went through everything," Dimon told me. "They said, we can handle this, we understand this, we don't understand these, we're going to do some more work on it."

The process was repeated with every division at Bear, right down to calculating the severance costs of a merger. The number of people going through the books and running the numbers had swelled by the next day, Friday, but this due diligence was the key to determining whether J.P. Morgan could buy Bear, regardless of government pressure. "Several times we were ready to walk away," said Dimon. "It had to make sense for us or we weren't going to do it."

On Sunday he came close to calling off the deal when Black and Winters presented him with their findings. They were bleak. Dimon said there were simply too many risky assets on Bear's books for J.P. Morgan to acquire the bank and not risk facing similar problems itself if the credit crisis got worse (which it did). That was when Dimon called Geithner. "I said, 'Tim, we can't do it. I'm sorry.' Treasury secretary Hank Paulson called me. I said, 'We're not doing it'. Then Tim said, 'What would you need to do it?' I said, 'If you really mean that, I'll tell you, but don't try to push me, because I have to try to do what's right for this company,'" Dimon said. "I called them back after a couple of hours and said, 'If you take this $30 billion, we can handle the rest.' Remember we were taking $350 billion." This was a shrewd move that allowed him to acquire the bulk of Bear but not the part that could be quickly worth half of its value—or nothing at all.

Dimon's second concern was price. How much was he going to pay for a firm that had some solid assets but also plenty of assets whose value could go to zero? The key to this figure was the margin of error. Bear had several well-performing divisions and some star employees. But in the process of the due diligence, Dimon realized that many of the assets on the books that were linked to mortgages could be worth less than their stated value. He was listening to what his lieutenants were telling him for the good of J.P. Morgan, but in doing so, he made it clear that they would be the ones running those desks if he bought the bank. This was a strong incentive for them to be honest with him. In the end, Dimon offered $1 billion for something that had a book value of $12 billion. It sounded like a steal. But embedded in that price was the assumption of risky assets. "We were more focused on the downside," he said. "We had to have the fortitude to get it done, but we also had to have the fortitude not to get it done the way the government wanted us to do it."

Throughout the negotiations, Dimon remained at his desk, listening to the heads of each division at J.P. Morgan. His concern was their concerns. Again, while he felt an obligation to the government, he also felt a strong responsibility to his employees and the firm he ran. If he had abdicated that, then J.P. Morgan could find itself hobbled and the U.S. financial system would be in worse trouble. "There were a lot of questions being raised," he said, but in the end the deal worked: "We did real due diligence with people we trusted. We had a real margin for error built into the price. And we had people who could run it the next day." This was the essence of the process that leads to clutch decision making. Throughout this, Dimon was surely clutch—focused on the merger, disciplined in how he assessed Bear's value, ready to adapt his plan and walk away if necessary, completely present throughout the process, and wisely fearful of hurting his firm. But he also personally accepted responsibility for what was happening. He knew he was ultimately accountable to the shareholders.

When the deal was announced on Monday, March 17, Bear's demise had been averted, but the focus was on how J.P. Morgan had done this. It had convinced the Federal Reserve and the U.S. Treasury to assume responsibility for $29 billion of the worst securities on Bear's books, and in paying $2 a share, it had bought the eighty-four-year-old firm for little more than the cost of its midtown office building. But this was an oversimplification. Dimon had assumed responsibility for over $300 billion in assets on Bear's books. The failed firm also had some thirteen thousand employees J.P. Morgan was inheriting. And he had taken all of this on in a wildly uncertain market. The mortgage problems that had gotten Bear into so much trouble were about to get far worse, and Dimon's reputation was riding on the outcome.

Six months later, on Monday, September 15, Bank of America announced it was buying Merrill Lynch for $50 billion. On that same day, a third firm, Lehman Brothers, filed for bankruptcy. At first, Ken Lewis looked heroic. Sure, he had just paid $29 a share, or a staggering 70 percent premium to where Merrill's stock had closed on Friday. It was a huge discount compared to the firm's high of $98 in 2007, but many suspected that Merrill would have been the next firm to fail and that B of A could have had it for much less. However, Lewis called the acquisition the "strategic opportunity of a lifetime," and it seemed to be just that. Bank of America had a network of branch banks across the country, but it did not have the same level of investment banking capabilities or the financial advisory business that Merrill had. On the face of it, this was a golden deal.

"First, obviously Merrill is much, much more than an investment bank. It is the best wealth management company in the world," Lewis said that day. "The frustration, I think, is we were in some ways in no-man's land. . . . This solves that, and creates the company instantly that would have taken decades to build. We would have been frustrated for quite some time, and this just changes that. I like it again."

Investors disagreed. From day one, they did not like the deal. While Lewis promoted a great fit and little overlap, investors saw problems. At the close of trading that Monday, Bank of America's stock was down over 20 percent, reducing the bank's value by $33 billion, or two thirds of the price it paid for Merrill. Reflecting Lehman's bankruptcy, the Dow Jones Industrial Average lost 504 points, or 4.4 percent of its value. B of A's announcement was supposed to be the good news. The firm, in Lewis's view, had saved Merrill from Lehman's fate—and helped the U.S. economy in the process. He was quick to point out that he had done the deal without government money—likely a jab at J.P. Morgan, which had pushed the worst of Bear's assets onto U.S. taxpayers—and noted in the celebratory press conference that there had been "absolutely no pressure" from the government to do the deal. This was a slap at the elite New York banks that had gone, hat in hand, to the U.S. Treasury and the Federal Reserve for taxpayer dollars. Bank of America, down in Charlotte, North Carolina, had done the deal alone. Suddenly the firm that had been cobbled together by acquiring a series of small Southern banks was a big player in New York.

The devil, though, was in the details. Looking at the Merrill deal through the lenses of price, integration, and due diligence, it was a very different process from what happened with Bear. One, Bank of America paid a premium for a firm that was considered vulnerable. Any price higher than where Merrill's stock was trading was too high. Two, the question of integration was dicey: Charlotte-based B of A had done a middling job of integrating the other firms they had acquired. Years after slapping their logo across Fleet Bank branches in Boston, it still took up to ten days for a check to clear when I lived there in 2007, while Citibank, with only a handful of branches in the city, could clear a check there the same day.

Then there was Lewis. He had long been seen as a man with a chip on his shoulder. Although he ran the second largest bank in the country by assets, he had always been outside the New York banking elite. He lacked their pedigree—a graduate of Georgia State who had started as a credit officer, not an Ivy League man who had gone into investment banking—and his bank made its money in the less glamorous business of taking deposits and making loans. This is where problems with the third measure—due diligence—arose. The Merrill deal had not been foisted on Bank of America, as Bear had been presented to J.P. Morgan, so the belief was that Bank of America's Charlotte-based bankers had thoroughly gone through Merrill's books. But a year after the deal closed, James B. Stewart, writing in the *New Yorker,* conjured up the hours before the papers were signed with damning detail. Merrill CEO John Thain and his lieutenants arrived at Bank of America's legal offices at 7:30 P.M. on Sunday to sign the merger documents. Stewart wrote:

> While lawyers continued working out the details, Thain and Lewis went to a small conference room to await the news that they could sign the merger documents. A bottle of chilled champagne and two glasses had been placed in the room to toast the completion of the deal. Thain felt that he had done the best he could for Merrill's shareholders. As the time passed, Lewis grew impatient, and called several times to ask where the papers were. Finally, just before 1 a.m., they arrived. The two men signed, and then poured the champagne. Neither one said anything about Thain's future with Bank of America. "I look forward to a great partnership with Merrill Lynch," Lewis said, raising his glass. He grimaced. The champagne was warm.

Why was Lewis not overseeing the last details of the most important merger of his career? Why was he standing around while lawyers worked on the crucial fine print of the agreement instead of making sure everything was right with the transaction? Lewis and Thain had been sent into the room because the signing was imminent, but obviously some-thing was holding it up. Lewis should have sensed something was amiss. Contrast this with Dimon, who never left his desk or stopped talking to his lieutenants, Geithner, and Paulson. He was not preparing to pop a cork before the deal was signed.

LEARNING THE WAY

In the year that followed, the two men handled the public and political scrutiny of their acquisitions as differently as they assessed the deals themselves. Dimon accepted full responsibility for the decision he made under extreme stress, while Lewis tried not to. What makes them an interesting comparison is not just the conditions of their banks before and after the crisis, but also their similar professional grooming. Both were understudies to two charismatic leaders who built giant financial services firms from nothing. Dimon cut his teeth at Citigroup under Sandy Weill, and Lewis came up under Hugh McColl at NationsBank, which became Bank of America. But the paths Dimon and Lewis took were as radically different as their mentors.

Sandy Weill, who built Citigroup from a third-rate Baltimore firm called Commercial Credit, rarely betrayed his Brooklyn roots—even if they ran through Cornell University. His goal with each acquisition that led to Citigroup—Gulf Insurance, Primerica (which owned Smith Barney), Travelers Insurance, Shearson Lehman, Salomon Brothers, and finally Citibank—was to cut costs, create profits, and do both in a bare-knuckle way. He did this first by operating the businesses more efficiently and then by creating economies of scale. When he was done, a client could deposit a check, sell stocks, and buy insurance all within the same "financial supermarket." The term itself became associated with Weill and Citigroup. When he began his acquisitions, the Glass-Steagall Act still prohibited banking services and insurance from being sold by the same company, so he pushed the successful lobbying effort that overturned it.

Hugh McColl had a similar acquisitive bent with what became Bank of America. Born in Bentonville, South Carolina, and educated at the University of North Carolina at Chapel Hill, he set out, essentially, to build a national branch network that would amass deposits and provide coast-to-coast commercial banking services. He used North Carolina National Bank as his platform to buy other small and regional banks around the South. He was a deal hunter, buying troubled banks from the FDIC as well as taking advantage of the savings-and-loan crash in the late 1980s by acquiring nearly two hundred failed S&Ls at bargain prices. His crowning achievement was buying San Francisco–based Bank of America in 1999, after the ninety-five-year-old bank hit a rough patch with a massive loan loss to a hedge fund. At the end of this streak, McColl had a giant commercial bank—an institution meant, at its core, to serve a local market of depositors and borrowers. The knock against it was always that none of the individual banks were properly integrated, that all of the parts did not add up to a well-functioning whole. The difference between the Weill and the McColl strategies was that Citi diversified itself with many different types of financial businesses, while B of A had essentially one business diversified geographically.

So what role did the lieutenants play in this? Dimon was the details man. He was charged with integrating the various firms Weill put together and making them work. Lewis was the apprentice, sitting at the right hand of McColl, a dealmaker who kept adding bricks to the wall without worrying if the colors matched. The big difference was, Weill fired Dimon a year after creating Citigroup, while McColl stepped aside in 2001 so Lewis could be promoted into the top spot. Did Dimon's being fired from Citi make him clutch? Did Lewis's smooth ascent make him more complacent and ultimately cause him to choke after the Merrill deal? It's not that simple. What is more indicative is how the two men acted at crucial junctures in their careers—Dimon's time in Chicago and Lewis's consolidation of power after McColl stepped aside.

It is well known in the financial community that Jamie Dimon does not mince words. Whereas most executives dance around sore subjects—such as why they left a firm—Dimon doesn't. He has repeatedly said Weill fired him in November 1998. At the time, it was painful. Dimon had tied his future to Weill straight out of Harvard Business

School in 1982 and been richly rewarded for it. When Weill took over Commercial Credit, Dimon was named the chief financial officer at age thirty. Together they had been a formidable team, with Weill conceiving the deals and Dimon working out the details. (Weill has never given a reason for firing Dimon, though it is widely believed to have stemmed from Dimon's refusal to promote Weill's daughter.)

Seventeen months after being fired, Dimon was hired to lead Bank One. He landed at the Chicago-based financial services firm in March 2000. It had been cobbled together a few years earlier from three regional firms, and it was in no way clear that this job would launch him back to the big leagues of Wall Street. Bank One had grown by combining with other banks in the Midwest, but it had not done it very well. The various businesses were not only underperforming, but employees' loyalties were to their original institutions, not to the merged entity. Dimon's first order of business was shoring up the balance sheet. He did this by going through each division and finding out what the assets were truly worth. He wanted to write down all of the inflated assets at once so the bank could take its lumps in one fell swoop and move on. He also cut reimbursements for country-club memberships and the bank's stock dividend, both of which proved very unpopular. When the dot-com bubble burst, he had to do a second round of write-downs, but he never apologized. He took responsibility and made it clear that not doing so would be more about ego than what was right for the company. "When we took that first write-down, I didn't know the economy was going to go to hell in a handbasket," he told me. "I wasn't going to say this was the end of anything. We had a lot of issues to deal with. I never promise, because I never completely know. You have to recognize reality as fast as you can in all things. Problems don't age well, and denial is no good." But despite criticism, he had shored up the balance sheet.

In doing this, Dimon drew on his experience at Commercial Credit as a thirty-year-old chief financial officer. Then, he had to scrutinize everything to find out where the waste and the risks were. "Risk comes in many forms," he told me. "My first question is always Can I trust you? Then it's Who's doing the job? and Are there controls in place? I was a real fanatic for controls and reporting on everything. When you sign a document, you'd better damn well know what you were signing. I read every legal contract. If you are moving phone numbers, how much should it cost to do this? If we were buying furniture, I'd ask, Can we get it cheaper?" This was because he felt personally responsible for the decisions he was making. He knew that a few bad moves could have brought down the operation, so no detail was too small. When he learned that caring for the plants on the executive floor at Commercial Credit cost $16,000 a year, he told me, he went ballistic—the plants were plastic. The same thing happened when he was presented with a $50,000 bill to lease a phone routing box. He went out and bought the same box for $5,000 and paid a retired phone worker $10,000 a year to move the numbers around. "I'd go over and over everything, and that's where you'd learn." For him, Commercial Credit was more like a mom-and-pop store, and he was as accountable as a proprietor would be.

Such thrift is an odd thing to hear about today from the head of one of the world's largest banks. But his detailed knowledge of his firm's assets points to Dimon's emphasis on details and ultimately the responsibility that he has. When he engineered the sale of Bank One to JPMorgan Chase in July 2004, he took no chances. He made sure the deal stated that he would succeed the current chief executive in two years. Dimon had learned the hard way from Weill that unless succession was spelled out in writing, he could be on the losing end. "You do learn," he said. "You develop over time." But just as he had taken responsibility for what he had done at Bank One, he took responsibility for his own future, refusing to leave it to chance again.

When the Federal Reserve approached him to buy Bear Stearns, he saw the proposition through the same lens of personal responsibility. Even though time was of the essence, he refused to acquire the firm, even at a bargain price, until his team had evaluated the assets. Six months later, when the FDIC approached him to acquire Washington Mutual, he moved more quickly because he had already gone through the company's books: J.P. Morgan had recently tried to buy WaMu. The problem had been the asking price of nearly $8 billion. Now he was getting WaMu for $1.9 billion. Even though the Seattle-based firm had been a huge issuer of subprime mortgages, Dimon was confident he could manage the bad assets in exchange for adding all of WaMu's West Coast branches. "There were other guys in the room with me all the time; there was a lot of give-and-take," Dimon told me. "But I was responsible ultimately."

By comparison, Lewis's acquisition of Merrill Lynch should have been a breeze. The only pressure in acquiring Merrill was of Lewis's making: He wanted it to happen quickly. Merrill seemed to make sense for B of A, which was still a web of regional banks. Its largest acquisition during Lewis's tenure had been the $47 billion purchase of Fleet Bank Boston. But it had also bought MBNA, a huge credit card issuer, U.S. Trust, and Countrywide. Merrill would fill a gap with its investment bank and, more important, its network of financial advisers. Lewis was sure it was a perfect fit.

That bankers and investors, people presumably in the know, saw the deal differently irked Lewis, a son of the South who seemed to finally have his seat at the Wall Street table. He had paid a 70 percent premium for Merrill when it might have collapsed, but he got a firm B of A had coveted. And yes, there would be integration issues, but that was always the case with a merger. He was doing what B of A had always done: growing by acquisition, just as his mentor, McColl, had. The financial crisis could get worse but B of A had the largest deposit base of any U.S. bank. Now it was finally the financial supermarket it had longed to be. Whatever premium it had paid for Merrill would be worth it in the long term. But then the real scrutiny of the deal began.

The first bombshell was over pay. It emerged that Merrill executives had seemingly paid themselves huge bonuses, $3.6 billion, as they walked out the door. Lewis portrayed the Merrill executives as speeding up the payments before the deal closed. Merrill CEO John Thain, with his Clark Kent looks and technocratic manner, was to blame. First, Thain tried to invoke a clause in his contract that would have paid him an additional $10 million. Given that he had only been the chief executive for ten months and had received a $15 million signing bonus, this was, at best, tone-deaf, in view of the severity of the economic crisis. Then it came out that he had redecorated his office to the tune of $1.2 million. Thain backed off the bonus request and reimbursed the bank for the decorating costs. But he had already been painted as the bad guy.

In reality, Thain had served his own shareholders well under pressure. The firm's financial advisory business had a great reputation, but other parts had made missteps. One of them was in collateralized debt obligations. These securities became the bogeymen of the financial crash when the market for CDOs—often securities created out of and tied to mortgages and other assets—evaporated. Then there was Merrill's stock price. When Thain joined, it was $59.06, down from its peak in early 2007 of $97.53. On the Friday before the deal was announced, it was at $17. The $29 that Thain got Lewis to pay was a boomtime premium. Granted, the stock was half of where it had been when Thain came in to turn the firm around, but it was a lot better than where Lehman Brothers' stock went on the day the Merrill deal was announced. And had he been the egotistical, tone-deaf financier he was being portrayed as, surely he would have balked at the blow to his reputation: He had been hired to turn Merrill around and instead sold it to a large but less prestigious commercial bank. He had saved the firm but not in the way he had anticipated.

This was where questions of responsibility began to arise. As the deal was closing, it surfaced that Lewis knew all about the bonus payments. Thain kept silent about this until almost a year later, and then he let loose. "When I got fired in January and they said 'John Thain secretly accelerated these bonuses,' they were lying," Thain said in September 2009, according to Bloomberg News. "And that has now trapped them into a lot of trouble, because there is a document that says yes, in fact, they agreed to this in September [2008]." Lewis had hinted at the opposite, perpetuating the notion that bonuses had been given out on the sly. Even if this had been how it happened, it made Lewis look either careless for not reading the deal documents or stupid for being duped by a Wall Street titan.

The second shock came over earnings. In January, B of A reported a fourth-quarter loss of $1.73 billion and blamed it on Merrill, which had lost $15.3 billion from securities it had on its books. Again, Lewis tried to present this as something he could not have foreseen, given how severely the economy deteriorated. He was blaming outside forces so he would not have to take personal responsibility. Then questions were raised about why Lewis had not alerted shareholders to such deterioration. Lewis tried to sound altruistic. "We just thought it was in the best interest of our company and our shareholders and the country to move forward," he said.

It is hard to believe this statement on all three counts. One, the company was now under intense scrutiny and went from being praised to being ridiculed. Two, shareholders had seen their wealth wiped out. By the middle of January, B of A had a market capitalization of $42.7 billion— meaning the entire firm was worth less than what Lewis had paid for Merrill four months earlier. This was an 80 percent drop in stock price. And three, there was the belief that the deal was good for the country. While Lewis could argue that Merrill would have gone bankrupt without B of A (more likely it would have been saved, like AIG, the insurer), he could not say that the government bailouts were good for the country's taxpayers. That month, B of A had received $20 billion in direct aid through the Troubled Asset Relief Program (TARP) to bring its total take to $45 billion, along with $118 billion in government backstops. These were similar to the now comparatively small $29 billion in guarantees J.P. Morgan received for Bear—and that Lewis had proudly said B of A did not need. The irony was that three quarters of the assets backed by that government facility belonged to Merrill, which Lewis, as a former credit officer, should have seen deteriorating. B of A went from seeming strong and well-managed for not taking any federal money in acquiring Merrill to being beset by rumors that it would be nationalized.

Personally, Lewis found himself fending off speculation that he had been strong-armed into completing the deal by Ben Bernanke, the Federal Reserve chairman, and Hank Paulson, the Treasury secretary. This was the third major issue. If proved true, it would allow Lewis to foist the responsibility for the transaction onto the government, yet it would also make him seem like a weak chief executive who could be bullied— never mind that such a level of government intervention was chilling. After all, Dimon had told Geithner and Paulson that he would only go so far and no further, to protect his shareholders. Lewis, if the allegations were correct, was a patsy. It all went back to the question Why did Lewis rush the deal?

WHERE RESPONSIBILITY MATTERS

In the aftermath of the Bear and Merrill deals, Dimon and Lewis had to backpedal on statements they had made.

In January, Dimon seemed to say that he would not cut J.P. Morgan's dividend, but a month later he reduced it to 5 cents a share from 38 cents. This was the first time JP Morgan Chase had cut its dividend since 1990. In doing so, Dimon said he saved the bank $5 billion a year and justified it by saying extraordinary economic times called for extraordinary action. "I made up my mind and said we're going to do it," he told me of his decision to make the announcement on a random Tuesday. "I was thinking what would happen if the country goes into not a Great Recession but a Depression. If you had known with certainty that we were going to have a mild recession, I wouldn't have cut the dividend. But we were looking into a potential abyss. I wanted to survive anything. That dividend over a two-year period was $10 billion." It was a tough decision, and he took full responsibility for it.

Lewis, on the other hand, found himself the subject of regular congressional inquiries. Each appearance allowed him to take responsibility for what had happened, but he never did. At one point, on June 11, 2009, Representative Dennis Kucinich, the Ohio Democrat, asked Lewis if he had requested a letter from the Federal Reserve saying the government had forced him to close the deal, in order to protect him against shareholder lawsuits for not revealing the depth of Merrill losses. Lewis had been dancing around the issue for six months, and instead of coming clean, he said he could not recall.

Kucinich exploded and read an e-mail from Chairman Bernanke to the Federal Reserve's counsel from December 23, a week after Lewis was alerted to the $13 billion in losses. "The e-mail says, 'He now fears lawsuits from shareholders. He still asked if he could use as a defense the government ordered him to proceed for systemic reasons. I said no,'" Kucinich read before pausing to lash out at Lewis. "We would hope that a CEO would have both a good memory and the integrity to take responsibility for his decisions." Lewis grimaced. Kucinich continued with the response from the Fed counsel: "'I do not think it is appropriate or necessary for us to give Lewis a letter along the lines he asked.' Is it still your testimony that you don't recall asking for a letter to absolve you of your responsibility for acquiring Merrill Lynch's huge losses?" Lewis's chin crinkled and pocked in frustration: "What I do remember is calling Chairman Bernanke and asking him if he could give us something in writing along the lines of what the solution would be." This was a classic dodge in corporatespeak, and Kucinich became indignant: "We're now updating Mr. Lewis's previous testimony. That may help you escape perjury, but it doesn't get away from the question of whether or not you were trying to absolve yourself of responsibility for acquiring Merrill Lynch's huge losses. I mean, we're talking about events that transpired only a few months ago. And your failure to inform your shareholders could constitute a fundamental violation of security laws." Lewis simply sat there.

Later in the same hearing, Peter Welch, Democrat from Vermont, asked who was ultimately responsible for telling B of A shareholders about the Merrill losses. Lewis tried not to answer the question. "I'd leave that decision to our securities lawyers and our outside counsel," Lewis said. Welch pushed back: "You're not CEO?" "I'm not a securities lawyer." "You're not ultimately the one responsible?" Welch asked. The back-and-forth provided supreme drama, and it would have continued, had Mr. Welch's time not run out. But this never would have happened if Lewis had taken responsibility from the start.

As the first anniversary of the merger approached, what should have been a celebration of a career-capping deal for Lewis was marred by increasing investigations. A federal judge threw out a settlement with the Securities and Exchange Commission in which B of A agreed to pay a $33 million fine but admit no wrongdoing over the timing of the Merrill bonuses. A congressman from upstate New York demanded that Lewis reveal when he knew about Merrill's enormous losses, while the state's attorney general was conducting a similar investigation into the merger. The bank also found itself battling the government over the $118 billion in guarantees it had been provided at the beginning of the year. In late July, B of A said it had never signed the agreement for the facility, so it owed the U.S. government nothing. The problem with this logic was that for the previous six months, the investing public had believed that such a guarantee had been in place. Lewis was not only *not* accepting responsibility, but he was doing so in a way that descended to the point of deception. Simply put, that rescue agreement, which everyone thought existed, had saved Bank of America.

PRESSURE REVEALS WHO HAS IT AND WHO DOESN'T

So why did Ken Lewis fail in the face of the worst banking crisis in modern memory and Jamie Dimon did not? The difference came down to how they perceived their actions. Dimon was the technocratic leader, the man sifting through the numbers and demanding accountability from everyone and himself. Taking responsibility for the good and the bad was at the core of how he lived. Lewis was a throwback to the imperial CEO, demanding respect by dint of his office and the standing of B of A. He ruled by fiat, from on high. His biggest acquisition had been Fleet Bank Boston, which had the oldest banking license in the United States and was run by Chad Gifford, the ur–Boston Brahmin. This had been a feather in Lewis's cap; it brought him closer to the respectability he yearned for. It fit Lewis's sense of destiny that he should be in the room with the bottle of champagne, not working out the last details of the Merrill merger. He thought that deal was going to be the crowning moment of his career, not the beginning of the end. When the deal was later questioned, Lewis recoiled. In the moment when he should have accepted responsibility, should have stepped in and said he either knew about the agreements or did not, he punted. It was obvious it would only get worse for him. Without taking personal responsibility, a leader can never be clutch.

The psychological literature around personal responsibility has two strands. The first veers toward self-help. Most books are geared toward getting people out of bad relationships and bad behaviors. They take a consoling route: *I did this; I should not have; and I'm going to stop.* The second is the objectivist philosophy associated with Ayn Rand. It advocates a form of enlightened self-interest that requires people to take responsibility for what they do and be rewarded for it: *I did this well, and I deserve to be compensated for it.* The psychology of self-help and Rand's enlightened self-interest share an emphasis on taking responsibility for what you have done, good or bad, and either becoming better or being recognized for it. The reward for the responsibility, though, comes after the fact. It's reactive.

The type of personal responsibility that is needed to be good in the clutch is different. It is always there, but under pressure it becomes purely focused and is the underlying force in the action: *I am doing this because it is the right thing to do, and if I fail, I know I tried.* Responsibility here is not an accounting for your actions; it *is* your actions. And however it turns out, you are the one who did it. You are in your office working on the deal; you are not letting someone else iron out the details. Lewis could have avoided many of the problems B of A had if he had admitted to knowing (or how he could possibly not know) about the bonuses and had disclosed the Merrill losses to shareholders as soon as he learned about them. That is responsibility. That is doing what is right and leaving the rest to be sorted out. If the shareholder reaction had been negative, the worst that could have happened to Lewis would have been getting fired. He would have left the bank with his dignity and reputation intact for having done the responsible thing. But once he started dodging responsibility, there was no way he was not going to choke. His actions made the immediate outcome of the Merrill deal worse on all fronts: government backing, shareholder ire, stock decline, and subpoenas from states, legislators, and judges.

In the financial crisis, Lewis was by no means alone. Just as rapidly falling stock prices flushed out Ponzi schemers like Bernie Madoff, it revealed leaders lacking the character to be responsible. Dick Fuld, who had been chief executive of Lehman Brothers for fourteen years, was another case of ego trumping shareholder interest. He adamantly refused to accept responsibility for the firm's demise, even after it filed for bankruptcy. He chose instead to blame the federal government for not engineering a sale of Lehman the way it had helped J.P. Morgan buy Bear. And a year after the collapse, he was still in the same denial mind-set when a Reuters reporter approached him outside of his house in Ketchum, Idaho. "They're looking for someone to dump on right now, and that's me," he told the news service. "The facts are out there. Nobody wants to hear it, especially not from me." But would Lehman have been the firm that got dumped on had it managed its risks better? No. And that's what Fuld missed. That is where he should have taken responsibility but could not. "He blamed the markets, blamed the short-sellers," said Lawrence McDonald, a former Lehman vice president who wrote a book about the Lehman collapse, called *A Colossal Failure of Common Sense*. "The truth is, qualified people warned him several times, and he wouldn't listen."

And here is the sad part with leaders like Fuld and Lewis: They thought they could do no wrong because they had had long, successful careers. They had become dangerously insulated. They were both imperial chief executives. And their closest advisers treated them with deference instead of presenting them with the truth. Fuld and Lewis believed in their importance to the U.S. banking system, that it would be acknowledged, and that everything would turn out fine for their firms. Their failure was a failure of perspective. Their separate testimony before Congress solidified their images as being completely out of touch with the reality of the recession. When they should have accepted responsibility, they blamed others for their firms' mistakes. This made bad situations worse. And it served to erode reputations built up over decades. In trying to burnish their images, they destroyed their reputations.

Dimon was different. He focused on making sure he had the information he needed to make the right decisions. "We have daily, weekly, monthly reports for almost everything—credit, risk, markets, sales, everything," he told me. "I don't read them every day, but I do actually read them. And then I call up the people and say, 'Explain this to me.'" And if his decision is wrong, he stands ready to correct it. "People should admit their mistakes—I do it all the time, of all different sizes, publicly," he said. "Clients don't mind that you made a mistake. They mind when you deny it." They are OK with the mistakes because someone has taken responsibility for what happened. This also helped to explain how during the same two-year period, Bank of America went from being worth $236.5 billion to $146.8 billion while acquiring a storied financial firm, and J.P. Morgan went from $161 billion in value to $167.1 billion after buying two failed institutions.

[8]

THE PERILS OF OVERTHINKING
Rehearsing the Speech
Before the Victory

THE BASEBALL WORLD was turned upside down in 2008. The New York Yankees missed the playoffs for the first time in thirteen years, and the Tampa Bay Rays, a perennial last-place finisher in the same league, made it to the World Series. This was baseball's equivalent of a black swan or thousand-year storm. Either of these events was unlikely, but together they were completely improbable. Many factors guided the two teams to victory and defeat, but two players came to represent each team's divergent fortunes: an experienced, highly paid choker and a rookie who was amazing in the clutch. Both had been number one draft picks in their respective years, but that was where the similarities seemed to cease. Just as the previous chapter looked at personal responsibility by comparing the approaches of Jamie Dimon and Ken Lewis in the Great Recession, this one will look at the second trait of chokers, overthinking, through how Alex Rodriguez and David Price saw themselves in big games.

Throughout this strange season, the Yankees and the Rays were a study in contrasts. Beyond their own fans, few felt sorry for the Yankees' defeat. The team had a long tradition of winning and receiving international renown from it. They had played in 39 of the 104 World Series championships and won 26 of them. Yet their critics derided them as the "evil empire" and attributed their success to the exorbitant sums they were able to spend on players. It was tough to argue against the effectiveness of the team's wealth: In 2008 its payroll was $209 million, or nearly $70 million ahead of the team with the second-highest payroll. Tampa Bay that year paid its entire squad a middling $43.8 million—or the equivalent of the annual salaries of Rodriguez, better known as A-Rod, and Derek Jeter. Given the Yankees' depth of talent, it was not surprising that they had played so well in thirteen consecutive postseasons. They were a clutch factory, always managing to win under extreme pressure with talented players at every position.

One of those players was A-Rod. But by the 2008 season, five years into his time with the Yankees, fans had lost patience with him. The highest-paid Yankee and the highest-paid player in baseball, at $30 million a year, had developed a reputation for being an unreliable performer and had compiled a woeful roster of statistics in his postseason appearances to prove it: 0 for 29 with men on base, 0 for 18 with runners in scoring position, 8 hits in his last 61 postseason at-bats for a .161 batting average. When the Yankees missed the playoffs, A-Rod became a lightning rod for the blame.

The Rays, on the other hand, should never have been where they were that fall. The mixture of veterans such as Cliff Floyd, Carlos Peña, and Eric Hinske with young prospects like Scott Kazmir, Evan Longoria, Dioner Navarro, and David Price had gelled into a winning team. Before the season began, the team's big news had been changing its name from Devil Rays to Rays. Now, as the season drew to a close, they were in the playoffs and advancing to the World Series. It seemed too good to last. Just as the Yankees won all the time, the Rays lost. It was the natural order of baseball: New York had the best players money could buy; Tampa Bay had rookies, middling players, and aged veterans cut from other teams.

But by October, the feeling had changed. The Rays beat the Chicago White Sox in the division series in four games and carried that momentum into the American League Championship Series against the Red Sox, the defending World Series champions. After losing the first game, they won the next three in a row and were one game away from going to the World Series. By all accounts, the Rays were too young to play against such an experienced team. They would choke, and that was what seemed to be happening when they lost the next two games and let Boston tie the series. Their magical run was drawing to an end. The only glitch was, the Rays would not let go. In the bottom of the eighth inning of the last game, Coach Joe Maddon brought in rookie pitcher David Price. The number one draft pick that year, he had breezed through the minor leagues and notched his first big-league victory in game two of the ALCS. Standing on the mound with a two-run lead but the bases loaded, he pitched as he always did. He struck out the batter and came back in the next inning and got the three outs the Rays needed. With that, they were off to the World Series.

OVERTHINKING WHAT YOU DO

How could a young, untested pitcher be so clutch in the most pressure-filled moment in his team's history, while a seasoned player, a three-time American League Most Valuable Player, could spend season after season choking when it mattered most? The answer lies not in how they went about doing their jobs but in how they *thought* about doing their jobs. Price threw the ball as he had been trained to do—hard and fast or with a curve to it—and struck out batters. At the most crucial times, Rodriguez was the one who struck out, hit into double plays, popped up weakly, or otherwise hurt his team when it needed their greatest player most. The reason was, in the clutch, A-Rod overthought his every move; in fact, he thought of most of his moves in their historic place in baseball. Price, on the other hand, channeled his college success but also his failures to get himself ready to pitch. Under pressure Price pitched normally, but A-Rod played differently, as if the weight of expectations was sitting on the end of his bat.

Team sports like baseball are where pressure performances can make a player immortal or reviled. This is where the fiercest debates occur over who is clutch and who is not. For a time during the late 1990s and early 2000s, when statistics reigned supreme, many wondered if clutch-ness existed at all. But no matter your point of view, sports fans and commentators crave heroic performances and need only the slightest mention of the great ones to stir their memories: the 1980 Miracle on Ice, Kentucky's championship year under Rick Pitino, Tiger's chip shot at the Masters that paused on the lip before dropping. These moments give fans the chills. And great athletes know it. Who wouldn't want to be remembered forever for a clutch play?

That was part of Rodriguez's problem. Since he was in high school, he had been considered not just the most gifted player at his position or even one of the most gifted of his era. He was labeled early on as one of the best ever, as an era-defining player like Babe Ruth or Ted Williams. It wasn't all hype. He had the stats to back it up. The problem was not just that he believed it—all great athletes are confident, and plenty are arrogant jerks. (In 2004, I interviewed Roger Clemens and walked away thinking, *You can either have blond highlights in your hair, or you can be arrogant, but you shouldn't be allowed to have highlights and be arrogant.*) The problem was that Rodriguez began to carry himself as if he were already one of the immortals in the Baseball Hall of Fame.

The greatest piece of insight into that mind-set was a 2001 *Esquire* profile by Scott Raab. It was one of A-Rod's few unguarded interviews, and he has spent years backing off from some of his statements. "It's hard to compete when you don't have a place in the game now as a short-stop, so you have to look years back to find someone to compete against," A-Rod said before signing the largest baseball contract ever. "That's what I do. I'm playing against guys like Ernie Banks or Hank Aaron or Ozzie Smith." Not only are two of the three men Hall of Fame shortstops, but all three are considered among the best to have ever played the game. His agent, Scott Boras, went so far as to put together a book called *Alex Rodriguez: Historical Performance*, which has become infamous for its grandeur. In it, A-Rod was compared statistically to his contemporaries but also to the greatest players the game has known. At every turn, he was ranked against those players over the course of their careers but also when they were the same age as he was, twenty-four. He almost always came out on top. On one level, the book served its purpose: The

Texas Rangers paid the twenty-four-year-old Rodriguez $252 million for ten years in 2001. But on another, it put A-Rod into a chronic state of overthinking: He wasn't just standing at the plate; he was batting in the shadow of Hank Aaron, chipping away at his legendary home-run record. In normal games, he did fine, inspired by these comparisons, but under pressure the comparisons would become too much. When Raab asked him about the pressure to live up to the comparisons in his agent's stat book, A-Rod parried: "I'm chasing all those things—internally. It's not good to talk about it." He may not have been talking about them, but he had surrounded himself with people who certainly were thinking and talking about them, starting with his agent.

David Price was different. Though he had been recruited by several professional teams out of high school, Price went to Vanderbilt University in the hope of improving his game before turning pro. Tim Corbin, the Vanderbilt head baseball coach, told me his goal with all of his players was to clear their minds of clutter. "You want to get them to a level where they could perform and not be restrained by other factors," he said. "They needed to focus on what was going on to compete." Price was fortunate, though, to have a coach and not an agent. Midway through his freshman year, Price told me, he was thinking of quitting and returning to his hometown of Murfreesboro, Tennessee. He didn't even think he was the best player at Vanderbilt, let alone the best of all time. But Corbin wouldn't let him quit. "He just told me my future wasn't in flipping burgers; it was in throwing pitches," Price said to me. "Everything he had told me up to that point had been true, so I stayed."

Corbin's usual pep talk was more than that. He has become known for not talking to his players about money and greatness but about marshmallows, jelly beans, and rocks. He holds each one over a flame. The marshmallow quickly turns gooey and burns up. The jelly bean, hard on the outside but soft on the inside, initially holds up better, but it, too, is melted by the flame. Only the rock withstands the heat intact. If anything, it comes out a bit shinier, a bit more polished after being washed by the fire. The point of the story, Corbin said, is to show his players what pressure does to them if they are not prepared. There are players, he said, who are soft all around and will melt with the slightest pressure. There are others who walk in cocky and tough and look as though they can withstand anything, but when the heat of a big game is on them, they dissolve. Only the rocks can endure real pressure. "Everyone wants to be a rock," Corbin said. "My thinking is not everyone who goes into the army, navy, or marines is a rock, but they become one." Under Corbin's guidance, Price's game improved as he had hoped, and three years after choosing college over flipping hamburgers, he was the top MLB draft pick.

Now think of the two players. Alex Rodriguez's mind was filled with lofty assumptions: He expected to make the clutch plays fans crave, to be the perennial subject of ESPN highlight clips, to leave glory in his path to the Hall of Fame. Three years before pitching his team into the World Series, David Price was considering a job at McDonald's. A-Rod imagined himself playing alongside Banks, Aaron, and Smith when he needed to think about hitting the ball. Price focused on trying to pitch as well as he could whether it was a Vanderbilt game or the World Series. That is the difference between thinking and overthinking.

FROM FAME TO DERISION

Alex Rodriguez had always been exceptional. In 1993, he was the number one Major League draft pick as a high school senior. Within three years, he was playing full-time for the Seattle Mariners, where he began compiling the monster statistics that he is known for. In 1996, he batted .358 with 35 home runs and 123 runs batted in and won the American League batting title. He turned twenty-one in the middle of that season. The next year, he was voted onto the All-Star team. The year after that, he had 213 hits, including 42 home runs. He also stole 46 bases, making him a complete offensive threat. In 2000, when he led the Mariners into the playoffs, he played under that pressure as if it was no different from the regular season. In the division series, the Mariners beat the Chicago White Sox, and he hit .308 with 2 runs batted in. When the team faced the Yankees, a far more talented team, he hit .409 with 5 RBIs in Seattle's six-game loss. A-Rod was the face of the franchise, and he handled it well.

He was great, but it wasn't clear how much he was thinking of his greatness until the next year. That was when he signed with the Texas Rangers and began talking about himself in the context of Hank Aaron and Ozzie Smith. In Texas, his personal stats were still great. He hit 52 home runs his first season there, 57 the next, and at the beginning of the third, he became the youngest player to hit 300 career home runs. That year, 2003, was also when he won his first American League Most Valuable Player award. But the Rangers still finished in last place—no better than before they signed him. So in 2004 the team traded him to New York.

This was when his greatness should have flowered. After all, in his *Esquire* interview, he had said how easy his rival at shortstop, Derek Jeter, had it: "Jeter's been blessed with great talent around him. He's never had to lead. He can just go and play and have fun." Enter A-Rod, the player who statistically would lead the Yankees back to their late-1990s glory, when they won four World Series in five years. In his first year, 2004, the Yankees went to the postseason, and in the first series A-Rod batted .421 over four games with 3 RBIs. The Yankees won, and all seemed fine. But in the next series, for the American League championship, something different happened. A-Rod had 5 RBIs, but his batting average dropped to .258. He embarrassed himself by trying to slap the ball out of a pitcher's hand in game six—something it was hard to imagine one of the immortals doing—and by the last game, which the Yankees lost to their archrivals, the Boston Red Sox, he stopped hitting.

Over the next three postseasons, his batting average plummeted: He went 9 for 63. In the division series, he hit .133 in 2005, .071 in 2006, and .267 in 2007. The Yankees never made it to the championship series in any of those years. Yet during the regular season in those same three years, A-Rod kept adding to his career stats in games when less was at stake. He won his second MVP in 2005. In April of that year, he hit three home runs in one game and drove in ten runs, one off the all-time record. The next season, he became the youngest player to hit 450 home runs and among the youngest to reach the 2,000 hits mark.

The highest-paid player in baseball, however, was failing to live up to New York's postseason expectations. He did so while producing one tabloid cover after another—strippers, arrogant statements, discussing his feud with beloved captain Derek Jeter, divorce drama, rumors of an affair with Madonna. Even though he won a third MVP in 2007, he was becoming a sideshow distraction. When Rodriguez continued to fail to perform in 2008, even with an increase to his already huge salary, not only Yankee fans but also his teammates turned on him. Behind his back, fellow players began to call him A-Fraud. The New York press dubbed him Mr. April—a reference to his great statistics at the beginning of the season when they mattered least, and an unflattering comparison to one of the Yankees great postseason players, Reggie Jackson, known as Mr. October. Perhaps oddest of all that season may have been the assessment of Harold Bloom, a famed literary scholar at Yale University best known for his study of Shakespeare. Bloom had been asked by the *New Yorker* magazine to comment on A-Rod's reported relationship with Madonna and her interest in Jewish mysticism, a subject Bloom had studied. After discussing Kabbalah, a mystical tradition in Judaism, Bloom offered his critique of the star third baseman. "The great Alex Rodriguez, the famous A-Rod, is not a clutch performer," Bloom said. "He compiles these enormous statistics, but every time I make the mistake of looking at a game, he comes up with two out and men on second and third, and does nothing."

A-Rod's failures were only magnified by his teammate Derek Jeter's success. Jeter, the captain and shortstop, was the face of pressure playing. Since the Yankees began their championship run in 1996, fans believed he would always get the hit or make the play when it mattered most. Jeter was the guy who played better in the postseason. He was a study in focus and discipline, and it was no surprise that he was clutch. As a boy, his father drilled line drives at him so he wouldn't be afraid of the ball, and this stayed with the Gold Glove Yankee shortstop. Jeter's father also showed him that if he flinched or closed his eyes he might get hit by the ball, but if he kept his eyes open and concentrated, not only would he avoid getting hit, but he might make a great play. What his father was really teaching him was to think about one thing, what he was doing, and not the glory that could come from making the play. This stayed with him as he proved his greatness on the team: He never walked out there as the "great Derek Jeter"; he went out there as one player among nine and played ball. The results were hard to argue with. From 1996 to 2007, Jeter had enviable postseason statistics. He had a .314 batting average with 17 home runs—more than he usually hits in a 162-game season—and 48 RBIs. He had the records for the most postseason hits (150), postseason singles (108), and runs scored (85). Jeter was hardened to deal with clutch situations. Teammates, opposing players, and fans expected him to do great things, and he usually did.

Comparing A-Rod and Jeter under pressure became easier in 2008 when Bill James, a renowned creator and compiler of statistics, came out with *The Hardball Times: Baseball Annual 2008*. For the first time, he quantified clutch hitting. In an essay in the book entitled "Mr. Clutch," James listed the seven elements needed to define a clutch hitter: the score, the runners on base, the outs, the inning, the opposition, the standings, and the calendar. His formula showed that the Boston Red Sox's David "Big Papi" Ortiz was just as clutch as fans suspected. In 2004, when the Red Sox won the World Series, he hit .339 and drove in 33 runs in clutch situations during the regular season. Big Papi was often held out as the anti-A-Rod—the player who would get the crucial hit when his team needed it most. So what did the evidence show for A-Rod? Pretty much what you would expect. In 2008, his batting average was an even .300. But with runners in scoring position, he hit .271. This would not seem like a huge change, but according to James's clutch measurements, his clutch coefficient was a negative 11.4. During that same horrible year for the Yankees, Derek Jeter had a clutch rating of positive 0.7, giving him a 12.1 percentage-point difference over A-Rod in clutch hitting. "It may be that most outstanding hitters tend to be even more outstanding when the game or the season is on the line," James wrote.

That wasn't the case with A-Rod. He was great, but his problem was what he was thinking when he stood at the plate with the game on the line. Jeter is so great under pressure because he is focused on hitting the ball or making the play, and he is completely in the present. A-Rod, on the other hand, has often looked like Ken Lewis at a congressional hearing: taut, stiff, not himself. What was worse was that the Yankees hitting coach had worked with him in the 2007 season, tweaking his swing to the point where he had an MVP year—at least in the regular season. That made the question more pressing: Could A-Rod ever stop comparing himself to great players and actually be great under pressure?

FROM A MARSHMALLOW TO A ROCK

David Price arrived in the major leagues in 2008 with none of A-Rod's thoughts of grandeur. Standing a lanky six feet six inches tall, Price had always been an imposing figure on the mound, but it took his time at Vanderbilt to make a rock out of a marshmallow. In his junior year, his last season in college, he won 11 games and lost 1 with a blistering 2.63 ERA. With his Major League–speed 95 mph fastball and his hard slider, he also had 194 strikeouts—the most in Division I—and was named the athlete of the year in the top Southeastern Conference. But still, was that preparation for pitching in the World Series?

When he was called in to close out game seven of the ALCS, he told me he thought about failing. "I took it back to the same preparation as college," he said. "I did my visualization. I'd envisioned myself failing now and again. It's human. When you've done that envisioning, you've seen it before. You don't always envision the good stuff because you're going to give up that home run, you're going to give up that go-ahead run or game-winning hit. It's part of the game." Failing was not his last thought, but it was part of how he prepared before the game.

This technique is a refutation of the power of positive thinking. Call it the empowerment of being realistic. What it certainly is not is overthinking. Price was not running out of the bullpen thinking he was going to save the game, pitch his team into its first World Series, and win glory. He had already won game two of the ALCS—getting his first postseason win in the major leagues before his first regular-season one. Once game seven was actually under way, though, he thought of nothing but following the game. He made sure he knew which players were up to bat. He described what he did as: "Stay loose, watch the game, pay attention to the score, get up and walk around, be ready." It was what he had done at Vanderbilt. When he got called in, he trotted from the bull pen like a Major League veteran and took the mound as he had in college. The winner of the game, which Price now controlled for his team, went to the World Series; the loser went home. "All the pressure was right there, but I wasn't going to think about it," Price told me. "Pressure is perceived. If I don't put added pressure on myself, I'll be fine."

This sounds like wishful thinking. But Price had never faltered in his year climbing out of the minor leagues. He was 4-0 at single-A Vero Beach with an ERA of 1.82; 7-0 for the double-A Montgomery Biscuits, with a 1.89 ERA; and 1-1 for the triple-A Durham Bulls with a 4.5 ERA. At that point, the Rays, looking at their best season in team history, called him up. But now with the season on the line, he was facing J. D. Drew, who drove in the winning run in game five to keep his team alive. It had started to look as though Tampa was falling apart. After leading the series 3–1, they found themselves in a do-or-die situation. Tampa had a two-run lead, but the bases were loaded when Drew came up. The previous year, he had hit a grand slam in a similar situation to propel the Red Sox to the World Series. "I felt in control," Price told me. "I tried to think about the same thing I normally do, the next pitch. That's a huge thing for a pitcher to be able to do. I was just focusing on that next pitch."

He struck out Drew. He then got the last three outs of the game in the next inning and sent the Rays to the World Series. He proved how clutch he had learned to be in the biggest moment in Tampa Bay team history. He was a rock. He did not think about the significance of the game. He just pitched—a hard fastball and an impressive slider. He maintained his resolve. He avoided choking by not thinking of what he was about to do and just doing it. This was textbook clutch behavior— the ability to do what you can do normally under extreme pressure.

Price told me Corbin's practices were what got him to this point. "Practice was definitely tougher than games," he said. "There was no walking once you got on the field; you had to run." Price said that at other colleges he visited before choosing Vanderbilt, the pitchers had it much easier. They generally just shagged balls hit to the outfield and worked on pitcher field practice—a routine in which pitchers throw the ball to one of the bases and run to first to help with an out. It was different at Vanderbilt. "There they call you to the mound and you have to work on your pick-off move [the throw to first]. You have to snag balls hit to your right or left," he said. "If there was only one guy on the mound, the other pitchers were going to run." Price described Corbin's method as constantly raising the bar "so you can't fail." "He expects everyone to be perfect all the time," Price said. This might sound as though Corbin was a demanding tyrant, but what he was trying to do was instill a competitive mind-set at a time when players might otherwise be standing around, dreaming of future fame or reliving great plays from the last game. He turned the pressure on high every day, so when they were in the actual pressure-filled environment of a game, they would not feel it the same way.

How did Corbin turn Price into a rock? The secret was in how he made the whole team practice. "I try to put pressure on everything they do," he told me. "You either rise up or you disintegrate. Through practice you set a high standard." The problem is often that players and other coaches treat practices as something that is not real, Corbin said. They think practice is one thing and the game is another. Corbin sees the two as a continuum. He refers to practices as "training" and said they are meant to get his players in a game frame of mind. A good part of this is the speed at which they do things, which is fast. He doesn't want them taking a ground ball in six seconds, but in four, as they would have to take it in a game. He knows that if they have to speed up in a game, their fundamentals will change. The same goes for pitchers. They couldn't hang around. They couldn't throw the ball and relax. They had to be moving as if they were facing an opponent, not a teammate. "I want a pitcher to field a bunt like he's in a game," Corbin said. "If you treat it like field practice, then don't expect it to transfer to the game." But there is a method to his madness: He tries to unnerve them, so when they face real pressure, they will hold up. "I try to get in their heads," he said. "That's what the game does all the time."

Yet when it's game time, Corbin trusts his players to play. Price said in his last year he had pitched the team into a jam. They had a slim lead, and he gave up a home run in the ninth inning. Price was not worried that he was going to be pulled from the game, even though Vander-bilt had a top reliever in the bullpen. By that point, he was allowed to pitch out of his own mistakes. "He let me work out of my head," he said of Corbin. "That was something I had earned." It was also part of the coaching he had gone through at Vanderbilt. "When I got there I thought my problem was just mental. But it was everything. My mechanics were nowhere where they used to be. I went there with good pitches but I came back with more solid pitches."

When I talked to David Price in 2009, he was in Murfreesboro for his best friend's birthday party. The Philadelphia Phillies, who beat his team in the 2008 World Series, were playing the Los Angeles Dodgers, but he wasn't watching on TV. As we were talking, he offered one of his friends a ride home, as any twenty-three-year-old would do—not one who played in the World Series or even one who received $5.6 million for signing a contract that would pay him $8.5 million. He apologized for keeping me waiting and showed no signs of fatigue when he went over things that happened years ago. He was perfectly relaxed and at ease. What struck me was how honest he was about almost quitting the game. He had doubted himself until he had incorporated that into his prepara-tion. He could give up a hit, but it would not be because the pressure got to him. It would simply be because he threw a bad pitch. It happened. He did not overthink any of it.

COMING BACK FROM ROCK BOTTOM

Alex Rodriguez's problem was that he treated the postseason differently from the 162 games of the regular season. He could seem like a rock then, when he was adding to his great statistics, but when the real pres-sure was on, he became a jelly bean. The game in 2005 when he hit three homers and batted in ten runs was against the Angels, a team the Yankees faced often in the postseason, but he never repeated that feat in the playoffs. Under the weight of his self-created comparisons, he choked again and again. He literally thought himself out of the game.

Like past seasons, 2009 was productive for him. And it ended far better than it had started. At the beginning, it was difficult to imagine A-Rod's image getting any worse than it was at spring training. Before the training camp opened, a magazine published a photo spread that featured him topless and kissing himself in the mirror. Then it was revealed that he had used performance-enhancing drugs from 2001 to 2003, which he had denied for years but now had to admit. His former manager Joe Torre wrote in his book that A-Rod was mocked by Yankees teammates. And then he was forced to undergo hip surgery and missed five weeks of the season while he was on the disabled list. He faded from the conversation, and many fans in New York were happy to have a break from him, even though the team struggled in his absence. When he returned in May, he hit a home run on the first pitch. He hit 7 more in his first 11 at bats. He kept hitting throughout the season. But no one was ready to believe that the great choke artist was becoming clutch.

For all of his mediocre performance in the clutch, A-Rod consistently hit homers and drove in runs during regular-season games. In each of his twelve previous seasons, he had hit at least 30 home runs and had at least 100 runs batted in. In 2009, it looked as though that streak was going to end. He had come close, but those weeks away from the game had given him fewer opportunities. But in his penultimate at-bat, he hit a home run that drove in two other runners for a total of three runs batted in. At that point, he had 29 home runs and 96 RBIs. The chance of his hitting the 30 and 100 marks was possible but not plausible. He would have to hit a grand slam—a home run with three men on base—to reach his marks. The next time he came to bat, there were three men on base. Better than a plain, old grand slam, he hit one with two outs, which in Harold Bloom's assessment was when he usually struck out.

"I just didn't think it was realistic at all, so therefore it wasn't a goal," A-Rod said in the press conference after the game.

That was a crucial admission. He wasn't trying too hard; he wasn't imagining the glory of pulling off the impossible. He wasn't overthinking. That improbable feat prompted a self-assessment that more than anything else had been what led to his incredible season. "I think it's fair to say I hit rock bottom this spring, between the embarrassment of the press conference [about steroids] and my career being threatened with my hip injury," he said. "My life and my career were at a crossroads, and I was either going to stay at the bottom or I was going to bounce back." It seemed as if he had stopped thinking of himself as "the great Alex Rodriguez, the famous A-Rod," and just focused on hitting the ball. Wisely, he had stopped talking to the press, and while he was seen around town with another pretty celebrity—Kate Hudson—he somehow managed to keep it from becoming a focal point. He played too well for anyone to care much about what he was doing outside of the stadium. He was finally earning his money on the field, and the fans were happy to forgive.

Still, the looming question was: What would he do in the playoffs, where he had failed so frequently in past years? Since coming to New York, he had been a postseason flop. By the time the 2009 division series rolled around against the Minnesota Twins, it had been five years since A-Rod had batted in a postseason run, since the second game of the 2004 championship series against the Red Sox. In the first game against Minnesota, that changed. In his third at-bat, he hit a single to left field and the runner scored. He ended his ignominious streak of going 0 for 18 with runners in scoring position and 0 for 29 with runners on base. His response was muted, more like his clutch teammate Derek Jeter. "It just feels good to contribute," he said. That was a far cry from holding forth on his struggles to compete against players already in the Hall of Fame; it was a far more workaday response. Yet A-Rod still had the 9-for-63 statistic to contend with. He began to chip away at that in the division and championship series. And in the eleventh inning of game two of the ALCS against the Los Angeles Angels of Anaheim, he hit the home run that tied the game, kept the Yankees alive, and allowed the team to win in the next inning.

So, what changed? It comes back to what A-Rod said when he returned from the disabled list. While he was still rehabilitating his hip, he spoke at spring training and admitted that his mistakes had been a distraction. He spoke of the time after his surgery in Colorado as a chance "to rethink things, recommit myself, and really understand my responsibility to my teammates and my team." The statement from his press conference that was more startling was the one that made him sound like a Yankee. "Ownership is committed to winning," he said.

"I want to be a part of something that I think will be very special this year." Few had believed him then. His personal and professional life had merged into one, indistinguishable mess, with each tabloid story seeming more outrageous and distracting. But after missing twenty-eight games, he returned and set a different tone. He hit a home run and kept going from there, focusing on playing great baseball, not on thinking about being a great baseball player.

As the postseason rolled around, fans allowed themselves to be swayed, as he had one clutch hit after another. For the first time as a Yankee, A-Rod let his innate ability come out in the chase for a World Series championship. In the first nine games, the ones that got the team to the World Series, A-Rod did not overthink, did not fear criticism or dream of glory. He just played baseball as well as he could, which is to say he played it at the highest level. He had 12 runs batted in, including 5 home runs. His batting average in the division and championship series was .438—triple what it had been during his postseason slump. He also had an eleven-game hitting streak, second best in postseason history, and set a record for hitting an RBI in eight consecutive postseason games—far different records than he had had before. In the World Series, he helped his team win its twenty-seventh championship. Through the entire 2009 postseason, he hit .365 with 6 home runs and 18 runs batted in, which was one off the postseason record. Brian Cashman, the Yankees general manager, commended him: "No one can say anything about him anymore. He's performed in October. He's performed on the biggest stage. He's got a World Series ring coming his way, and he deserves it." But the highest praise for A-Rod came from Hank Steinbrenner, the team's managing partner, who had publicly rebuked him for opting out of his contract in 2007 to get more money: "He was amazing. He proved himself in the clutch. No one can ever question him again. Period."

A-Rod did not suddenly become clutch in the 2009 postseason. He had been performing in the clutch all year. How he summed up his play after the Yankees won the game that sent them to the World Series was telling. "For me, with no expectations and trusting my teammates and taking the walks and doing the little things, you end up doing big things," he said. And he reiterated this sentiment in the moments after the Yankees won the World Series: "I had nothing to lose this year. I hit rock bottom. There's nothing else that could happen to a human being. I just said, 'Let me go out and be one of the guys.' It takes a lot of pressure off you just to go out and play, and your talent sometimes shines even more when you don't worry about individual stuff. I've been humbled. I've been through a lot." In other words, he played without dreaming of greatness. And by doing that, he proved that he was great and could play at the top. He showed that he could be clutch.

THE LESSON OF A-ROD

There was something so painful about watching A-Rod struggle over the years. Even if he did himself no favors in his personal life, I used to cringe like Bloom whenever A-Rod came to the plate. The Yankees, I feared, were going to lose again because of him. He reminded me of how a former colleague described the editor of a newspaper we worked for. He said the man walked into work every day playing himself in the movie version of his life. It was so true. Instead of being inspired by him, we rolled our eyes at his pronouncements. Like A-Rod, he was incredibly smart and gifted, a polyglot who had all the skills needed to run a newspaper. But his conception of himself as a great editor, which he was, made him a horrendous decision maker under pressure. He would reassign the wrong people, never fire the right ones, and let many talented journalists go. This is the tragedy of overthinking. It keeps people from rigorously hewing to the five traits that would make them clutch because they think they have those skills inherently. No one does. But A-Rod's case shows that there is hope of reining yourself in and actually learning to perform under pressure. To avoid the perils of overthinking, a person needs to just do what he does—and not think of what he could, would, or should do in that situation.

[9]

OVERCONFIDENCE STARTS THE FALL

What the Worst Factory in America
Cost GM and Taught Toyota

IN 1982, GENERAL Motors closed its manufacturing plant in Fremont, California. The location, far from Detroit auto suppliers, was considered among the worst-performing assembly lines in the company's system. Occasionally, insiders would argue the quarterly performance reports and say that another plant in Framingham, Massachusetts, was actually the worst, but it was a parlor game. Neither plant was a model of industrial engineering. They were known for wildcat strikes, union hostility, and abysmally low rates of productivity. Roger Smith had become GM's chairman the year before Fremont was closed, and he had begun to think of ways to reorganize the car company. He knew there was a problem; he just wasn't sure what it was, exactly, or how to fix it. Then along came Toyota looking to strike up a joint venture with an American car company as a way to expand into the U.S. market. GM offered them Fremont, and at the time, it seemed Toyota had been stuck with a lemon.

In 1984, Fremont was reopened as New United Motor Manufacturing Inc., or NUMMI. Toyota had retooled the space, but as part of the agreement, it had rehired many of the same five thousand employees who as members of the United Auto Workers had made it an unruly and inefficient place. (This was not an act of generosity but part of Federal

Trade Commission approval of the deal.) While GM provided the plant and a dysfunctional workforce, Toyota agreed to teach GM executives the Toyota Production System, its management technique that had gained popularity through the 1970s. It would also show the company how to build, finally, a small car that people would buy.

On the surface, it looked as though Toyota was giving away the two most important things it had as a company to the world's biggest automaker—TPS and compact-car know-how. It seemed liked a decidedly uneven deal, tilted in GM's favor. It looked even worse when you judged Toyota against its Japanese competitors, who had opened stand-alone plants. Honda was in Marysville, Ohio, and Nissan was in Smyrna, Tennessee, both closer to Detroit. (Fremont is 2,400 miles away.) Their competitors' plants could also start from scratch without an entrenched UAW way of doing things. Toyota was aware of all of this, but as a cautious company, it preferred signing on with a partner to going it alone in a market that it did not fully understand. Then, in December 1984, the first Chevrolet Nova rolled off the assembly line. It was an exact copy of the Toyota Corolla, a light and basic box with wheels. That spring, cars made at NUMMI went on sale. The Nova would eventually be marketed under the tagline "Imported from America."

In the process of making cars at NUMMI, something strange happened: The UAW workers went from obstructive to productive. The wildcat strikes were gone, and productivity was up. In 1988, Elmer Johnson, an executive vice president vying for the top job when Smith stepped down, wrote a memo to the executive committee detailing the company's challenges. At the outset, he praised what was happening in Fremont. "The NUMMI joint-venture dramatized GM's determination to open our eyes to the current state of the art in production systems," he wrote. "In one sense the experiment has been a great success. A historically troubled workforce was turned into a role model for all of GM in terms of teamwork, product quality and productivity gains."

For sure, Toyota did things differently. It did not promise workers life-long employment, as an American carmaker would, but when demand sagged in 1988, the company did not lay anyone off. It took some workers off the line and gave them additional training. Toyota called this *kaizen,* a tenet of TPS: With it, workers would be better when capacity increased again. The next year, NUMMI produced its five-hundred-thousandth car. A year after that, it began producing light pickup trucks, which proved to be wildly popular. The millionth car rolled off the assembly line in 1991. Most important, Toyota had learned to work with the union autoworkers and understand the American supply chain. The company was now confident about its prospects in the United States.

NUMMI had not been a success for both halves of the joint venture, however. GM, while still the world's biggest carmaker, had not gotten as much out of the deal. For one, it had not learned to market a small car. The Nova was a flop compared to the Corolla, and this made no sense to them. Before the Nova was discontinued in 1988, the two cars were the same. They were made at exactly the same plant, by exactly the same workers. One had a Toyota nameplate, the other said Chevy. Yet consumers treated them differently. There was still the perception that Toyota made a quality compact car and GM did not. For once, there was absolutely no basis for that opinion.

Moreover, there were other, straight GM models that were doing no better than the Nova. Smith, who became chairman in 1981, had set out to reorganize the various GM divisions for the first time since Alfred Sloan, the iconic automotive thinker, had split them in the 1930s. While Sloan's efforts are still revered because of what they did for brand identity, Smith's decisions were largely seen as disastrous. One thing that came out of his 1984 plan was the Cadillac Cimarron, the brand's first compact car. It became a running joke in the industry, essentially a Chevy Cavalier with leather seats and a higher price tag. As the years wore on, GM continued its well-chronicled decline, in fits and starts. As part of the Chapter 11 bankruptcy filing, in the summer of 2009 GM pulled out of NUMMI, and one month later Toyota did the same thing. By this point, Toyota had a dozen of its own assembly lines in North America, most of them in closer proximity to Detroit parts suppliers. It had gotten everything it could out of the joint venture. The two cars it produced at NUMMI—the Corolla and various models of the Tacoma pickup truck—were solid sellers, but the Corolla was also being made at a plant in Ontario—less than two hundred miles from Detroit. The

one car GM made there—the Pontiac Vibe—had been discontinued
along with the entire Pontiac line.

Failings with the NUMMI joint venture were not the reason GM
ended up in bankruptcy. But NUMMI was one of the many small and
large mistakes executives made at the automaker over decades. The root
problem it illustrated was a persistent overconfidence, a belief despite evidence to the contrary that GM was the best carmaker in the world and
would always remain so. This shows what happens when executives stop
believing failure is a possibility and cease making the difficult decisions
a company needs to prosper. Overconfidence in the day-to-day operation
of a business leads to choking in the clutch. GM, at the end of the day,
became a frog in a boiling pot of water: It did not realize it was getting
cooked until it was too late. Rick Wagoner, the company's last prebank-
ruptcy chief executive, had resisted the Chapter 11 filing until he was
forced out by the U.S. government as part of its increased bailout. He
will be forever linked to the collapse of the company, but this is not
entirely fair. While he made some mistakes—defending the Hummer
brand, failing to sell underperforming brands sooner, starving Chevy of
new models—he was just the last overconfident man in a long line of
overconfident GM men stretching back beyond Roger Smith.

The more important issue is the cause of GM's long, slow slide into
bankruptcy. Overconfidence pervaded the entire company. Why GM
failed to adapt to the changing U.S. auto market—and was overtaken by
Toyota as the world's largest automaker—stemmed from the attitude of
its executives going into NUMMI some twenty-five years earlier. (Roger
Smith was there at the official opening to shake hands with Eiji Toyoda,
his counterpart at Toyota.) While GM executives seemed confident
about the deal they struck, they were actually overconfident. And the
difference between the two is the difference between being clutch when
the pressure increases and choking.

Confidence is the ability to execute a plan even with the knowledge
that it might not work out exactly as you suspect: Toyota wanted to make
cars in the United States as part of its plan to become the largest carmaker in the world, but it wanted to tread carefully in entering the U.S.

market. This is similar to how Larry Clarke, in chapter 4, learned to prepare for his auditions. Confidence was feeling self-assured, being prepared, and mixing in a dose of humility. To him, it was the opposite of being cocky, when he was self-assured but not sufficiently prepared. Overconfidence is different from both confidence and cockiness. It is the belief that the plan you have worked hard to create is infallible, even when faced with evidence to the contrary: GM had always been the biggest carmaker, and so it always would be. Despite abundant signs that GM's place in the auto world was less secure, Smith and successive chairmen right up to Wagoner failed to act on this reality. That they would choke in the clutch had been preordained. GM's overconfidence blinded the company to the economic realities that Toyota had been dealing with all along. A closer look at NUMMI provides a cautionary tale of the perils of overconfident executives.

THE UNDERCONFIDENCE STRATEGY

John Shook figured the only reason Toyota hired him was because of NUMMI. In 1983, he became the first American to work as a regular employee—as opposed to a translator or teacher—at the company's Toyota City headquarters, and he would eventually become the company's first American manager. He had convinced company management that he could help them with their U.S. strategy. Born in Tennessee, Shook had just completed his MBA at the University of Hawaii, but he had been fascinated with the Japanese management style since his university days in Knoxville. That was when his goal became to work at the "most Japanese company" he could find. After he bounced around Tokyo for nine months trying to convince someone to hire a skinny thirty-something American in a work culture that was mostly closed to non-Japanese, it turned out he was in the right place at the right time. "In the 1980s, Toyota's challenge was globalization," Shook told me. "They could make Corollas and make them more efficiently and with better quality in Toyota City, but all of the suppliers were right there, within twenty minutes of each other, so 'just in time' was easy. But they didn't know how to do what they were doing globally."

That was where NUMMI came in, and Shook, who had a better grasp of American geography than Toyota, thought it was an odd starting point. "For Toyota, why would you want to do this?" Shook asked. "No one produced cars in California anymore, and there were good reasons: Land costs are high, labor costs are high, energy costs are high, no one else is there." But Toyota saw it as a chance to learn. "At this time, Toyota was sitting there saying, 'Do we know how to build cars in the States? Of course not.' So they didn't try to fool themselves. They didn't try to solve the problem sitting in a room and trying to guess." The company had the resources to do a stand-alone plant, like Honda and Nissan, but then it would have had to figure out both the American worker and the American supply chain on their own. "They always want to know their strengths and weaknesses first," he said. "And one of their weaknesses was that they did not know how to do this. They admitted that." Going into a joint venture would speed up the learning curve. The biggest risk, though, was giving away its management system, but executives felt the best way to get into the American market was through a partnership.

Shook was based at Toyota City and flew regularly to California as a liaison. He said the pressure on Toyota to succeed with NUMMI was immense, but what struck him was how Toyota executives handled it. They used it to focus their work and did not allow it to cause stress. "Most of our quintessential American leaders—like a Lee Iacocca or a Jack Welch—have this image of deciding from your gut: You know what to do and you're going to show people how we get this done. The Japanese don't play that game. It's a silly, stupid game. It's much smarter to realize you don't know what's going to happen tomorrow." So Toyota tried to learn and to be, if anything, underconfident in its venture.

Their goal was to overtake GM and become the largest car company in the world. They had been working toward this since after World War II. Patience and diligence were ingrained in the corporate culture. But in the early 1980s, GM sold three times as many cars as Toyota in the United States. NUMMI was going to be a beachhead in America to see if Toyota could become a global brand. It was also a way for Toyota to get around an import agreement between the United States and Japan. The quota for all Japanese carmakers was set at 22 percent of U.S. car sales and was meant to stop imports from eroding the market share of GM, Ford, and Chrysler. In this sense, a joint venture was incredibly shrewd on Toyota's part, because it circumvented the quotas. Despite the need for protectionist measures, GM still saw itself operating from a position of strength. It had been the dominant automaker in the world since World War II and was sure this would continue, even if its model—a line of cars for every price range, from Chevrolet to Cadillac—was starting to strain. And while there may have been voices of concern in the company, like Elmer Johnson's, most executives in Detroit were confident that GM, with a few tweaks, would remain at the top. Such a belief, however, was leading the company and its executives down a dangerous path. Their confidence in their abilities was evolving into overconfidence that they would always be on top.

The first concern Toyota had at NUMMI was about American workers: It was not confident they could actually work to Japanese standards. The perception was that the American autoworker was lazy. But the bigger concern, Shook said, was whether they could be taught Toyota's management style. "Plans are useless; planning is everything," Shook said. "Planning means knowing where you stand, knowing where you want to go, and all the contingencies between here and there." The big-picture plan for NUMMI was for Toyota to understand the U.S. market, build cars Americans wanted to buy, and expand their brand. But for the line workers, the plan was to teach them to be more involved in the details of making cars. Toyota did not want them to mindlessly execute whatever tasks they were charged with but to play a role in improving the designs themselves. What this meant was real quality control, not just slogans. The NUMMI workers were told that it was their obligation to stop the assembly line if they saw something wrong with a car. The goal was not to get the car through the line as fast as possible, come what may, but to make sure it left the plant properly engineered. This was how it worked in Japan, but Toyota executives were not sure it could be translated. That was Shook's job. How Shook—who knew nothing about cars beyond having liked them growing up in Tennessee—got to teach unionized autoworkers the Toyota style of Japanese management showed in and of itself that an American could be taught TPS.

After being hired, Shook was put to work as an autoworker in Toyota City. He started by building Corollas. He rotated through the whole process from body welding to production control. In his months on the line, he saw firsthand how a manager would respond when Shook pulled the rope to report a problem. A sign lit up over his workstation, and one of the team leaders came over. He told me he did this particularly often when he was installing seat belts. Although this slowed the process down, it increased the quality, and by the early 1980s Toyota was becoming known for the quality and not just the low price of its cars. At NUMMI, Shook helped implement the same process. "When GM was told about this, they said, you're crazy," he said. "GM looked at us as if to say, 'This workforce would stop the line anyway, and now you give them the right to pull a rope and stop the line?' We said, 'No. We give them the obligation to do that.' That's their job to see those problems and call someone over to fix it. Their job is not to get the car out of the door even if it's bad." To some surprise, the new system worked. The idea of teamwork, imported from Japan, took hold at the California plant. Part of the reason was that both sides had something invested: Toyota needed to succeed in America, and the five thousand workers knew that NUMMI was providing the only autoworker jobs in California.

As Toyota's philosophy took hold with the line workers, Shook said, managers were pushed to do more as well. The expectations were different. The goal was to challenge them. For example, if Shook told a manager to cut 20 percent from the cost of a cup holder, he did not expect him to actually cut 20 percent. In fact he would be upset if he came back with 20 percent cut from the cost. "We don't understand causality well enough to know that there is exactly 20 percent worth of savings," he told me. "If I say you need to get 20 percent and you hit it, that's insane. C'mon! There is no way I can sit here and guess there is 20 percent savings in something." He would be happier if the person came back and said the cost could only be cut by 5 percent—or maybe it was

50 percent. The request was an exercise; it was done to see if something could be made better. "At the end of the day, I don't care if you make it for 20 percent less. The goal is to make it better," he said. "This is playing with ideas so we can learn."

This might sound logical but it stands in stark contrast to one of the dominant American management systems: Set a target and meet it. In that school of thought, the 20 percent reduction was the goal—not the improvement of the thing itself. And the person charged with making that reduction would be judged strictly on whether or not she accomplished it. If she did, she had succeeded; if she did not, she had failed, even if she had tried harder. As absurd as this sounds, it was what Steven Rattner, the man who was briefly the U.S. car czar in the Treasury Department, found when he went into a nearly bankrupt GM in 2009. "Everyone knew Detroit's reputation for insular, slow-moving cultures. Even by that low standard, I was shocked by the stunningly poor management that we found, particularly at GM," he wrote in *Fortune*. "From my first day at Treasury, PowerPoint decks would arrive from GM (we quickly concluded that no decision seemed to be made at GM without one) requesting approvals. We were appalled by the absence of sound analysis provided to justify these expenditures."

At NUMMI, and Toyota in general, the Toyota Production System was designed to prevent the overconfidence that comes from an ingrained way of doing things. What drove the company was the desire to make the cars they produced better, even when they were already good. And this meant competition within the company itself. As a case in point, Shook pointed to the first Toyotas made after Lexus was launched in 1989. The challenge of having a designated luxury line made Toyota engineers think even harder about design quality, to the point where models in the early 1990s were "outrageously overengineered." While that is an extreme case, it highlighted the culture that kept Toyota from growing complacent. "You have to get used to the idea that the plateau will never come," Shook said. "Your job is that process along the way of doing those little improvements. You're truly never done. It's actually only when you come to terms with that that you can relax and the pressure no longer bothers you." In other words, there is always something to improve and improvement itself, not a fixed goal, becomes your job. There is no time to sit back and be complacent.

ALL OVERCONFIDENT LEADERS KILL COMPANIES IN THE SAME WAYS

Overconfidence is the bigger, more destructive cousin of overthinking. It might be the most pernicious form of choking for one reason: its magnitude. When someone like A-Rod overthinks the situation, he fails personally, but other teammates can make up for his shortcomings. When the leader of a company becomes overconfident, his choking can be systemic. (The opposite is also true: A company that overthinks things may miss out on a deal and lose market share, but it can probably correct things. And a person who is blithely overconfident on his own most likely spirals into ineffectiveness—or barroom solipsism—without doing greater harm.) But the collapse overconfidence brings about is a complicated thing. It usually starts off as a feeling of unease, and that uneasiness may manifest itself as a sense that something is not sustainable, perhaps even at the top. Then, it abates, with months, years passing before anything more happens. But when the collapse comes, it is usually swift. And those left in its wake start to wonder how they missed something so obvious. The lies, the tales, the trumped-up reports were, of course, too good to be true. If it was fraud and not mismanagement, the sense of betrayal is worse. And if it wasn't, then the steps to arrest the decline become obvious in retrospect.

That was the situation GM found itself in after years of ignoring that things had to change. Elmer Johnson, who had praised NUMMI, tried to draw attention to this in his 1988 memo. "In the four or five years we've been at it, we have made only slight progress toward our visionary goal of a new GM production system. We simply appear unable to execute the plan." What made Johnson's assessment so interesting was that he looked at GM as an outsider: He had worked for twenty-seven years at a Chicago law firm before Smith hired him as legal counsel. Within five years, he was promoted to executive vice president and named one of four executives from whom the next chairman would be picked. And that perspective allowed him to see clearly where GM struggled and point it out: "We have vastly underestimated how deeply ingrained are the organizational and cultural rigidity that hamper our ability to execute ['clean slate' strategies]." Two years later, he was passed over for the chairmanship for a consensus builder, Robert Stempel, a lifelong GM executive.

One common characteristic of overconfident executives is that they do not think failure could ever be an option. "Too big to fail" was the label used by the U.S. government to defend its actions in saving Wall Street banks during the Great Recession. What's different is that most overconfident executives run companies that could very easily fail—and be allowed to go under. Yet they do not realize this. When something comes along that forces that executive to face the reality of the situation, he is not equipped to do it. Yet the miscalculations are so common—and consistent across industries—that they have spawned an entire industry: restructuring. And Tony Alvarez and Bryan Marsal, two of the go-to guys in the business that cleans up when leaders fail under pressure, said one of four reasons always causes the overconfidence.

The least pernicious reason is the business cycle. If your business is built on oil trading no lower than $30 a barrel, when it is at $50 a barrel, you're fine; if it goes to $20 a barrel, you could be in trouble. That was the case when Alvarez & Marsal was founded in 1983. The U.S. economy was humming along, but oil companies started to scramble. They had been focused on growth, on expanding their companies while oil prices increased steadily through the late 1970s; but these higher prices led to more exploration, and prices fell. A similar thing happened with the first wave of Internet companies, where "eyeballs" were everything and revenues and profits something to be considered later. In both instances, the people running the companies grew overconfident because they thought they were living in an environment where their businesses would always grow and they would not have to make contingency plans for a time when they could shrink. Demand for oil and Internet pet food companies would always be strong, and then suddenly it wasn't. Part of the problem was the chief executives who got hired for those jobs: people who considered themselves visionaries with a mission of rapid, dazzling growth. "Their strength is not managing the costs to coincide with the revenue; their strength is being bold," said Alvarez, a compact man with a quick smile. When boldness is no longer required, their companies are in trouble.

The second state that creates overconfident executives is easy money. "It's like candy," said Alvarez. And it brought his firm a lot of work in the late 1980s and early 1990s when the deals put together by leveraged buyout funds had to be unwound. After the credit crisis of 2008, A & M entered another boom time, as firms began to go bust. "Three years ago [in 2006], we were saying this is crazy. They're getting money for nothing. These are going to be clients of ours because it was so easy." That was exactly what happened. When Lehman Brothers filed for bankruptcy, a victim of too much debt and misplaced bets, Marsal, the more physically imposing of the team, was named the company's chief restructuring officer. He told me the company's problems were simple and obvious: "They shouldn't have had so much leverage. They shouldn't have had such a disproportionate concentration in real estate assets. And they should have been smarter about using short-term debt to finance long-term assets." Sorting out the company's bankruptcy has been a situation that required coming up with a plan focused on the goal of getting the most money for creditors.

The last two areas where leaders grow dangerously overconfident are specific to a company's management—when it is bad and when it is fraudulent. The bad manager thinks he knows more than he actually does. This was the case with GM. It was also the situation with Warnaco, a holding company for Calvin Klein and other clothing brands, and its chief executive, Linda Wachner. "She was a brilliant leader who did not surround herself with a strong team," Alvarez told me. "She had a hard time holding on to good people. She could overcome that problem when the company was smaller, but when it got bigger, it was too difficult to manage." He was brought in as the chief restructuring officer but became the chief executive within four months, after the board pushed Wachner out. Alvarez's job was to sort out the company after it found itself unable to pay debts and the licensing agreements for its various brands.

Then there's the fraudulent manager who is uniquely and supremely overconfident: He thinks he can get away with something and never be detected. When Richard Scrushy, the chief executive of HealthSouth, and eighteen of his top lieutenants were indicted on charges of accounting fraud—on the order of $1.4 billion—Marsal was brought in to right the company. In 2003, the federal government charged Scrushy with directing his subordinates to inflate earnings as far back as 1996 in an attempt to keep up with Wall Street expectations. Marsal said this was far tougher than his work on Lehman Brothers, where he was simply trying to sell assets at the best prices for creditors. "We had to bring that company back to life," he told me. Scrushy had been a flamboyant and charismatic leader, the big man in Birmingham, Alabama, so when he was indicted and the viability of the company was put into question, employees descended into a state of shock. They had believed in what Scrushy was doing, which was what makes the fallout from the overconfident fraudster the hardest to handle. "I'd walk the floor and yuck it up with the troops," he said. "Then I'd go back to my office, close the door and say, 'Oh, my God, what have I gotten myself into.'"

He was trying to maintain calm so he could keep employees on board. So, like other clutch people I've discussed in this book, he hunkered down, focused, and began making decisions. He recalled that shortly after he was named the company's chief recovery officer, a group of doctors who ran a surgery center in Tuscaloosa came looking for a bigger share of the revenues. Under its contract with the center, HealthSouth split the profits fifty-fifty. At the time, HealthSouth had three hundred similar surgical centers around the country, and he knew that if he let one renegotiate its deal, the others would soon follow. "I said, 'To be honest with you docs, with no disrespect to you, I'd rather burn this facility than give you what you want.' I always remember what one of the docs said. 'This is the damnedest thing I've ever seen. The first guy they put in there was a crook cooking the books; this guy is an arsonist.' But they left. Word got out that this guy is crazy and if you're going to have a beef, it had better be a legitimate beef." In addition to being a funny story, particularly when you picture Marsal's football-player build, his response illustrated the difference between overconfidence and confidence: Marsal made his decision based on the facts of the situation and the risks and ramifications of cutting a deal with one group and not another. After all, HealthSouth's problem was not in the services it provided, which were legitimate, but in one overconfident chief executive's fraudulent accounting.

Regardless of the trigger, Marsal said the initial reactions of the leaders was the same. "Almost all of these companies are in denial like an alcoholic—'I don't have a problem, just sprinkle holy water on this and I'll be fine.' You see so many similarities of denial in crisis. You have to solve your problems from within, from what you control. You can't always solve your problems on the revenue line." And this is where, regardless of how an executive's overconfidence brings a company to its knees, the cure begins the same way—with a need for leadership. "What we realized was, managers were paralyzed," said Marsal. "They would sit in their office and say, 'Oh, my God, what do we do? How did I get here? What am I going to do now?' Then the people beneath them say, 'If that guy's paralyzed, should I be looking for a job?'" And that is the most morale-busting part of an overconfident leader's failure. Workers believed in him, and when that belief is shattered, the workforce becomes quickly and severely underconfident. "You've got to get someone in there to control the process," Marsal said.

Just as executives grow overconfident in the same ways, how they try to wiggle out of their predicaments is often just as predictable. It goes back to Marsal's alcoholic analogy: They want an easy way out, and they want to stay in control. The two typical strategies a chief executive in crisis tries first are looking for a way to increase profits quickly and, when that fails, selling assets to raise money. They do those things because neither fundamentally changes their position at the company. "By the time we come in, they've exhausted these options," Alvarez said. Yet because of the predictable nature of overconfident leaders, Marsal said, their firm is usually able to get a handle on the situation quickly. On one side are creditors who want to get paid and, just as important, want to know that if they cut a deal with an executive who owes them money, he is going to make every effort to pay them back. This part is fairly straightforward. It is on the company side where there needs to be tougher conversations. "They'd tell us they had already cut everything they could," Marsal said. "Then I'd go through the books. Was the tea lady needed? Was the plane needed? I'd have to tell them, 'Never show up in a corporate jet, never show up in a limo when you owe somebody money.'" Wagoner and his fellow auto executives could have used this advice before they flew on private jets to Washington, hats in hands, to ask for billions in November 2008. Instead, one congressman shot the quip heard round the world: "Couldn't you all have downgraded to first class or jet-pooled or something to get here? It would have at least sent a message that you do get it."

In taking control of a company, any restructuring firm reins in overconfidence. Alvarez equated how they do their job to a game of golf. "In golf, I'm not thinking so much about how I'm going to beat you in this match and thinking about that outcome. I'm literally thinking about How am I going to play this hole?" he said. "In a workout [of a company], I'm not thinking this has to become this kind of answer. I'm thinking this is what has to be done then."

PUTTING THE BRAKES ON OVERCONFIDENCE

If there is one thing that sets off John Shook, who is now an automotive industry consultant, it is when someone implies that Toyota beat GM because it did not have the same union baggage and health-care costs. He believes talk about the legacy costs is a crutch to excuse decades of bad management. And it is another manifestation of GM's not taking responsibility for what happened, of the overconfidence that it would always be on top regardless of the bad decisions it made: "It wasn't just that Toyota had less baggage than GM. There were automakers all over the world that did," Shook told me. "GM could not respond under pressure because of the 20 percent it was always trying to cut, and it didn't see beyond that." The real problem was they didn't adjust to the changing landscape of the 1980s and '90s. The mentality that created the "job banks"—rooms where laid-off workers went to collect GM paychecks—was set in motion by that 1950s mentality. There was no *kaizen* in it. In its heyday, GM quite literally needed to build as many cars as it could, across the range of its models, and it could be confident that Americans, in the postwar flush, would buy them. They had a 60 percent share of the U.S. market then, so GM didn't blink at paying workers high salaries and giving them lifelong benefits: They were making so much money it didn't matter. "That," Shook pointed out, "sent them on a binge which they possibly never recovered from. It was not that they had so much baggage from the 1950s; it was that the decisions they started making in the 1950s set them on this course." It was the difference between plans and planning.

The notion that forces outside of GM's management were to blame persisted until the end. "Rick [Wagoner] and his team seemed to believe that virtually all of their problems could be laid at the feet of some combination of the financial crisis, oil prices, the yen-dollar exchange rate, and the UAW," Steven Rattner wrote. But what shocked the car czar was the company's proposal to make things better: "GM's February viability plan was more 'business as usual' and not the aggressive new approach that we felt was essential." This mirrored what Alvarez & Marsal found about companies put into a crisis of overconfidence: They want the quick fix; they do not want to do the hard work that's necessary.

Shook, who since leaving Toyota has consulted for Ford and GM, said he prefers to compare Toyota and Nissan. He argued that at the start of the race to beat GM, Nissan was equal to Toyota or perhaps had a slight advantage because of its closer relationship with the Japanese government. But by the end of the 1990s, Nissan was worried about its survival and agreed to a partnership with France's Renault to stay in business. At the time, Toyota was profitable, having introduced the Lexus line that became a luxury standard. The bigger question now, Shook said, was whether Toyota would slip into the same overconfidence that hobbled GM once it became the biggest carmaker in the world. For over fifty years, Toyota's goal was to surpass GM. Their energy was focused on it, and it was what informed their planning. They could never grow over-confident while they were underdogs. But then they passed GM, and their challenge ended. Not only did GM file for bankruptcy and become a ward of the U.S. government, but Toyota became an industry leader in hybrid technology. When we spoke in the spring of 2009, Shook was worried that this would not be enough for a company whose corporate culture had been built around reaching the next level. He said the company desperately needed to tackle a far bigger question than hybrid technology to remain the company it had been. He suggested a suitable project would be the idea of mobility itself in the future.

Akio Toyoda, the company's chairman and grandson of the company's founder, seemed to realize as much. He said the company needed to define new challenges and set new goals. In an interview with *Fortune* in the summer of 2009, before announcing the closing of NUMMI, he admitted that Toyota suffered from "big company disease." But he said the company was focused on what would come next:

> I believe the auto industry is now trying to face the challenges of presenting a solution to this once-in-a-century change. And what is clear to me is that what is going to happen will not just simply be an extension of the past . . . these conditions that supported the prosperity of the auto industry started to disintegrate. I believe it is an important time for Toyota to present some answers for the coming 100 years. It is Toyota's mission to find out how we can utilize available energy resources and technology for the future.

Before it had a chance to do that, Toyota had to initiate its biggest vehicle recall in company history. The issue was faulty accelerators on some 8.5 million automobiles. It seemed the great underdog had become overconfident.

Shook told me the recall had not changed his basic thinking on Toyota's need to take on a bigger project, but the company was being forced to confront the issue far more quickly than he had imagined. As he wrote in a blog post in February 2010, "If this can happen to Toyota, it could happen to you." He said what was most at stake was the trust and confidence Toyota had engendered with its customers over three decades.

With its accelerator problem, Toyota showed that even the best can become hobbled by overconfidence. Their crisis also reinforced the fact that clutch traits are not permanent. Just as Alex Rodriguez found a way to stop overthinking, Toyota grew complacent.

PART III

||||||||||||||||||||||||||

HOW TO BE CLUTCH

[10]

HOW TO BE CLUTCH WITH YOUR MONEY
Knowing When to Quit

FREDERICK PETERS IS not the type of man you would expect to have financial problems. He owns Warburg Realty Partners, which sells the most expensive apartments in Manhattan to people with unimaginable wealth. These are dream homes, Park Avenue penthouses once occupied by Vanderbilts and Whitneys, Tribeca lofts that should be in movies, exquisite brownstones that evoke an American grandeur that scarcely exists anymore. These homes often cost over $10 million, but many climb higher to levels that boggle the average person's mind. It's a rarefied but lucrative niche. And over its hundred-year history, Warburg has done a fine job of servicing its demanding clientele.

Peters was born into this world, though you wouldn't guess that at first glance. Dressed in a black shirt and black pants, with close-cropped hair gone thin in spots, he looks like an avant-garde musician, not a business owner and certainly not a real estate wheeler-dealer. He appears far more downtown edgy than uptown elite. And he certainly does not look like the descendant of a trifecta of legendary banking families—Warburg, Rothschild, and Schiff—which he is. He has the height and aquiline features associated with the very wealthy, but he comes across as a slightly distracted, overworked New York everyman. Had I not been told beforehand, I would have never guessed that a few months earlier he had been forced to make decisions under extreme pressure to keep his firm afloat.

The main Warburg office is old-money shabby. Above Peters's desk hangs a gigantic flat-screen television, mounted like a prized elk. As big, black, and shiny as it is, it does not fully cover the faded spots of yellow wallpaper around it. Nor does it hide the holes from whatever was hanging there before. In all its newness, the TV looks out of place, as if it were hung there as a prank. The rest of the office is like the wallpaper, tired. Peters's desk is cluttered in a way that is unbecoming to the president of one of New York's major real estate brokerages. (It is more excusable if you know that his first career was as a musician and that he studied toward a doctorate in composition.) There are photos of his wife and two children, but they are obscured by stacks of real estate binders. His view onto East Seventy-sixth Street, a beautiful block of well-kept brownstones, is through two soot-stained panes on a wall so long it could accommodate three times the number of windows. The public areas are no better. The waiting room, where the city's great and good enter, consists of two chairs wedged into a corner between the elevator and the reception desk. These walls are also pocked with holes that are only half covered by what is hanging there now. Even though the office is across from the Carlyle Hotel, one of the city's grand old meeting spots, the place looks like a used-car dealership in a depressed town. An advertisement for the space in the cheery code of real estate agents might read: "Prime location, great bones. Bring your decorator and your imagination." A civilian would call it a dump.

"I don't believe in owning your office space," Peters told me, sipping his tea from a glass cup marked PESSIMIST MUG. "If you have to change locations, it makes it tough."

Peters has worked in this office for twenty-nine years and owned the business for the last two decades. He has also lived in the same apartment on Central Park West for thirty-two years; he bought it the year he was married. ("If everyone was like me with real estate, I wouldn't have a job," he said.) Peters doesn't "do change," but he likes to have the option. And having options like that came in handy when in the financial crash the Manhattan real estate market seized up. "My business pretty much ran into a wall on Lehman Brothers Day," he said.

That day—September 15, 2008—was when the once-great trading house ceased to exist. While thousands of bankers lost their jobs, the firm's collapse had a ripple effect. It was a boulder dropped into a bathtub: It shocked the global financial system and caused otherwise wealthy, savvy investors to immediately think they were broke. Even when they realized they weren't, they started to rethink how they were spending money and what they were spending it on. Suddenly, they seemed to be acting cautiously, whether or not it was warranted. On that day, the Dow Jones Industrial Average closed at 11,220.68, down from its high of over 14,000 a year earlier. Investors were in a state of shock: Their portfolios had been crushed, and they began to cling to the money that would have financed purchases of luxury homes. Peters grew distant as he remembered that day. Quite simply, sales of high-end real estate stopped, he said. They didn't slow; they didn't pull back; they came to a grinding halt. "There were no transactions to be done," he said.

Peters had been through real estate contractions before. He bought the business in 1991, just as New York entered a real estate slump. And he had seen prices plateau several times in the past thirty years. In many ways, he had been more fortunate than most. His niche was akin to selling waterfront property: Just as there is a limited amount of beach, there are only so many prewar buildings on Park Avenue and no more can ever be built. At the highest end, prices did not swing as they would in a development outside of Phoenix; they slowed, but there was always an underlying value in the desirability of the addresses. So when the market froze, Peters grew concerned. He had never seen this happen.

In November, two months into the real estate slump, Peters was already feeling anxious when he read a story about businesses failing in difficult times because they typically do not cut back quickly or deeply enough. This was on his mind as he went into a meeting with his board of directors. Instead of talking about the prospects for a recovery in the coming year, the chief financial officer ran through doomsday scenarios: What would happen if the business went down 30, 35, or 40 percent? When he heard the answers, Peters was shocked by not only how much he could lose but also how quickly he could lose it. "I told my CFO, 'Let's see where we are at the end of the first quarter,'" he told me. "A week later, he came to me and said, 'I know you don't want to have this conversation, but I don't think we can wait that long.'"

The collapse of the U.S. economy—and with it wealth in many forms, from property and retirement savings to ongoing income—was something that seemed inevitable in hindsight. The economy—as much as people's expectations about it—was a house of cards that had to collapse at some point. But the people who were building that flimsy house kept talking about new paradigms, historical returns on equity, the housing markets, and most of all, the unprecedented wealth in America. Seemingly smart people allowed themselves to be convinced that this time was different, that this boom would last forever. Yet with the Great Recession, even people who said they were prepared for a "market correction"—the polite euphemism for losing money in various securities—were not prepared for it to correct as much as it did. Peters was no different. At first, he wanted to believe that this recession was going to be short and shallow and that business as usual would resume in 2009. But his CFO, the guy running the numbers and calculating the profits and losses, saw something different. He told Peters that he had to make cuts immediately if he wanted to keep the rest of the business afloat. This was overwhelming to Peters. From his ramshackle head-quarters on the Upper East Side, he had added four more locations to become a dominant player in the city's luxury real estate market. Making the hard choices his CFO demanded—namely, closing an office in Harlem—was too much for him to bear. "I needed to think about it," he told me, still agitated months later. "I went out for a walk. I know myself, and I needed to wrap my arms around it."

What Peters struggled with was not entirely a financial decision. After all, he came from not one but three storied banking families. He was not going to be living on the street if his business failed. He was wrestling with something that inhibited clear thinking much more—and causes people of all wealth levels to make the wrong decisions under pressure. "The biggest problem for me was pride," he admitted. "We all knew what the marketplace was like, but if I closed an office, I was going to be publicly acknowledging that my business sucked."

BEING CLUTCH WITH MONEY AND IN SPORTS

So far, *Clutch* has shown why some people excel under pressure and why many more choke under similar circumstances. I have discussed the traits of each. But now I want to show how two highly skilled professionals, people who possessed the underlying foundation to be clutch, actually found themselves in high-pressure situations and prevailed. They were able to do what they do in everyday conditions but under extreme pressure. In Peters's case, this meant running a successful real estate business. In the next chapter, I tell the story of Mat Goggin, a professional golfer who has played well on the PGA Tour for many years but never won a tournament. Peters found himself in a financial crisis that threatened the future of his firm. Midway through the last round of a major tournament, Goggin was in the lead. How they performed in these quintessential clutch situations will help you think about your own struggles in these two areas—money and sports.

More so than in the previous chapters, I have gone through these stories from an evolutionary point of view. This, I hope, shows how these men made the crucial decisions they needed to make under pressure and offers some takeaways for readers in their own lives. Peters and Goggin responded under pressure well because they had applied the principles of being clutch to their lives: focus, discipline, adaptability, being present, and a bigger dose of entrepreneurial desire than fear. This gave them a solid foundation to make the decisions they needed to make when the repercussions for not doing so were stark. They also avoided the three traits of those who choke. As soon as they found themselves tested, they took responsibility, did not overthink their situations, and most certainly did not grow overconfident. They kept thinking and acting as they would have if the pressure had not been as great. They were presented with a problem, and they set out to solve it.

While it will be easy to see how each man relied on the five clutch traits under pressure, I have also provided more specific guidance in making financial decisions and playing competitive sports. I did this because these are two areas where every person could benefit from becoming better under pressure. Wouldn't we all like to make better financial decisions? And who wouldn't want to win the weekend golf or tennis match? The way Peters and Goggin handled their situations can serve as a guide for anybody.

PRIDE CLOUDS DECISION MAKING

Peters was self-aware enough to know what was holding him back. But that was no guarantee that he could make the correct decision. Pride is an emotion that inhibits many people's ability to make all kinds of necessary decisions. In financial matters, pride acts like a smoke screen. It keeps people from making the right choice at the right time, from looking at what the numbers say and acting rationally. Pride lets you lie to yourself and believe that whatever financial situation you're in will get better on its own. The truth is, this has never been the case. Most people know the saying "Pride comes before the fall," but not as many know that its full version is found in the Bible. Turn to Proverbs 16:18 and behold: "Pride goeth before destruction, and an haughty spirit before a fall." In simpler language: Take comfort—you're not the first person to spend too much and go bust. Yet had more people in the Great Recession made quick, hard decisions, their financial lives would have been better. That was what Peters did.

During his walk, around some of the nicest streets in New York City, Peters thought his way past his reservations. He remembered the 80/20 rule—that 80 percent of his firm's revenue was generated by 20 percent of his agents. That was comforting because if he closed an office and let some less productive agents go, he could eliminate costs, not revenue. His goal now was to keep his business afloat, so he had to adapt. It was then that he realized he could close not only the Harlem office but also the one in the West Village. "I realized I could retain all of my income production with fewer people and less space," he said.

When he returned to the office, he shocked his CFO with his decision: He was ready to close two offices. Peters had gone out unsure if he could do anything but came back focused on making tough cuts. Within weeks he had the discipline to close one office and then the second one two months later. He laid off 15 percent of his agents in the West Village and half in Harlem. But his real savings came from rents, office costs, and marketing, which he had eliminated from those branches. "It was very hard for me," Peters told me. "I'm very bad at firing people. There was a lot of it that was very painful. I'd invested a lot of money in these offices, and that was very painful." Then he caught himself and came back to the thing that still bothered him, four months later. "My big struggle was with pride, with how it was going to be seen in the marketplace," he said. "I walked my way through that. Now I feel relieved. I took the steps I needed to take to bring my overhead down." He had made his decisions based on the present situation—an unprecedented collapse in the real estate market. They were the right decisions under those circumstances. He had feared his business would collapse, but he also feared the social stigma of making cuts. In this case, his desire to save what he had built over thirty years prevailed.

What Peters did may not seem remarkable—cutting costs is an obvious way to save money—but it is, because so many people cannot do it. For that matter, small-business owners and consumers saddled with debt often show the same inability to recognize their problem, let alone deal with it. They can exhibit a version of Alvarez & Marsal's alcoholic syndrome with overconfident executives: They want the easy fix that leaves the world as it was. In the recession, many people looked for ways to hang on to what they "owned" when in reality they were barely renting all those big-screen televisions, leased luxury cars, and condos in warm locales. They should have cut, not tried to renegotiate; they should have admitted their big-spending ways caused their woes, not the high interest rates on their credit cards or the teaser rates on their mortgages.

Peters's life had a different outcome. His hour-long walk saved his company almost 20 percent in costs. That is a significant number at any time, but it was even more so when two other figures were considered. One, his CFO's predictions were wrong. At the beginning of 2009, he had to revise his worst-case scenario: The firm would be down 47 percent for the year, led by property prices dropping nearly 30 percent in five months. Two, high-end confidence had been severely shaken: On the day in March 2009 when Peters and I spoke, the Dow closed at 6594.44, over 40 percent below where it had been on Lehman Brothers Day. Under the extreme pressure of choosing between saving the business he had built or enduring the askance glances of Upper East Side society, Peters put his ego aside. He not only made a clutch decision, but he did it without hesitating. What made him able to look at his situation objectively? Why could he see what needed to be done when others might have resisted too long and found their company out of business? The answer lies in his poorly decorated office and an old friend. From what they did, anyone can learn to put himself in a position to make better financial decisions under pressure.

RICH ADVICE FOR ANY PERSON

Peters had been primed for the decisions he had to make by a lunch with Alec Haverstick II. The two men had been friends since the third grade, when they met at the Buckley School, an exclusive all-boys preserve on the Upper East Side of Manhattan. Taking separate paths through the country's best private schools, they ended up at Yale together, where they could not have been more different—Haverstick was the angry young man and Peters was an affected music student. Yet however they comported themselves then, their pedigrees said these men had every benefit in life and would not fail. While Peters was a descendant of the Warburg family, which was running banks in Europe before the Rockefellers existed, Haverstick's grandfather had been a banker for Coca-Cola in Atlanta and sallied into New York society. The two men came from a moneyed culture that not only endured but maintained its wealth and influence through wars, market crashes, divorces, boozy nights, and all manner of breakdowns that inherited money can cause.

Haverstick suggested we discuss what his firm did over lunch at the Yale Club, the university's alumni clubhouse across from Grand Central Terminal. On a crisp, blue winter day, the club harked back to a different time. Depending on your point of view, that time was either more decorous, proper, and understandable or more exclusionary, snobbish, and stultifying. Haverstick strolled into the lobby in an elegant gray top-coat with his business partner Arthur Bingham IV, a tall, fit man in a fur hat.

The two men had recently founded Boxwood Strategic Advisers, a firm that focused on clients' liabilities, or debt, more than on their assets. Haverstick summed up what they did as managing personal balance sheets. This was revolutionary in the wealth management business, where most advisers made their money by taking a commission on products they sold clients or receiving a fee based on the amount of money they managed. While traditional advisers might help people secure a mortgage or other type of loan, they generally do not get paid much, if anything, for doing so. This created a negative incentive for them to do more than manage the person's assets. Boxwood's idea was to look at the other side of the ledger and help people sort through all that they owned or owed. The idea had come to Haverstick several years earlier, but he had not acted on it until that summer. It turned out his timing was perfect: When Lehman Brothers Day hit and stock prices began to fall, even wealthy people were suddenly worried about their fiscal soundness, not least of all because of how much they had borrowed against their portfolios. I wanted to understand Boxwood because I had a hunch the firm's prescriptions for the wealthy would shed light on how people of average means could make clutch decisions when they found themselves under financial pressure.

Haverstick and Bingham, a storied New York name with oil money behind it, had sold Peters on an old-world notion of discipline and thrift as the only way to extricate himself from a tough financial situation. Their advice would work for anyone because it was not based on having a lot of money so much as being smart with the money you had.

Peters had agreed and reduced expenditures until he had cut enough to be within his comfort zone. "This is about structuring and restructuring. It's about How do I pay my bills?" Haverstick told me. "Those who capitulate early, seek help, and get out early live to fight another day. The rest will face an economic Armageddon. You've got to get out."

While said in the heat of the Great Recession, the advice was something anyone struggling under the weight of personal expenses can benefit from. And there was nothing terribly complicated about what they proposed: You are not entitled to own anything you cannot afford, and if you cannot afford something, you need to sell it. No tears, no moaning, just action. If things improve, you can buy it back. It seemed simple, but their strategy took tremendous discipline to pull off. At their level, Haverstick and Bingham were counseling clients to sell vacation homes they could not afford, even if the prices were less than they thought the properties were worth. This would free the owners from the associated costs—mortgages, upkeep, utilities, security. If they bought the home by taking out a loan against company stock they were restricted from selling—a common practice—and it had lost a lot of value—also common at that point—then they could avoid having to sell other assets to meet a margin call. Consider an example Haverstick gave me: A banker at Goldman Sachs made tens of millions of dollars in salary and stock year after year. Instead of selling his shares in what was considered the best-run investment bank in the world, he borrowed against them to fund his lifestyle. This included buying primary residences, second homes, yachts, and planes, as well as nontangible assets, like paying for household help, shopping, dining out, and generally living a lavish life. Then the value of that stock plummeted, and soon a bank was demanding more collateral because the ratio of what was borrowed had outstripped what was pledged to secure it, the Goldman stock. If you had the cash to meet the margin call, no problem; if you didn't, you were in trouble, and this was where Boxwood would step in.

The public reaction to wealthy people who found themselves in financial straits during the recession was some combination of anger, scorn, and mockery. But that missed the underlying argument of the example: In a recession unlike one that anyone had lived through, people who were overleveraged needed to act quickly, and it was better to shed things you did not need so you could stockpile cash. In Peters's case, he said his apartment and business were the only things sacrosanct, and he was willing to do what needed to be done with the rest of his assets. That meant closing offices and laying off employees. But he knew he had to do it because the real estate market had changed so drastically. This took discipline along the lines of what Ari Kiev worked to instill in SAC traders. It was clear Boxwood's advice to clients was stern stuff—bereft of the modern American sense of entitlement. If people could no longer afford what they had, they needed to keep a stiff upper lip, take their medicine—however bitter—and sell assets until they reduced their debt to a serviceable level.

In the case of the less wealthy, the choice was starker: People who bought homes by lying about their incomes and taking out mortgages they really couldn't afford might have been best served by defaulting and moving on. This wasn't Boxwood's demographic, but it became clear in 2008 that allowing people to go into foreclosure was politically unpalatable. The average person who bought a $500,000 house using an artificially low interest-only mortgage may have really liked that home, but he should have never bought it because he could not afford it. Instead of accepting responsibility for a bad decision, he blamed the mortgage broker for selling him the dream, and then he wanted the federal government to help him keep it. This is the anti-Boxwood strategy, and it almost guarantees choking under pressure. Even if the person received relief on his mortgage, chances are he was going to find himself in debt down the road: He would have kept his house for the time being but the debt would still be a burden. The choice should have been simple, even obvious: Sell while you still can.

The trouble is, when financial pressure mounts, most people do not and cannot think dispassionately until it is too late. They choke. They wait too long, thinking their situation will improve, and when it doesn't, they have burned through their reserve funds and are still going to lose what they were struggling to keep. Boxwood provided a calculus to prevent this: When you have less than twelve months of cash left to cover your debt payments, you needed to start selling assets. Yet in the first global recession of the twenty-first century, what they were advising clients to do was radical. It came across as a new austerity when it was really a simple formula on how to make financial decisions under pressure. Boxwood was providing a tool that could take the passion out of financial decision making. Their prescriptions applied to anyone who got himself in over his head. Instead of being clutch in this situation, too many people took the chokers' path: They did not take personal responsibility for what was happening, and they were overconfident that someone would bail them out.

HOW TO CUT UNDER PRESSURE

Fred Peters was a guinea pig of sorts. He and Haverstick happened to have lunch just as the stock market was falling and Peters had begun to worry. "Alec helped me look at the corporate and personal picture as one," Peters told me. "In a way, one of Alec's premises is, if you're a business owner, then a business is just one of your assets." Peters knew there was nothing he could do about the magnitude of the financial crisis. He could only control the decisions he made, and he knew they would be crucial ones. The social embarrassment of closing two offices would pale in comparison if he did not act and watched his business fail.

The starting point was an honest examination of Peters's business and personal debt. What did he need to do to get through a calamitous real estate market? Haverstick, Peters said, helped him see that if he paid off the debt from his business and rolled it up into his personal account, his costs would go down—by some $400,000 per year. Because Peters had a relationship with a private bank—the white-glove equivalent of the commercial banks most people use—he said his personal cost of borrowing was less than his corporate cost. He saved 4.5 percentage points in borrowing the money himself, because of a lower rate on a personal line of credit. More important, assuming the debt personally gave him greater control over how the loan would be paid back. "The risk isn't that much more, even though it's a personal loan," Peters said. "Other than my wife and my kids, there is nothing more important to me than my business. I've devoted endless hours to it over twenty years. I needed to do something to keep it going."

The immediate savings were crucial, but Peters believed he bought himself "a couple years of wiggle room." Given the shakiness of the U.S. economy at the end of 2008, he could not be sure that that would be enough, but it was a good place to start. "We're sailing in uncharted waters," Peters said. "No one has a clue about what happens next."

Haverstick saw Peters's swift action a different way. "If you have cancer, you take chemo," he said. "It's now a practical problem. You do what is necessary to cure it." If you fear being unable to cover your overhead, you start cutting until you can. This is where those who inherited wealth have a psychological advantage: They have seen how family fortunes ebb and flow and how some relatives made the right choices and, in Haverstick's phrase, lived to fight another day. They have also seen others who succumbed to the pressure and watched their fortunes dissipate.

Peters had also shown prudence before the crisis. He had left cash in his business. Many business owners are tempted to use their companies as an ATM to fund their lifestyle—just as homeowners refinanced their houses and blew the equity on vacations, electronics, and fancier cars than they needed or could really afford. Peters was clearly wired differently than most. He is, after all, a Realtor who has lived in the same apartment for thirty-two years, which is like meeting a bartender who doesn't drink. Moreover, while his ancestors were leading bankers of their time, his father was a journalist. Peters had never known poverty, yet he inherently understood that a cash cushion was a good thing. In circumstances beyond his control, he did what he could, and it gave him room to breathe. "We're under huge pressure, but what are you going to do?" he told me. "I'm not worried every day that I'm not going to get to the other side." It turned out that our interview took place only five days before the stock market hit bottom.

LESSONS TO LIVE BY

Boxwood's philosophy could help everyone, rich or poor, straighten out his finances. Yet making clutch decisions when it comes to money can be the most difficult thing in this book to master. This is because money is much more than a means of exchange for so many people.

"Money is the most powerful secular force in the world," Brad Klontz, a financial psychologist and author of *Mind Over Money,* told me. "Money is linked to everything—safety, health, relationships, creativity and spontaneity, social belonging. It's the one thing that intersects everything, and as soon as I'm talking about money, all the family dynamics come out."

When many people saw their portfolios plummet in the Great Recession, loss led to anger and, worse, blame. They waited too long to take action. They took baby steps when decisive action was needed. They choked when it came to making decisions about what they had left. However, there are lessons to be learned and clear ways to be clutch with financial decisions in the future. Here are five specific steps to take when the pressure you face is financial:

Accept

The first step to getting out of a tough financial bind is to admit that you're in one. That's not as easy as it sounds. Americans are generally a future-focused group. Our country is predicated on the belief that tomorrow will be better than today. If that's the case, why do what Peters did? The reality is different. If you sell the vacation home—or get rid of the expensive leased car—you will feel crummy tomorrow. But if you hold on to it and it goes into foreclosure or is repossessed, you're going to feel worse. You will have been weighed down by the burden of those payments on something that is no longer yours. While many people sought to blame others for the downturn that began in 2007 and wreaked havoc through 2008 and 2009, the reality is, if you couldn't make your payments, you had not planned well personally. Where were your reserves? Accept that your financial situation is not as you thought and the longer you wait to act, the more pressure will be on every decision.

Psychologically Readjust

The faster this happens the better. You have to become aware of the feelings you're having about your money. In a crisis, it may be gone, and that's not good. But obsessing about it is not going to make it come back. You could have made better decisions ahead of time, but you didn't. Still, you have a chance to save what you have and, you hope, to make better choices the next time around. What holds people back is the powerful emotional force that the decision-making part of the brain exerts over the rational part. Klontz equates it to an elephant and his rider: When things are going smoothly, the two work together; when something spooks the elephant, there is little the rider can do but hang on. From a purely financial point of view, Bingham suggested people look at their excess assets in terms of economic rent—or what you need to pay to use something. Since you can't rent a horse farm, you have to buy it. But in actuality you are paying economic rent to whoever lends you the money. The same was true for the lease payments on your BMW or Mercedes. In a crisis, it's time to stop and drive a cheaper car.

Prioritize

Once you have come to terms with what has to be done, you have to decide how to divide things up: What do you need, what do you want to keep, and what needs to go immediately? Getting rid of what you can't afford in a crisis will go a long way to bettering your financial position. This realization was at the root of Peters's decision. His family and his business mattered to him, so he could close two offices, remain solvent, and slough off any pride issues. This is a tough thing to do. "People don't change their lifestyles easily," Haverstick said. "Circumstances change several years before people change their lifestyles. Look at a widow or a retiree." But the person whose finances are under pressure does not have the luxury of time.

Take Responsibility

No one made you buy a house or anything else you could not afford. Regardless of what kind of deal or incomprehensible mortgage you were offered, the ultimate responsibility lies with you. But not selling that house, car, or other big-ticket item, taking the loss, and moving on with your life is a worse decision. You cannot let emotion trump rational thought. And those who do not take responsibility for this are at risk of developing what Klontz called "money-avoidance disorders" that can ruin a family. A simple version of what he calls a "money script" is "Money is bad; rich people are shallow and greedy; people become rich by taking advantage of others." You can think that all you want, but it is not going to make your financial situation any better.

In terms of irresponsible behavior, the overextended California homeowner became the poster child for financial choking, but he has plenty of company among the wealthy people who show up in Boxwood's lobby. Among their clients' biggest liabilities was their lifestyle expenses. Unlike a house or car, which will be paid off at some point, the cost of funding a lavish lifestyle is of infinite duration. And changing the mentality that created this is not easy. "No one guarantees a good outcome for life," said Bingham. "This is a group that's lived without consequences for a very long time."

Focus on the Outcome

This comes back to Haverstick's mantra: You want to live to fight another day. Your goal is not to sell one thing to buy another. Your goal is to shore up your personal balance sheet, the way Jamie Dimon did with J.P. Morgan. Once you have restructured your cash flow, you will be better positioned to make money decisions under less pressure. But timing counts. Remember, if you find yourself with only enough money for less than twelve months of expenses and no income, you need to begin restructuring what you have.

Ultimately, being clutch in a personal financial crisis means embracing thriftiness to keep yourself out of such crises in the first place. If that fails, you need to dispassionately sell off assets to keep from losing everything. People should live within their means, but they should also plan for the possibility that the present will not continue. Do this and you may avoid being in a pressure situation where you will have to make clutch decisions. Those who do all these things and still find themselves in a tough spot need to act quickly. "People who are clutch have been tempered by various things that have happened to them," Haverstick told me. "They're optimists. They know what's going on." In other words, if the ship starts to take on water, don't wait for it to start sinking before jumping off.

[11]

HOW TO BE CLUTCH IN SPORTS
Trust What Got You There

MATHEW GOGGIN WAS chatting with me as he walked to the seventeenth tee at the Tournament Players Club at Sawgrass. He stopped only long enough to rest his club on the ground and swing. Before the ball landed in the center of the famous island green—130 yards across a pond—we were talking again. The mortgage crisis was a favorite topic that day. Goggin had little interest in discussing his round, even though he is a professional golfer and was ranked 47th in the world at the time. He was chatting to stay loose. While he had just hit the perfect shot to the most psychologically intimidating hole in professional golf, he had expected to do so. Goggin simply trusted his swing. Few recreational golfers could imagine that that shot could be so easy for anyone.

The seventeenth at Sawgrass, just outside of Jacksonville, Florida, is one hole that even nongolfers know. It is postcard beautiful and utterly distinct. And it is one of three finishing holes that are meant to impose the maximum amount of pressure in the final stretch of the annual Players Championship. What makes these three holes so tough is they are a series of intertwining optical illusions. The par-five sixteenth skirts the same body of water that the seventeenth floats in, forcing players to decide between going for the green on their second shot or hitting it

200

short for an easy third shot. The par-four eighteenth is even tougher. A lake runs along the entire left side of the hole, coming into play on the drive and approach shot. But it is the seventeenth that is the purest test of whether someone will choke or be clutch.

It should be an easy shot for the best golfers in the world. Its length is minuscule by PGA Tour standards, and the clubs pros use to reach it are the most accurate in their bags, wedges to 8 irons. If it were three hundred yards away, it would be pure luck to hit it. Still, the hole unnerves even the best. In 2008, 65 balls landed in the water during the tournament— down from 93 the year before. It's even worse for the recreational golfer who plays the course at other times of the year: Some 120,000 balls find the water, not the green, annually. When the tournament starts, the area around the seventeenth hole is packed with spectators who sit there like silent NASCAR fans: They want to see a crash, or, in this instance, a splash. And generally there are plenty. In 2008, Sergio Garcia won the tournament after Paul Goydos hit his shot into the water. It was the first hole of a sudden-death playoff, and all Garcia had to do at that point was hit the ball anywhere on the green, which was what he did.

"Under normal conditions, it's an easy shot," Goggin told me as we walked to the green during the practice round the day before the 2009 tournament. "You just have to hit a nice, quality shot. The toughest part is, there is no place to miss it. A poor shot means you have to hit the shot again."

The smart shot is always to hit the ball to the middle of the green, which allows room for error on both sides. Even if the player is trailing, the center should still be the target; he could make up a shot or two on the final hole. "Sometimes the mentally toughest guys are the ones who can stand there and be one shot back and not push," Goggin said while two-putting for his par from pretty much the center of the green. "It's not being negative. It's living to fight another day. But on Sunday, you feel like you have to make up ground, so you hit it right at the flag. It's a ridiculously stupid shot. You can end your tournament right then and there. But some days you think you have the shot."

Goggin was having a solid run on the PGA Tour while amassing a small fortune. To that point, he had earned over $6.5 million without winning a tournament in four seasons. His best finish was second place in 2008. Yet he believed he had the ability to win. "You always see yourself as the guy who can win, who can win majors," he said matter-of-factly. "Because you haven't done that doesn't mean you don't believe it won't happen. You have to have the mind-set, or you wouldn't get into that position."

His statistics in May 2009 neither supported nor refuted his belief in himself. He was lurking in the sweet spot of the PGA Tour money list, where at any time one of the top 75 players in the world could win a tournament, even a major, and leave golf fans scratching their heads. There were players with tournament victories who were ranked lower than he was on the money list. And he hit the ball almost flawlessly. He was statistically straighter off the tee than Tiger Woods, and better than average with the length of his drives and how often he hit the green in the required number of strokes. In fact, in every category but one he was better than average when the average was derived from the best 125 golfers in the world. So why hasn't he won? His one weak spot was putting. He needed 29.32 putts per round when the average was 29.10. A difference of a quarter of a stroke per round might seem insignificant, but on the PGA Tour the difference in scoring average from the second-ranked player to the last full member on tour, number 125, is only 1.7 strokes. If Tiger is included in this, the difference widens to 2.86 strokes. In other words, everyone but Tiger was packed tightly together. Giving up a quarter of a stroke on the greens meant something.

Such statistics show just how equally matched professional golfers are. But as we walked to the eighteenth tee, Goggin had a different idea as to why some win on the tour and others don't. "Everyone chokes all the time out here. The guy who chokes the least wins," he said. "If you have this feeling that you have to be perfect, you're going to struggle."

THE ESSENTIALS OF THE MATCH

If the best golfers in the world succumb to pressure, is there any hope for a recreational player? There is, but not through the ways people have typically tried to get better. While this chapter is focused on golf, the lessons here apply to all people who play sports and find themselves frustrated by how they perform under pressure. The reason is that too much emphasis has traditionally been placed on the wrong things, from quick fixes to the thoughts running through someone's head. Negative ones cause choking, the thinking goes, positive ones don't. This belief is misleading and could result in more frustration. If it was just positive thinking or psychology that was needed to excel, Goggin would have won a tournament by now. He believes in his ability completely, like any professional athlete. The problem is his ability: He is a tremendous golfer, but his game has one deficiency, his putting.

Under pressure, sound fundamentals matter more. I came around to this belief through the time I spent with Goggin but also with his coach, Dale Lynch. Lynch believed Goggin was finally in a position to handle the pressure of winning a tournament. He got to this point through a method that did not involve any of the tropes of sports psychology, or some new swing style with a faddish name. Lynch's method was simple but more difficult than the cure-alls golfers embrace. It is something any recreational sportsman can understand and apply.

Lynch sees frustration under pressure as a result of too much emphasis on the mental game and not enough on perfecting the skills that would naturally make someone mentally tougher. In his view, the only way to get better under pressure is to fix your problems on the driving range. This may seem obvious—and players may roll their eyes, as if to say, "I always hit it great on the range." But Lynch has found that most players don't hit it as great as they think in practice. While shelves sag under the weight of books promising a quick fix to what ails a person's golf game through mental exercises, Lynch does not see any of this as being truly helpful. He differs from better-known swing gurus in his belief that sound fundamentals are more important than a radical new swing or time on the sports psychologist's couch. But above all, he knows there is no one physical or mental exercise to make someone instantly better.

"People who want the quick fix are deluding themselves," he said as we walked with Goggin in the practice round. "It's not that difficult. You need to look at the aspects of the game and say, 'Where do you rank in those areas?' Then you keep improving all the different areas. It's not rocket science. You just have to be honest with yourself."

Lynch speaks from experience when it comes to choking under pressure. Having taken up golf at age twelve, he played on the Australian PGA Tour for seven years, but frustration with his skills drove him from competition and into teaching at age twenty-eight. "It was a failed-player-turned-coach scenario," Lynch, fifty-one, told me matter-of-factly. But it became a quest for redemption. He was frustrated because he felt he could not get the assistance and instruction with his game that he needed. Instructors told him he just was not as good as he used to be, which only made his swing flaws worse. So, as much for himself as anyone else, he began figuring out what had gone wrong with his once promising career. "I was in Melbourne, and I fairly quickly developed a reputation of being a radical," he said. "What I was teaching was very different and in some cases the opposite of what was being taught. But I had started getting results with some pretty established players in Australia."

His own breakthrough as a coach came when the mechanics of the golf swing began to make sense to him. It would seem that a professional golfer should understand this. But he meant it more deeply. He began to think about the plane the club is swung on, the angle of impact, the trajectory of the ball's flight, and how they all worked together. One discovery led to another and kept him moving forward on his quest. What he found was how crucial it was for a player to have sound fundamentals and a complete game. Again, this is obvious, but even great golfers have been able to get by on natural talent and a persistence that allowed them to compensate for their shortcomings. Ben Hogan, considered one of the greatest golfers of all time, struggled his whole career with putting but made up for it with mystical ball striking. The same could be said for Lee Trevino, who won every major except the Masters: He had an ugly, looping swing, but it worked for him.

Making a player's game complete so he had no weaknesses under pressure became Lynch's goal. The player could still hit bad shots or get lucky or unlucky, but when he stood over the ball, he would feel confident that he could hit whatever shot was required. To get to this end, Lynch started to simplify everything in order to dissect the different shots. Then he measured the results so he could quantify what a player needed to work on. How many shots landed where they were supposed to? How many missed the target? This way the player could know where he was strong or weak. His work was noticed by the Australian government, and in 1991 he was hired to start a golf training school at the Victorian Institute of Sport (VIS), an Olympic-level training center.

From the start, there were five areas that Lynch emphasized: technique, physical conditioning, simulated pressure, an unwavering routine, and success on the road. Working on these areas will help every golfer get better under pressure, but they will also help any person who plays a recreational sport that involves pitting himself against another player or a challenging terrain:

Technique

This was first and foremost. If a player was not technically sound, his swing would break down under pressure. "Without great technique, the rest falls over," Lynch told me. "Our method is to make the golf swing simple and effective and repeatable, with no compensations. When there is no compensation, there is less going on in the swing, and the swing holds up under pressure." A tic that was a signature move under normal conditions would fail in the clutch. That technical soundness extended from the full swing to short shots around the green to putting. The goal was to have no weak area, so a player could always hit a shot with the feeling that he would strike it well. It might not turn out as he had envisioned it, but he would have hit the shot many times before and not be second-guessing himself. This mastery of technique would allow the player to commit fully to every shot. He would be playing from a position of strength, not out of a fear of missing the target. It would be one buffer against the natural pressure of tournament golf.

"There were technical deficiencies in my own game that would break down under pressure," Lynch said. "If your chipping is really poor, that puts more pressure on your iron play. Your target becomes narrower. You feel that you have to hit the ball closer each time because you're afraid of chipping the ball. That pressure will build on you. If you're competent in all areas, then under pressure there is a lot less stress on your iron play. Once you can chip better, you can hit the ball in there and feel better."

Physical Conditioning

By the early 1990s, the era of flabby golf pros—exemplified by even the great Jack Nicklaus in his pudgy prime—was coming to an end. Golfers, like other professional athletes, had begun to recognize the need for fitness to sustain them through the rigors of a tournament. Golfers needed to be both strong and flexible to swing a club the right way. But they also had to be able to bear up to the physical strain of walking six miles a day in the hot sun for upwards of five hours. Being fit is de rigueur on the tour, but it is something the recreational golfer may struggle with: If you run out of steam on the fifteenth hole, no theories or tips are going to help you win.

Simulated Pressure

Unlike so many who preach sports psychology, the VIS did not promote mental toughness under pressure through visualization. They did it— and this is key—by simulating pressure in every aspect of practice. This was akin to what kids do in their backyard—*if I chip the ball into the can, Sally will kiss me.* The difference was in the restrictions the VIS imposed. Instead of letting students hit a particular shot twenty times, the coaches forced them to hit it right the first time or not at all. They began to emphasize quality over quantity. This involved certain skills tests throughout the practice session, making the shot the focus. The mental aspect came through creating what Lynch called internal pressure. The belief was that if enough pressure could be put on hitting a single shot to wherever they were told to hit it, then this would mirror the external pressure that comes from leading a tournament. "If someone was practicing for two to three hours, the quantity of balls they were hitting was quite low," Lynch said. "But the quality of shots was very high."

An Unwavering Routine

At the crossroads of all this was a routine that was built into practice. This was what allowed players to move their game from the driving range to the course, but it wasn't the same for everyone. As Lynch noted, some players run hot and some run cold. Those states needed to be harnessed and understood. The player whose mind was racing when he went to bed with the lead in a tournament and the player who slept soundly in the same situation both needed a routine to keep them thinking shot by shot the next day. But those routines were very different. Here there was no set plan—other than the routine had to be repeated before every shot, from driving range to golf course, from tee to green.

"When we work with young players, part of the coping package is working on their routine and making it consistent," he said. "That helps their mental skills to cope." Not surprisingly, Lynch said the people who cannot sleep before the last round of a tournament in which they are playing well were often the ones getting ahead of themselves. They were rehearsing their acceptance speech before they had won, which was a sure way to choke under pressure.

Success on the Road

The fifth element of the VIS program is a softer one. Because of Australia's distance from the rest of the world, all young players had to travel. But this allowed Lynch to test their progress. Many amateur golfers shoot low scores on the course they play every day but find themselves flailing on new courses or under conditions that are less familiar. The main reason is that their game has not been truly tested and is not as complete as they thought. They had been able to rely on their knowledge of every bend and rise in their home course to compensate for weaknesses in their game. On unfamiliar terrain, their deficiencies become apparent. This quickly increases their frustration and puts pressure on their game.

"Whatever limitations you have with your game, you can compensate for them on your home course," Lynch told me. "You get to a new course, and the feel of the shots and the picture of the course doesn't immediately come to you. You feel uncertain. You don't know what you're doing. The weaknesses in your game get magnified. That's a very common thing, and what it means is, the guy who is a six handicap at his home club is not really a true six handicap because he doesn't possess the tools mentally or technically to play to that mark at another venue."

With all five points, Lynch's goal was to create a complete player. Breaking down a defense against pressure into its component parts was necessary for him to show that golf at the highest level could be taught just like the violin: Before you could be the concertmaster, you needed to master the scales. This process was also where expectations must be managed, particularly for the nonprofessional player. "A guy who wants to go from 100 to 80 but can only practice once a week doesn't have a lot of hope," he said. "If someone wants to bring his handicap down, you break down what he has to do. You set up a plan and you continue to build from that. You get yourself conditioned to the one-putt, one-shot mentality."

The training is not easy. Goggin was receptive to it because of a desire to prove himself. He said some of this came from being born in Tasmania, where players were always comparing themselves to their counterparts on the mainland of Australia. He said the "false constraint" of his birthplace made him less likely to make grand comparisons and more focused on his game. "A Californian wins the State Junior Amateur and walks around thinking he is the best junior amateur in the world," Goggin said. "He's never left the state. He wouldn't know if the guy in Nevada could beat him. He'll say, 'I'm the greatest player in the world.' The kid who wins the Tasmanian Amateur doesn't think he's the best player in the world—he doesn't even think he's the best player in Australia. That's a very different mind-set."

Goggin was focused on improving, and that meshed well with the inherent discipline the VIS program demanded. Whereas other players resisted the changes that temporarily made them worse, Goggin embraced them. He did not have a great teacher in Tasmania to fall back on, so he looked at the VIS as a way to advance himself. He knew he was talented, but that talent was raw. His goal was to get better, whatever way that happened. Two years after entering the VIS, he won the Australian Amateur and the Tasmanian Amateur, and then he went to the United States and played well there. "It cemented my desire to take the long view of things," he told me. What that instruction gave him was a foundation. He learned how to hit every shot he could imagine, so when he found himself in an awkward position on the course, he could feel comfortable: He had hit a low shot over the water in practice countless times, so he could now do it on the course just as he had on the range. That confidence in his game allowed him to assess every shot in the present, without bemoaning how he got there or thinking ahead to the next one. Throughout all of this, Goggin's desire was to continue moving up the professional ranks.

Still, his greatest struggle was making sure he was present. Not doing so was his equivalent of choking. The weekend golfer imagines choking as losing the last three holes of a match with his buddy and going home a few dollars poorer. A pro like Goggin equates it to not committing to the shot he has selected. This is the golf equivalent of not being present, and it is often what happens to players on the seventeenth hole at the TPC. They get over the ball and wonder if they should be hitting the 8 iron when they're hitting the 9 iron, or vice versa, and the next thing they know, their ball is in the water. If Goggin fully committed to a shot, hit it as he wanted to, and it got caught by a gust and bounced over the green into the rough, he could still be happy because he did what he wanted to do under pressure. A choke for him would be if he was standing in the fairway with a share of the lead, the perfect yardage, and he eased off the shot at the last moment. The ball landed on the green but forty feet away, and he still had the lead after holing out. Then two groups later, the player he was tied with hit a similar shot but to eight feet and rolled the putt in to win. "You didn't fully commit to the shot," he said. "You weren't hitting the shot you set up to hit. That might not be a choke for you, but it's a choke for me, when you get to this level."

ROUTINE AND REALITY

On the first day of the Players Championship tournament, Goggin looked as relaxed as he had the day before when we had walked eighteen holes talking about everything but golf. Starting his round on the tenth hole, a tight but straight par four, he hit second and drove the ball into perfect position. It was the same repeatable swing and ball flight I had seen the day before. He looked like the calm center between his two playing partners. Billy Mayfair, who won five tour events in the 1990s, was a bundle of nervous energy, waggling the club all around the ball before finally hitting it into good position. Thongchai Jaidee, an up-and-coming Thai player, looked calm, but he proceeded to duck-hook the ball nearly out of bounds, making him look more like a weekend hacker than a man who has won over $5 million in a decade as a professional golfer. Yet all three parred the hole.

For the next nine holes, Goggin hit the ball perfectly. His setup was the same. He two-putted for most of his pars, chipped up and one-putted for a few more. I was reminded of something he told me during the practice round. "In golf, pressure is all perceived," he said. "You look at the leaderboard and all of a sudden there is the perception that I have do something more. Instead of hitting it to twenty feet, I have to hit it to ten feet."

He equated this to what players do when Tiger Woods is leading on Sunday. Even though in almost every tournament, players shoot lower single-round scores than Tiger, he regularly puts together four rounds that add up to the lowest score for the week. Yet his last round may be the most conservative. "What Tiger is going to do is hit it in the middle of the fairway, middle of the green, two-putt, and shoot two under, taking no risk, knowing you're going to fuck it up," Goggin said. "Tiger proves that the goal is really to have one less than everybody else in the field."

This was the game Goggin seemed to be playing. On the signature seventeenth hole, he hit his ball the closest of the three and made his par. Mayfair, on the other hand, was struggling. He hit the ball into the water on one par three, whacked a few other shots into the trees, and generally made a hash of things. At times it looked as though he was talking to himself. Jaidee was worse. His errant tee shot on the first was a harbinger for his round. He kept hooking shots way left of the target until he sliced his drive into the hospitality tent on the sixteenth hole. It was a performance that would have lifted any weekend warrior's spirits and prompted the judgment *I can hit the ball better than this guy.* But in golf there are no style points. And after nine holes, Goggin was even par and so, remarkably, was Jaidee. Mayfair, on the other hand, was one under par, having made two birdies, including a sidewinder on the sleek island green. Goggin had outhit both of them, knocking the ball down the fairway and onto the green. But none of that was reflected on his scorecard. "For him mentally, he has to deal with the frustration that he should be scoring better than he is," Lynch whispered to me midway through the round. "The other guys have hit a couple of really rank shots, but they're scoring better. He has to work on this so he doesn't get frustrated."

When Goggin made the turn for his second nine holes, it looked as though he was about to get something going. On the first hole, his tenth, he hit two great shots that set him up with a three-foot putt for birdie. After Mayfair and Jaidee putted twice for pars, Goggin stepped up to his putt. He stroked it and watched as it horseshoed around the cup, leaving him a second putt longer than the first. It was then that something changed. He looked tighter. It was as if right there he remembered that putting was the weakest part of his game. While he parred the next two holes, he did not do it with the same crispness. On the fourth hole, his thirteenth, Goggin cracked. On the tee, his preshot routine was not his. Instead of taking two slow, arcing swings, he stubbed the ground once and then addressed the ball. This was not the preshot routine that had so impressed me. Normally his routine was smooth and simple; now it looked choppy. Still, his tee shot was the best of the three, sitting in the fairway 120 yards from the green. His caddy paced off the exact distance and gave him the club. The pin was in the front of the green, just over a creek. Goggin set up and swung. I watched as the ball floated in the air, falling in what would have been a perfect arc—if the shot had not been three yards short. Instead of sneaking onto the green, it splashed into the water. The smart play was to the center of the green; he had taken the riskier one to make something happen. He had pushed, just as he said golfers shouldn't do.

By the rules of golf, he could have dropped the ball at the point where it entered the water. That would have left him with a short chip and guaranteed him no worse than a bogey. Instead he walked up a few paces and dropped another ball. Again, his preshot routine was different, and after he swung he watched as what was now his fourth shot landed in the water. I cringed when Goggin immediately dropped another ball where he was standing and swiped at it. That shot, his sixth counting the penalty strokes, landed behind the pin and rolled back to inches from the hole. He tapped it in for a triple-bogey seven. He would add one more bogey to the round to finish four over par and tied for 133rd—out of 144 players. Jaidee was two shots ahead of him with a 74, while May-fair, who looked so hopeless on the front nine, was in contention with a round of two-under 70.

"The game of golf, like all sports, is momentum," Lynch told me. "If you make a few birdies and you make the turn at four-under, you're great. The problem is not waiting for it to come. Players inevitably try to force something, and they get away from their normal game plan."

This was how Goggin's triple bogey happened. He had deviated from Lynch's steadfast emphasis on a routine that was the same on the driving range, the practice putting green, on the course with friends, and in an important tournament. It also spoke to Goggin's belief in committing to a shot. He did not commit to two shots, and it put him out of the tournament right then and there. With Goggin that day, one error led to more. The missed birdie putt on the tenth hole may have rattled Goggin, but what it really did was make obvious that his putting was not good that day. Because Goggin knew putting was already his weak area, it affected other areas of his game. As Lynch had said about any weaknesses, this lack of confidence in his putting made Goggin's target smaller. He had to hit the ball impossibly close to give himself a chance at making the putt. So by the time he reached his thirteenth hole, he felt he had to hit his shot from 120 yards to within a foot to make the birdie. This was why he didn't go up and drop a ball after hitting one in the water; it was why he hit three shots from the same spot. He felt he had to get the ball impossibly close, but he also needed to know he could do it.

Such snowballing happens all the time in golf. The weekend player who is making a mess out of his one round of golf that month might be surprised to know that he shares something with the professional struggling to make the cut on Friday. Sure, if the professional makes the cut, he will get a large check for four days of golf. But at this level, the prize money is so high that a good living is guaranteed to anyone with a PGA Tour card. After all, Goggin won nearly $2 million in 2008 without winning any tournaments, and the last full member of the tour, number 125, made $662,000 that year. At this level, winning is the only thing that matters, just as beating a friend or shooting a personal best matters to the recreational player. Once either player starts to push, starts to try to force something to happen, the round can easily get worse. "From a coaching perspective, you want to give them the tools to compete," Lynch told me after Goggin missed the cut on Friday with a 77. "But there is a responsibility on the player's part for them to learn from their mistakes. They need to make the necessary adjustments to compete on the world stage."

DOES LYNCH'S STRATEGY WORK?

Given Goggin's performance at the Players Championship, his belief in his ability to win a tournament on the PGA Tour might seem quixotic, and Lynch's method faulty. Maybe there is a need to spend less time on the range and more on the sports psychologist's couch? But before Geoff Ogilvy, another of Lynch's players, won the U.S. Open, the same could have been said about him.

Ogilvy had been stuck for four years around the same spot in the world rankings where Goggin was. He had played well, but he was little known beyond the tour. Anytime he placed high in a tournament it surprised fans. This changed in 2006. Ogilvy began the year ranked forty-ninth in the world. Six months into the season, he was ranked seventh. This jump was almost completely attributable to his victory at the U.S. Open—a victory that has often been overshadowed by the collapse on the last hole of Phil Mickelson, then the second-ranked player in the world. Mickelson certainly choked under pressure, but of all the players with a chance to win that day at Winged Foot, only Ogilvy made par on the final hole.

Playing in the second-to-last group, Ogilvy left his approach to the eighteenth hole short, then watched it roll off the green and down into the fairway. He had a tough chip up the hill for his third shot, and he knew he needed to make whatever length putt was left to have a chance at even a playoff. Yet what an average golfer might think was running through his head at the time was not. "We all practice all of these shots a lot," Ogilvy told me. "I just went back to what I had been practicing in my head. I was trying not to kid myself about the situation—this was the last hole of the U.S. Open, and I really wanted to get the ball up and down. I wanted to just chip it as I did in practice." Ogilvy described the moment to me as "high intensity but a little blasé." He had to be focused to give himself a chance to win, but he could not be focused on winning itself. "When you hit a chip shot on Thursday, you want to get it up and down, but if you don't, it's not a big deal," he said. "On Sunday it gets more black and white." Three years after his victory at Winged Foot, he could joke about that six-foot putt that would be his margin of victory: "It's kind of hard to admit it, but I just wanted it to be over. If I'm being completely honest, I just wanted to hit it. I've made that putt a lot. A part of my brain just said, 'Please hit this putt and let it be over.'"

He did, and an hour after it dropped, he was hoisting the U.S. Open trophy in victory. He had been working with Lynch for decades and subscribed to his philosophy of becoming mentally tough through pressure-filled practice sessions. "Lynchy will argue, Get the fundamentals right and the rest will come," Ogilvy said. "It was a build-up of what we had done. It works so well for me because it's not in the here and now. I remember doing something we did four years ago and I'll bring it back.

It's like you read a book and you remember it a year later." That Sunday in June, all of that work paid off. Ogilvy became the U.S. Open champion and has not looked back.

Lynch believes Ogilvy put himself in the position to win the U.S. Open by what he had done a year earlier at the British Open. The tournament was played at St. Andrews, the birthplace of golf. Ogilvy teed off that week ranked fifty-second in the world and got off to a slow start. After he finished playing on Friday, it looked as though he was going home, until other players faltered and he made the cut. Instead of relaxing, Ogilvy went to the driving range with Lynch and practiced some shots that had not been working. Lynch recalled that Ogilvy couldn't hook the ball into the wind. This might not have hurt him at another course, but at St. Andrews, a player needed to be able to hit every shot—particularly one that played off the wind that always blew. "We worked on a few things that night," Lynch said. "He went out and shot the low combined score for the weekend. The thing he did on Friday night, really, was to trust. He trusted his game. When he left on Sunday, he had a new belief in himself as a golfer and a player."

That was Lynch's way to handle pressure. Get your fundamentals solid, and you'll know you can rely on them under pressure. Have any weaknesses, and they will haunt you when your adrenaline is pumping and you are struggling to stay focused. The same can be said for any recreational sport, from tennis and squash to skiing, rowing, or any number of activities in which you pit yourself against the elements: If your fundamentals are sound, you will do better under pressure. In tennis, you won't worry about hitting the ball into the net, because you'll have practiced that drop shot hundreds of times; in skiing, you won't fear the black diamond run because your turns are true. In seeing how fine-tuning allowed him to play so much better on Saturday at the British Open, Ogilvy gained the confidence to play even better on Sunday when the pressure was really ramped up. After finishing fifth—Tiger Woods won the tournament—Ogilvy realized Lynch had been right: He had the skills to compete at the highest level.

"Realistically, is he any different as a player missing the cut or tied for fifth? No, he's not a different player," Lynch said. "But within himself

mentally, he now believes he is a better player. From a coaching perspective, there are things you can do to help develop that belief, but for most
players, they need to go out and do it."

Ogilvy does not disagree with Lynch's assessment of what it took to
get him to a higher level. "He's probably right," Ogilvy told me. "It was
my first top ten in a major. At the PGA [the next month], I finished
sixth, and I said, 'This isn't a fluke.' I thought maybe I can play. Self-
belief is pretty important—not crazy confidence." That belief came from
doing it. Even though he felt he could win a major, Ogilvy said he did not
think it would actually happen until after his high finish at the British
Open. "The term that is used a lot is, 'The player needs to relax,'" Lynch
told me. "I disagree. Relaxed is not a competitive mind-set. Geoff tried
to relax, and he couldn't break 80. You don't want to put the competitive
fire out; you just want to control it."

PUTTING THEORIES TO THE TEST

On a typically blustery Sunday afternoon at Turnberry, Mat Goggin
stood on the tenth hole with a one-shot lead in the British Open. It was
three months after the Players Championship, and his playing partner
was Tom Watson, five-time Open winner, who had just lost the lead to
him. The 138th Open had been an idiosyncratic championship to that
point. Tiger Woods had missed the thirty-six-hole cut for only the second
time in a major. (The first was at the U.S. Open won by Ogilvy shortly
after Woods's father died.) And Watson, fifty-nine, had been leading
the tournament since the first day. None of the other big names were
anywhere near the leaderboard. But with eight holes left, Goggin, then
ranked fifty-eighth in the world, was right there. "I knew what position I
was in. I was comfortable," Goggin told me afterward. "You feel comfortable within yourself. I was probably less nervous than I was the first hole
or two. You get settled and into the rhythm of the day."

Goggin had stayed close to Watson the entire round. While Goggin
only led for a few holes—he bogeyed holes fourteen, fifteen, and sixteen,

taking himself out of contention—he told me three weeks later that he was happy with how he played those closing holes. "I hit good shots into fourteen and fifteen and made bogeys," he said. "They just didn't turn out. I didn't mis-hit them. They weren't rank shots. You were playing in 30, 40 mph breezes, and you were out by a foot on both of them, and I got punished. It would be different if I hit horrible shots and you felt like you weren't controlling the moment." Goggin committed to his shots and made the best swing he could. His fifth-place finish was his best in a major tournament. The result was almost as good as a win: He gained the confidence that he could play with the top players in the world and beat most of them under immense pressure and difficult conditions. He showed himself that he could commit to shots and control the moment.

"It was a very intense situation," Goggin said. "On top of being in the final group, I was playing with Tom Watson, and everyone else in the world wanted him to win. You take a lot away from it, namely the confidence that you can do it. You think about what happened, but you take away from it that you played well and you can do it again."

Golf has a term for what happens when a seemingly great shot ends up in an impossible spot—rub of the green. That was what happened to Goggin's shots on fourteen and fifteen. And it was another such rub of the green that cost Watson the victory. On the final hole, from the middle of the fairway, he hit a shot that flew just a bit too long. Watson bogeyed the hole and fell into a playoff with Stewart Cink, who, like Ogilvy at Winged Foot, had been on no one's radar until that point. Watson's magical week ended when Cink, as much a journeyman as Goggin, beat him in a four-hole playoff. On the second of those holes, it looked as though Watson suddenly realized what was happening, and his fine shot-making left him.

Did Goggin do anything differently to prepare for the Open? He insisted he didn't. He brought along an old putter because he had not been putting particularly well all summer, and he tried to play his normal game, something he had not done previously in big tournaments. "I went in relaxed," he told me. "I played as I normally played. That's not to say if you play your normal game you're going to win the British Open.

I was striking the ball nicely." And he also remembered something from his last major. "I learned a lesson at Augusta when I was way too intense. You want to have a great week and you put too much pressure on yourself. You end up playing poorly. On a scale of one to ten, I was ten out of ten at Augusta. At the Open, I tried to take it down to three."

Goggin, most important, kept his mistakes in perspective, and he was conscious about maintaining his routine. Then he simply played, confident that his solid ball-striking skills would matter more that week than his sometimes inconsistent putting. "Even if I had played badly, I would have taken something away on Sunday," he said. But playing well was essential to raising the level of confidence in his own skills. "He now knows he has the game," Lynch texted me after the Open.

At the British Open, Goggin's performance was a triumph of skill over past experience. And it carried a lesson for the amateur player. "It's not a matter of taking lessons," Lynch told me. "The golfer needs to learn more about the game and the swing. That's a big, big difference than to say, 'You need to feel your arm doing this.' That's a Band-Aid."

Lynch pointed to the work Goggin had put in up to that point and what it said for professional golfers outside the elite top twenty. One, Goggin continued to improve his technique—not just how he swung the club but how he hit short shots, putts, anything he could imagine. Two, he was in good physical shape, so he wasn't going to run out of steam on the sixteenth hole. Three, by the time he was playing in the British Open, he had tested his skills at every level of professional golf on courses all around the world. Four, he had decades of playing under pressure, so the Open was just the next step. And five, unlike at the Players Championship that spring, Goggin maintained his routine for every shot. He may have been walking down the fairway with Tom Watson, one of the greatest British Open champions of all time, but his routine kept him focused on just hitting the shot. And that for Lynch is the most important thing.

"When you don't call it a bad break, it just becomes the next shot you have to play," Lynch said. "It would be a disaster if you thought, *I can't believe I hit that shot,* and it's in the rough. Then it compounds. The most important shot is the next shot, not the one you just hit." It was clear Goggin had worked hard on the five principles that will get any athlete to the point where he plays to the best of his ability under normal conditions and can transfer those skills to pressure-filled moments. But it all starts with a know-thyself moment followed by hard work on the fundamentals of the game.

CONCLUSION

THE TIGER CONUNDRUM
Is He Still Clutch?

A YEAR BEFORE his private life became a public spectacle, Tiger Woods walked into a clubhouse in a remote part of North Carolina and shook my hand. It was a clear, autumn evening, and the sun was setting on a golf course designed by the man whose legacy he was chasing, Jack Nicklaus. I had been as nervous for the interview as any in my career. Tiger has always been extraordinary on the golf course, possessing a physical skill and mental ability that placed him far ahead of his competitors. To call him a golfer, even an athlete, seemed to diminish what he was doing in tournaments; he was like a jazz great, improvising his way around a course, leaving his competitors stunned. I knew going into the interview that he had little time for writers like me. I didn't take it personally. He was one of the few people in the world who had absolutely nothing to gain from publicity. Plus, I respected him for not trying to play both sides of the media game—he did not push his family out there one moment and complain the next if something negative was written about them. He kept his family private, and he just competed—or so it seemed then.

That summer, he had just added to his reputation for invincibility under pressure by winning the 2008 U.S. Open on a broken leg. It was his fourteenth victory in a major tournament—four shy of Nicklaus's all-time record—and it seemed to confirm his status as the most clutch athlete of his generation. Nothing could stop him, either on the course or in his budding business life. In addition to nearly eighty worldwide victories at the time, he was an endorsement magnet, earning some $90 million a year from corporations ranging from traditional athletic sponsors like Nike and Gillette to more buttoned up brands, like Accenture and AT&T. The public could not get enough of him, whatever he was doing.

Before our interview, I witnessed this adulation firsthand. He was in North Carolina to break ground on his first golf course in the United States. It was going to be the centerpiece of a new development in a chain of gated communities. In an otherwise economically depressed area, Tiger's image was selling vacant lots starting at $500,000—when that amount of money would have bought up vast acreage outside of the gates. For believing in these imagined communities, residents were given the chance to watch Tiger turn some earth. He stood there, smiling with a polished shovel in his hand. As he flipped a bit of dirt, the crowd looked rapt, studying his every move as if they might learn something life-changing from how he did this. Their fixation with Tiger was a testament not only to his skill as an athlete but to the American fascination with thriving under pressure. We are a nation that wants to be clutch and hates it when we choke.

Then, right after Thanksgiving 2009, Tiger crashed his Cadillac Escalade in front of his house, and secrets from a sordid personal life spilled out to everyone's amazement. After a lifetime in the public eye—his first television appearance happened when he was two—the most platinum image in sports looked tawdry. Who was this guy? In the shock about his past, people started to question every bit of Tiger. The inevitable conclusion was that he would never be the same. He could not be as clutch as he had been before. I took a different view. Tiger's sexual exploits were what they were. The more interesting juxtaposition was how he handled pressure on the course versus how he handled the pressure to respond to the allegations against him. The most clutch athlete of our time showed he was not clutch in every area of his life. That is the

Tiger conundrum: How could he be unshakable in his professional life but so awful at handling a crisis in his personal life?

What Tiger told me that day in North Carolina about his ability under tournament pressure still made sense. "I've put myself there, in that situation, more times than anybody else," he said. "Along the way you do succeed. The whole idea is to put yourself there more so than anyone else, each and every time you tee it up. You're not going to win every one. Golf shows us that we fail far more than we succeed. The whole idea is to keep pushing and put yourself there." When I asked how he always seemed to make the right decisions when he was in contention, he answered just as matter-of-factly: "Well, I don't do anything quickly. I think through it. That's one of the attributes I think that golf has allowed me to learn. It's thinking through the process and looking at all the different options. Golf is not a reactionary sport. There's a lot of time to think."

As I wrote in the beginning of this book, Tiger made being clutch seem too simple. Consider the 2008 U.S. Open, which was only four months earlier when I spoke to him. Tiger was standing on the eighteenth tee at Torrey Pines needing a birdie on the last hole just to tie and get into a playoff. It was no easy feat, given how hard U.S. Open courses are. But standing over his third shot on a course he had played hundreds of times, Tiger struck the ball well, to twelve feet from the hole. Then he hit his putt and watched as it curved slowly down into the cup. The crowd went wild.

In a moment like this, Tiger showed he was a remarkable combination of all the elements of clutch performance. He was focused on what he was doing. He was disciplined with the shots he hit. When one went astray, he concentrated on the next one, not on what should have happened. He was always in the present, from anger to elation. And while some people may be motivated by fear of failing, he was driven only by a desire to win. This record of winning gave him a free pass in many areas of his life, even on the golf course. "It's at the point in golf that whatever Tiger does is the right thing to do in golf," Mat Goggin told me at the Players Championship. "He'll hit it in the left rough, and you'll hear a commentator say it was too sunny along the right side, so he hit it to the left. No he didn't. He hooked it!"

Beyond the sports world, though, Tiger quickly found out he did not enjoy the same level of unabashed adulation. When his life off the course became known, he appeared suddenly and publicly to lose all of his clutch instincts. Watching him stumble, what came to mind was his answer to my question about his weaknesses in golf and business. "In business, it's probably just overall experience, and that takes time," he told me about his fledgling golf course design company. "It's just years and years and years of doing it. If I look at how I was five years ago, ten years ago, to where I'm now, I've changed infinitely. I hope I'll change infinitely more over the next five, ten years and on down the road." That was a thoughtful, honest answer. It was an admission of inexperience, if not vulnerability.

His answer to his weaknesses in golf was different. "Golfwise, I don't know. Maybe I don't win enough." He did not say this flippantly, but thoroughly confidently. And I could not argue with the logic behind it. He practiced every shot anyone could imagine, so when he hit the ball someplace it should not have been, he was ready for it. He did not have to guess what shot to hit next, and he certainly did not bemoan the bad break. He accepted that he hit the ball there, and now he simply needed to hit it out. So he did. This ability, more so than any confidence or mental toughness, allowed him to continue to play at the highest level even when the pressure was on. This was Dale Lynch's point. If Tiger had hit hundreds of low shots out from under trees and onto the fairway in practice, why wouldn't he be able to do the same in a tournament? He knew he could do it. And that's clutch: the ability to do what you need to do under pressure just as you would do it in practice.

Tiger's life off the course suddenly seemed a lot more like his business pursuits: plagued by weaknesses. The difference, though, was that he tried not to admit this at first. Obviously, a married sports star should not cavort with a string of cocktail waitresses and porn stars. If that was what he wanted to do, he probably should have passed on marriage and the marketing potential that went with it. He could have been like any other single athlete who avails himself of the perks of fabulous wealth and celebrity, and his liaisons would have existed as gossip. Yet having gone through a two-month vetting process to secure my twenty-minute interview with Tiger, I was not surprised by how Tiger let his protectors handle the scandal. He turned out to be just as bad a chief executive of his billion-dollar brand as Ken Lewis or Dick Fuld had been of their companies. He made the same mistakes they did: He surrounded himself with yes-men and tried not to accept responsibility for what happened. Tiger could have minimized the damage to his reputation and business interests—which were predicated on his image—by admitting some of what happened immediately. It might not have prevented the release of the voice mails, the text messages, and the allegations from dozens of women who claimed to have been his mistresses, but it would have muted their impact.

Like Lewis and Fuld, though, Tiger was living in a cocoon. On the course, he was his own man, in total control of his abilities. In his personal life, he was made to believe that he could do anything and get away with it. The people he employed were not going to tell him otherwise. They feared losing their lifestyles if they upset him. His agent, Mark Steinberg, owed nearly all of his professional success, personal wealth, and standing in the golf world to Tiger. How could he be an honest broker? Bryon Bell, his childhood best friend, was in an equally inflated spot. He was running Tiger Woods Design, a job he lacked the skills for and would not have had at any other design firm. He was also allegedly booking the hotel rooms and plane flights for at least one of Woods's mistresses, so what could he really say to his friend?

But it was Glenn Greenspan, Tiger's head of communications, who was the least qualified to advise him in the clutch. Greenspan had been in charge of communications for the Augusta National Golf Club at the height of its battle to exclude female members. At Augusta, he could get away with saying no and explaining nothing. He was working for a wealthy membership, and whatever one thinks of their policy toward women, it was their choice as a private club. Plus, the Masters golf tournament was such a draw that he could take a hard line and be confident that golfers would still play there, fans would watch, and sponsors would line up. But how he handled the issue of female members was not crisis management. It was stonewalling. And the allegations against Tiger showed that Greenspan had no idea how to conduct public relations in a real crisis. My one memory of meeting him was when he leaned around a corner to tell me my time with Tiger was nearly up. He was a bean counter ill-equipped to react well in the clutch. He was focused on the plan, not the fight. That was why his Augusta-like strategy with Tiger failed miserably. By the time Tiger took real responsibility for what he had done, through a televised speech three months after wrecking his car, his carefully cultivated image was gone. He had choked.

But does this mean he will no longer be clutch on the golf course? Not at all. If anything, he will be more focused and disciplined when it comes to competing. It's the one thing he can control totally. Barry Bonds and Kobe Bryant have less-than-stellar personal reputations, and they mismanaged their own scandals—alleged steroid use for Bonds, the home-run king; alleged rape for Bryant, the basketball great—but they remained dominant in their sports. Just because Woods let the biggest personal story of his career get away from him does not mean he won't continue to win more golf tournaments than anyone else. The reason, as he told me, is that he has put himself in a position to win tournaments more than anyone else. He is used to that pressure, and he has the skills to manage it. He knows what he is doing on the golf course. His personal life is another issue. Revelations of infidelity on a massive scale thrust him into a brave new world of tabloid scrutiny that he had no experience with and was utterly unprepared to handle. And he lacked the honest advisers to tell him what to do. This made choking a foregone conclusion.

WHO'S THE MOST CLUTCH?

The question I was most often asked while writing this book was Who is the most clutch person you interviewed? Everyone expected me to say Tiger Woods before the scandal and delete all mention of him after it. Both expectations were wrong. Yet it forced me to think of how to rate ability under pressure across professions. I thought of Bill James's clutch-hitting index in baseball, with its combination of seven crucial elements: the score, the runners on base, the outs, the inning, the opposition, the standings, and the calendar. In other words, there had to be something at stake when the player drove in a run. Someone who got a hit with two outs in the bottom of the ninth that drove in two runs would not be considered clutch if the action was meaningless—if, say, his team was already winning or losing by seven runs or was in last place at the end of the season.

I applied a similar reasoning to clutch performance. The answer was, soldiers leading in battle. What they did and where they did it involved life and death. After all, when Tiger wins in the clutch, he gets richer and adds another trophy to his collection, while fans get a good show and some watercooler chat. Yet when he choked at the 2009 PGA Championship to little-known Y. E. Yang, he still took home $810,000 for four days of playing golf, and fans had even more to talk about: It was the first time Tiger had the lead on the last day of a major championship and lost it.

Still, to think you have to be in a life-and-death situation or even to be perfect in all situations to be considered clutch is too high a bar. Trying to emulate what Fred Peters and Mat Goggin did will not be easy, but they are at least within the realm of possibility. They showed how becoming clutch is a process. It is for Tiger, too: In golf he has over thirty years of experience; in his private life, though, he has just begun.

DESIRE AND REALITY

At the end of my conversation with Tony Alvarez, the restructuring expert, he told me a story about when he used to bowl with his children. He was rolling the ball so well one day that he needed just one more strike to shoot 300, a perfect game. This would have been a remarkable feat, because it requires such persistent skill. On that last roll, he missed hitting a strike and came up short. A little later, he found himself in that position again. This time, he told himself that all he needed to do was throw another strike, and he concentrated on doing that. But he choked a second time. He was obsessed with bowling and practiced and played in his free time. He kept at it, and that brought him a third chance at a perfect game. This time he figured out how to fix what he had done wrong in the past. "In the last shot, the two times before, I was so conscious I was going to shoot 300 that I changed my release. I kept thinking, *Just hit the pocket.* I was thinking about my mechanics," he said. "The third time it happened, I had figured it out. I had been hitting the pocket, so I thought, *Just pick the dot on the thing and release, and you'll hit the pocket.* And I made it." What he had been doing all day had gotten him to that point, so he did it one more time.

Alvarez was able to bowl a perfect game because when the moment arose, he had confidence in his skills. He did what he could do in normal circumstances but he did it under pressure: He threw a strike. This is the definition of being clutch. He was focused on rolling the ball the way he had all of the others. He was disciplined to the end. He was able to keep the goal in mind and, perhaps most important, given his past failures at rolling a 300 game, he did not start dreaming of the victory before he had achieved it. He did not choke because in those moments he did everything that people who are good under pressure do.

This is where it would be natural for me to say that the time I spent with Dale Lynch and Mat Goggin made me clutch in golf. I have no doubt Lynch could do it if I put in the time to work on my shortcomings. I can't do that right now. But at least I know why I have choked over the years. It wasn't because the pressure got to me and eroded my mental game, as I told myself. I choked because I didn't have the skill. Then I did the three things chokers do. I grew overconfident on my home course, which was not very tough. I overthought what I was doing or where I was. And I didn't take responsibility for how badly I played. Instead, I blamed my poor performance on the pressure of the tournament or, worse, the condition of the course, which was the same for everyone. The truth was, I couldn't hit all the shots that a top player needed to hit.

Now if I mis-hit a shot, I realize I may not have the skill needed to hit the next one. If I couldn't hit the shot on the driving range, I should not expect a miracle on the course. But I don't dwell on that bad shot. I go up and hit the next one. The good news is, I enjoy my rounds much more. I accept that for how little I play these days I'm doing fine. I still concentrate hard and try to hit every shot the way I do in practice. I know that being clutch means performing at your best under pressure regardless of what that pressure is: For me these days, it's the knowledge that it might be weeks before I get another chance to play golf. I console myself, knowing there are other areas of my life where I have been clutch that matter far more in life than golf. Still, on those days when I get grumpy and wish I was winning my match, I remind myself: Being clutch is not a mystical state; it takes work.

ACKNOWLEDGMENTS

|||||||||||||||||||||||||||||||||||||||||||||||||||||||||||

This book would never have happened, quite literally, if not for a dinner with Tom Trettis in Naples, Florida. He introduced me to Jack Hoeft, who recommended me to his friend David Gernert, who in turn put Erika Storella in touch with me. At that point, Erika, as I have told her often, became the best agent I could have ever hoped for.

I would like to thank the team at Portfolio—Adrian Zackheim, Brooke Carey, Adrienne Schultz, and Amanda Pritzker—for helping me take *Clutch* from an idea to a book. Don't stop now!

I want to thank all of the subjects who agreed to talk to me. I also want to thank the people who helped get me in touch with many of these people: Nick Ragone, Dawn Schneider, P. J. Johnson, K. C. King, Lewis Goldberg, Colonel Brian Tribus, Steve Naru, Herb London, Sharon Marshall, Matt Card, Darin Oduyoye, Joe Evangelista, Kirk Paluska, John Margaritis, Barrett Wood, Paul Galley, and Denise Taylor.

Several editors and colleagues helped this process along in various ways. At the *New York Times,* I would like to thank Ron Lieber, Phyllis Messinger, Kevin McKenna, and Claudia Payne. Joe Nocera deserves special thanks for early guidance. I'd also like to thank Kyle Pope and Jacob Lewis—editors at Condé Nast *Portfolio* who sent me on trips that made two of these chapters possible—and Dan Roth, who introduced me to them.

Jay Parini and Alastair Reid have been my mentors and friends for the past fifteen years. I thank them for their unwavering belief in me as a writer. I also want to remember my grandfather, Papa, who told me stories when I was a boy and piqued my interest in writing.

I want to acknowledge my three assistants: Lucy, a retired breeder for the Guide Dog Foundation; Mark, a guide dog flunky who tried hard to be her sidekick; and Ricky Ricardo, the feline leader of the bunch.

Most of all, I want to thank my wife, Laura. I could not imagine a more supportive, encouraging, and honest partner. During the writing of this book, she carried, gave birth to, and single-handedly cared for our child, Ginny, in the first months of her life so I could finish writing. I love you so much, Sweet Potato Pie!

NOTES

||||||||||||||||

Introduction: What's Clutch? and Conclusion: The Tiger Conundrum

I interviewed Tiger Woods on November 8, 2008, at the Cliffs at Walnut Cove, a gated golf course community in Arden, North Carolina. Parts of our interview appeared in the February 2009 issue of Condé Nast *Portfolio*. I interviewed Mark Steinberg and Bryon Bell on October 31, separately, and Bell again on December 4, 2008.

Chapter 1. Focus

The quotes and facts in this chapter are based largely on my access to David Boies. I spent a month in the summer of 2009 attending the *AIG v. SICO* trial in New York City, where I watched Boies do battle with Ted Wells, an equally formidable litigator. After it was over, Boies sat for an interview with me at the Four Seasons in New York. We talked late into the night. The other details come from the court record. The video of Bill Gates's testimony is uploaded to YouTube. I also consulted two excellent profiles of Boies: "The Thorn in Microsoft's Side," by David Segal, *Washington Post,* October 19, 1998; and "Get Me Boies!" by Mitch Frank and Daniel Okrent, *Time,* December 25, 2000.

Chapter 2. Discipline

The facts and quotes involving Mark Branson and UBS are based on the reporting I did for a story about Bradley Birkenfeld, the whistle-blower who revealed the bank's offshore accounts. "UBS and the Diamond Smuggler" ran in the October 2008 issue of Condé Nast *Portfolio.* I interviewed Ari Kiev several times before his death in November 2009. I have long been fascinated by Steven Cohen's success and secretive life. The quotes attributed to him came from *Stock Market Wizards* by Jack D. Schwager, Harper Paperback, 2003. To verify other facts of his life, I consulted two other pieces: a July 21, 2003, *BusinessWeek* profile by Marcia Vickers entitled "The Most Powerful Trader on Wall Street You've Never Heard Of," and a September 16, 2006, piece in the *Wall Street Journal* by Susan Pulliam entitled "The Hedge-Fund King Is Getting Nervous." I interviewed William Mumma in his New York office on January 27, 2009. For information on the problems that would lead to the firm's takeover by Deutsche Bank, I also consulted a July 2, 1996, article in the *New York Times* by Saul Hansell, "Review Finds More Deception in Trading at Bankers Trust."

Chapter 3. Adapting

I learned about Willie Copeland's story from several interviews with Michael Paulovich during the summer of 2009. Subsequently, I filled in the details from Copeland's Navy Cross citation and an Associated Press article from April 22, 2005, that reported on his receiving it. I interviewed Chris Falkenberg for the first time on July 7, 2009, at the Campbell Apartment in New York. We met and talked several more times that summer and fall in New York City and Greenwich, Connecticut. I interviewed Colonel Thomas Kolditz in his office in Thayer Hall at the United States Military Academy at West Point on July 28, 2009. I met Matthew Bogdanos at the Explorer's Club in New York in April 2004. I later interviewed him on October 15, 2004, at Uncle Nick's Restaurant in the Hell's Kitchen neighborhood of Manhattan, for a profile that ran in the Weekend edition of the *Financial Times* on November 26, 2004. Subsequently, he published a book about his adventures, *Thieves of Baghdad,* Bloomsbury, October 2005.

Chapter 4. Being Present

On Valentine's Day 2009, I took my wife to see *The American Plan,* a play by Richard Greenberg, in New York. Sitting seven rows in front of us was David Rabe, the Tony Award–winning playwright. His daughter had the lead role in the play. I had interviewed Rabe several times for the *Financial Times,* and at intermission I went up to him. I was well into writing this book, and in telling him about it, I realized I had overlooked the most common form of excelling or failing under pressure, performance anxiety. While living in Boston, I had seen the revival of his play *Streamers,* and I was well aware of its tumultuous history. I decided then that I wanted the play and Rabe to be the focus of the chapter. He demurred and insisted I talk to Larry Clarke and Scott Ellis. I interviewed all three of them many times, particularly Clarke, who supplied me with all manner of supplementary material. I interviewed Joyce Ashley in her apartment on Central Park West on March 19, 2009. Her book is *Overcoming Stage Fright in Everyday Life,* Clarkson Potter, 1996.

Chapter 5. Fear and Desire

I first met Mark Stevens through a phone interview for my "Wealth Matters" column in the *New York Times.* He was promoting *Rich Is a Religion*

(Wiley, 2008). In the course of talking, he told me the story about his father. That led to three or four subsequent interviews for the book. I initially interviewed Bernie Marcus in early 2006 for a profile that ran in the *Financial Times* on March 3, 2006. I interviewed him again on January 11, 2010.

Chapter 6. Double Clutch

I do not know why I've known the story of Billie Jean King and Bobby Riggs since I was a child. My mom took tennis lessons, but that was it. But when I was thinking of this book, the Battle of the Sexes was one of the first examples of clutch performance to come to mind. To get the facts right, I've relied on Billie Jean King's book *Pressure Is a Privilege: Lessons I've Learned from Life and the Battle of the Sexes* (LifeTime Media, 2008). I was drawn to Daniele Paserman's paper by a February 9, 2007, article on Slate.com. It was called "Women Are Chokers" and written by Steven Landsburg; this also contained Ian Ellwood's post. Paserman's paper "Gender Differences in Performance in Competitive Environments: Field Evidence from Professional Tennis Players," January 2007, was downloaded from the University of Connecticut Department of Economics Ideas server. I interviewed Marianne Bertrand on November 13, 2009. Her paper "Dynamics of the Gender Gap for Young Professionals in the Corporate and Financial Sectors" was published by the National Bureau of Economic Research in Cambridge, Massachusetts, in 2009. I interviewed Sallie Krawcheck on January 13, 2010, in her office on the forty-second floor of 2 World Financial Center, in New York. I read about Jack Welch's beliefs about women under pressure in a July 12, 2009, piece in the *Wall Street Journal,* entitled "Welch: 'No Such Thing as Work-Life Balance'" by Cari Tuna and Joann S. Lublin. As with Tiger Woods, I have long been fascinated with Michelle Wie's career. I've followed it and no doubt drew on years of reading *Golf Digest* and the *New York Times* sports section for material.

Chapter 7. A Leader's Responsibility

I interviewed Jamie Dimon on September 10, 2009, in his office at 277 Park Avenue in New York. Before meeting him, I read Patricia Crisafulli's *The House of Dimon: How JPMorgan's Jamie Dimon Rose to the Top of the Financial World* (Wiley, 2009). I later read two *Fortune* pieces on Dimon by Shawn Tully, one from March 29, 2006, and the other from September 2, 2008. The data on the values of J.P. Morgan and Bank of America was compiled by the *New York Times* and ran in the Sunday Business section on September 13, 2009. The champagne story about Ken Lewis came from James B. Stewart's excellent piece "Eight Days: Behind the Scenes of the Financial Crisis," which appeared in the September 21, 2009, issue of the *New Yorker*. I was familiar with Sandy Weill's story from my years as a business reporter at *Institutional Investor,* Bloomberg, and the *Financial Times*. I was less familiar with Hugh McColl and am indebted to one story in particular, "*Forbes* Faces: Hugh McColl Jr.," which ran on Forbes.com on January 24, 2001. I kept track of the ups and downs of both banks through my daily reading of the *New York Times* and the *Wall Street Journal*. When I have quoted directly, I have noted the date and publication in the text. If there was a primary document involved, I found it online. Otherwise I am indebted to the beat reporters who followed the stories, particularly on Bank of America, as they unfolded. Other facts on both banks came from press releases on their Web sites. Like most journalists today, I consulted Wikipedia to check dates and various facts. The John Thain quote about Lewis's knowing about his bonus was in a Bloomberg News story on September 18, 2009. The Dick Fuld quote came from a Reuters story that ran on September 7, 2009. As to the congressional testimony, I watched it on television, viewed it on the Web, or downloaded the transcripts.

Chapter 8. The Perils of Overthinking

Since moving to New York in 1996, I have cheered for the Yankees, and I try to make it to a half-dozen games a year. I am an unabashed fan of Derek Jeter and was long skeptical of Alex Rodriguez's value to the team. That may have changed after the 2009 World Series, but it will depend on how well he performs going forward. I pray he doesn't return to overthinking his every crucial plate appearance. That said, the germ for this chapter was actually the first phone call I had with Tim Corbin on March 4, 2009. I had read about the marshmallow, jelly bean, and rock story in the *New York Times* (October 21, 2008) as I was putting the proposal for this book together and sent Corbin an e-mail once the book sold. We talked for nearly an hour while he ate breakfast at a Waffle House near Vanderbilt. He gave me David Price's cell-phone number. Price and I spoke after the 2009 baseball season was over for his team, on October 16, 2009. I spoke to Corbin again on October 22, 2009. I also read Lee Jenkins's piece about Price, "Young, Gifted and Black" in the August 4, 2008, issue of *Sports Illustrated*. As for A-Rod, the *Esquire* story by Scott Raab is required reading on the man. It ran in the April 2001 issue. The Harold Bloom quote ran in a "Talk of the Town" piece by Ben McGrath in the July 21, 2008, issue of the *New Yorker*. The document "Alex Rodriguez: Historical Statistics" is widely available on the Internet for download. A-Rod's own Web site, www.arod.com, is a wealth of information, statistics, and milestones on all things A-Rod. I would not have been aware of A-Rod's streak of 30 home run/100 hit seasons if not for Tyler Kepner's piece in the *New York Times* on October 5, 2009. I also relied on his daily coverage of the Yankees for press-conference quotes. Bill James's *The Hardball Times Baseball Almanac 2008* was published by ACTA Sports in November 2007. The 2008 stats on Ortiz, Jeter, and Rodriguez come from the *Hardball Times* Web site. Other stats on payrolls, hits, batting averages, etc. came from the Web sites of Vanderbilt University, Major League Baseball, the Yankees, the Rays, or baseballreference.com.

Chapter 9. Overconfidence Starts the Fall

I had been looking for a way to tell the story of GM's overconfidence when I got a lead at a birthday party for a three-year-old. One of the parents worked for the Lean Institute and told me about John Shook. I e-mailed Shook and interviewed him on June 29, 2009, at a diner around the corner from the Chelsea Hotel, where he was staying on a visit from Michigan. We talked for quite some time and continued to e-mail afterward about NUMMI. I also consulted his blog, on www.lean.org/shook, and his most recent book, *Managing to Learn* (Lean Enterprise Institute, 2008). I also relied on the historical production figures on NUMMI's Web site. (Full disclosure: My second car was a 1987 Toyota Corolla that Shook was sure had been made at NUMMI. It was a good car. My childhood best friend's father owned a Cadillac Cimarron, which was not a good car.) I downloaded the Elmer Johnson memo from the Web. The stories of Alfred Sloan and Roger Smith are well known. I interviewed Tony Alvarez and Bryan Marsal at the Capital Grille in New York on August 10, 2009. Akio Toyoda's comments appeared in *Fortune* magazine on June 26, 2009. Steven Rattner wrote about his experience with the auto bailout in *Fortune* on October 21, 2009.

Chapter 10. How to Be Clutch with Your Money

I interviewed Frederick Peters on March 5, 2009, in his office on East Seventy-sixth Street. I first interviewed Alec Haverstick II and Arthur Bingham IV for my January 24, 2009, "Wealth Matters" column. In addition to meeting with them to discuss Peters at the Yale Club, I spoke to Haverstick several more times over the spring and summer of 2009. I originally interviewed Brad Klontz for a "Wealth Matters" column that ran on February 7, 2009, and have interviewed him several times subsequently on the subject of the psychology of money.

Chapter 11. How to Be Clutch in Sports

This chapter came about because I was killing time before my Tiger Woods interview and played a round of golf with Brett Lachem, an instructor at the International Institute of Golf, and Barrett Wood, a sports agent who represented Mat Goggin. The IIG is run by Dale Lynch and Steven Bann. I told Lachem and Wood about my book, and we started talking about pressure. I followed up with Wood and had my first conversation with Lynch on February 18, 2009, and another the following week. I met Mat Goggin on May 5 at the TPC at Sawgrass and spent the week of the Players Championship talking to him and Lynch. I interviewed Goggin after the British Open on August 10, 2009. I chatted with Geoff Ogilvy at the Players but interviewed him on May 21, 2009.

INDEX

||||||||||||||||